Additional Praise for
Service Ready

"*Service Ready* is both a beautiful memoir and smart business guide that chronicles Molly and Meherwan's trials and triumphs into their successful mini-food empire. Their attention to detail, unique management style, and transformative hospitality have redefined the restaurant industry."

—Steven Satterfield, chef/owner of Miller Union and Madeira Park and author of *Root to Leaf*

~~~~~~~~~~~~~~

"In her remarkable book, *Service Ready*, the marvelous and inspiring Molly Irani has given the business world a great gift. Finally a business book that shares stories of love, generosity, kindness, and dignity, in which the money has to work out, but money is not why Molly, her husband Meherwan or the team at their restaurant, Chai Pani, work so darned hard every day, and a restaurant book that really gives an honest—and loving and effective all at once—look at what life in the food world is really like. In the Epilogue of *Service Ready*, Molly shares that "We decided to not worry about making the right decision. Instead, we committed to make the decision right." She has done just that with this beautiful book!

—Ari Weinzweig, co-founding partner, Zingerman's community of businesses and author, *A Revolution of Dignity in the Twenty-First Century Workplace*

"We first got tuned in to the joys of Chai Pani through our palates, from the precision, piquancy, and sheer deliciousness of its Indian street food. And reveling in the restaurant's warm room of riotous colors as vibrant as the cooking was an experience so holistically hospitable it seemed effortless. To learn that Chai Pani's genesis was in fact scary-precarious, requiring intense boot-strapping, layers of grit, and tense collaborations (something we know a thing or two about!) came as quite a shock! But therein lies the magic of hospitality, and in *Service Ready* Molly Irani distills her inspiring mid-life pivot and journey from the brink of failure to the pinnacles of success into ten fundamental principles. The lessons in this volume about building teams with care, attention, and empathy are as applicable to day-to-day relationships as they are to the hospitality industry. This is a book for everyone readying themselves for service: to a job, a creative partnership, a friend, spouse, family member—to *LIFE!*"

—Matt Lee and Ted Lee, authors of
The Lee Bros. Charleston Kitchen

"Molly Irani is an expert in dealing with employees, particularly younger generations. Her secret sauce is kindness, transparency, truthfulness, and an abiding sensitivity to the needs of others—all of which will be apparent to readers of this book. *Service Ready* will help you become a more 'successful' human without sacrificing your humor and humanity. Copy her ways, if you can."

—Peter Coyote, actor, author,
Zen Buddhist priest

SERVICE ✷ READY ✷

A STORY OF LOVE, RESTAURANTS, AND THE POWER OF HOSPITALITY

MOLLY IRANI

SCRIBNER

New York   Amsterdam/Antwerp   London
Toronto   Sydney/Melbourne   New Delhi

Scribner
An Imprint of Simon & Schuster, LLC
1230 Avenue of the Americas
New York, NY 10020

For more than 100 years, Simon & Schuster has championed authors and the stories they create. By respecting the copyright of an author's intellectual property, you enable Simon & Schuster and the author to continue publishing exceptional books for years to come. We thank you for supporting the author's copyright by purchasing an authorized edition of this book.

No amount of this book may be reproduced or stored in any format, nor may it be uploaded to any website, database, language-learning model, or other repository, retrieval, or artificial intelligence system without express permission. All rights reserved. Inquiries may be directed to Simon & Schuster, 1230 Avenue of the Americas, New York, NY 10020 or permissions@simonandschuster.com.

Copyright © 2026 by Molly Irani

All rights reserved, including the right to reproduce this book or portions thereof in any form whatsoever. For information, address Scribner Subsidiary Rights Department, 1230 Avenue of the Americas, New York, NY 10020.

First Scribner hardcover edition March 2026

SCRIBNER and design are registered trademarks of Simon & Schuster, LLC

Simon & Schuster strongly believes in freedom of expression and stands against censorship in all its forms. For more information, visit BooksBelong.com.

For information about special discounts for bulk purchases, please contact Simon & Schuster Special Sales at 1-866-506-1949 or business@simonandschuster.com.

The Simon & Schuster Speakers Bureau can bring authors to your live event. For more information or to book an event, contact the Simon & Schuster Speakers Bureau at 1-866-248-3049 or visit our website at www.simonspeakers.com.

Interior design by Kathryn A. Kenney-Peterson

Manufactured in the United States of America

10 9 8 7 6 5 4 3 2 1

Library of Congress Cataloging-in-Publication Data has been applied for.

ISBN 978-1-6680-5299-0
ISBN 978-1-6680-5301-0 (ebook)

 Let's stay in touch! Scan here to get book recommendations, exclusive offers, and more delivered to your inbox

For Aria and Meherwan,
who brought my greatest dreams to life.
And for our team,
who took a dream about a restaurant
and made magic.

Do your little bit of good
where you are; it's those little
bits of good put together
that overwhelm the world.
>   —Desmond Tutu

CONTENTS

Introduction — xv

Section One: Why We Built It

Chapter 1: Finding Your Bliss, and
    Other Accidents of a Midlife Crisis — 3

Chapter 2: How to Start a Restaurant with $60K — 9

Chapter 3: How We Got Here — 19

Chapter 4: Our Paths Merge — 29

Section Two: How We Built It

Chapter 5: Leadership Lessons from Dancing Guy — 41

Chapter 6: Moms (and Craigslist) to the Rescue — 55

Chapter 7: Opening Day: The Art of Jugaad — 65

Chapter 8: Year One: Finding Our Roles — 75

Section Three: What We Built

Chapter 9: Our Core Principles — 93

Chapter 10: "Mindblasting" Hospitality — 99
    The Way of the Mindblast — 101
    Fine Dining Attention in a
        Fast-Paced, Fun Atmosphere — 102

CONTENTS

    Etiquette 101 of Mindblasting Hospitality   105
    Mindblast the Mistakes   109
    Communication Strategies That Unite   111
    The Joy of High-Functioning Hospitality   114

Chapter 11: Building a People Company   119
    Prioritizing Our People   121
    A People Culture   123
    The Impact of Check-Ins   128
    Active Listening as a Management Tool   130

Chapter 12: Meaningful Growth   135
    Creating Rules of Engagement   139
    Criteria for Evaluating Growth Opportunities   141
    A Flat Company Chart   143
    Working with Friends   144

Chapter 13: Mastery in Servitude   153
    Establishing Our Zones of Responsibility   157
    Our Company Ethos   159
    Give People Something to Believe In   163

Chapter 14: Fostering Connection, Inclusion, and Belonging   169
    A Collective Journey   170
    Inventing Jobs for the Right People   171
    Identifying Our Highest, Greatest Impact   175
    Getting Creative to Allow for People's Greatest Impact   177
    Strategies That Support a Story of "We"   178
    The Importance of Psychological Safety   182

Chapter 15: The Elegant Solution   183
    Returning to Our Core Ingredients   187
    Transparency and Timely Communication   188

CONTENTS

Chapter 16: Designing Our Own Systems:
    The Birth of Botiwalla and Spicewalla   193
        Systems Create the Stepping Stones for Growth   194
        Over-the-Counter Service   198
        Adjusting to Scale   201
        Being an Industry Disrupter   203
        Just Start   204
        Teaching Our Teachers   205

Chapter 17: What to Do When Things Fall Apart   209
        The Role of Vulnerability in Leadership   212
        When Associates Become Comrades   215
        Reinforcing Cultural Values   216

Chapter 18: Finding Where the Love Lies   223
        Creating Go Forward Plans   225
        Utilizing Metrics   227
        Bright Shiny Things   230
        The Power of Visioning   235

Chapter 19: Storytelling with Food and Culture   241
        Connecting Leadership to the Company Ethos   242
        The Necessity of Reinvention and Trusting the
            Process of Change   247
        Representing a Culture with Authentic, True Stories   249

Epilogue: Then Came the Flood   255

A Love Letter to the Hospitality Industry   271

Acknowledgments   277

SERVICE READY

INTRODUCTION

I was sitting next to my husband and business partner, Meherwan, at the 2022 James Beard Awards in Chicago. Decked out in a tuxedo and a ballgown, we were surrounded by chef friends and seated alongside our cherished team members who'd been with us on our restaurant journey for thirteen years. Our COO, Charlotte Stack, started working for us at age twenty-one as a server. VP of growth, Isaac Clay, was our first investor and manager. Daniel Peach, Culinary Director, was one of our first hires and began as a line cook at age nineteen. Rose Dodds, GM, started out as a server while she was in college. I looked around the grand hall, full of so many restaurateurs I admired, all dressed up and glowing with excitement. Admittedly, I was a little aggravated that Meherwan was distracted by writing a last-minute, "just in case" acceptance speech on his phone—but nothing could dim the thrill of that moment. We were over-the-moon honored to be in that company. Being nominated for such a prestigious award seemed an improbable turn of events for our restaurant, which started with profoundly humble beginnings. After hours of watching the awards ceremony, we finally relaxed into the experience.

And then, I heard Chai Pani's name, along with the other restaurants nominated in the national category of most "Outstanding Restaurant." Our little scrappy Indian street food spot in the mountains of North Carolina was there alongside well-established, successful restaurants we looked up to. Lights circled the hall, and TV cameras swooped all around

INTRODUCTION

us. Meherwan and I held hands; I smiled at our team and attempted a deep breath. Then I heard, "And the winner is . . . CHAI PANI!"

The shock we felt in that moment was evident on all our faces as we sat for a beat, still clutching hands, unable to move. Our friend Vish, who was seated in front of us, somehow lifted Meherwan up out of his seat and into a bear hug. Then Meherwan and I sank into each other. It was the same embrace we'd fallen into thirteen years earlier when we'd stumbled home after Chai Pani's opening day. Time stood still. All the years of struggle and hard work culminated in that moment. We'd made it. Not only our business, but our marriage.

I realized that my husband was uncharacteristically frozen, and I knew it was my job to get us up on that stage. I signaled our team to follow us and, taking Meherwan's hand, guided him through the cheering crowds and into the spotlight. There we were: Meherwan, myself, Charlotte, Isaac, Daniel, and Rose. A small sampling of our sweet team who'd grown up with us and were now running a flourishing company. Each of us were accidental restaurateurs, starting out in a business we didn't expect to fall in love with. None of us could have imagined this night. We held on tight to each other as Meherwan bowed to have the James Beard medal draped around his neck. The pride I felt to be there alongside the team that I helped build was indescribable. Meherwan delivered a beautiful acceptance speech with raw emotion, in a quivering yet powerful voice, about how through the mastery of service, hospitality can change the world. Before leaving the stage, we fell into a big group hug as the audience cheered.

This is the story of a husband and wife who turned a midlife crisis into a mini food empire. We started our first restaurant in 2009 during the Great Recession and survived a global pandemic and historic flood—all while redefining the notion of what a restaurant can be. We built and ran our business as a married couple, not the easiest thing for any

INTRODUCTION

relationship to endure. Nevertheless, our greatest challenges turned out to be fundamental assets. I share the personal story behind the scenes that shaped our restaurant adventure. And why, at the late age of thirty-nine, we reinvented ourselves and found our bliss in a difficult business that has more than its fair share of stress.

The road wasn't easy, we constantly had to innovate, and just when we thought we'd made it, the pandemic hit. Faced with losing everything, we grew. Ours is a story of how we built a successful business without killing each other. It's about changing the norms of an industry to include a new understanding of management, building and nurturing a team of young people, manifesting a dream, and staying true to ourselves along the way.

Our restaurant group and spice company have received accolades ranging from being included in *The New York Times*' "America's 50 Favorite Restaurants" list, to being one of "Oprah's Favorite Things," to receiving many James Beard nominations, but we consider our biggest success to be the longevity of our company culture. Some of our first hires are still with us today and now head up our rapidly expanding business.

Women are told to "lean in" to a man's world, and this is particularly true in the historically male-dominated restaurant industry. We shifted that narrative. We created a team culture built on a clear ethos, weaving together our individual strengths as partners and those of our team. Not only did this help us improve the typically dismal restaurant retention rates, we rewired the ways we think about retention. My focus has been on creating a culture of care that ripples out into all aspects of our business and impacts our communities.

The foundation of care at the heart of our mission is what lifted a casual street food restaurant to being named the most outstanding restaurant in America. Finding the opportunities for human connection amid the swirl of a fast-paced restaurant is at the core of how we differentiate our businesses. We were not on that stage because everything

INTRODUCTION

always worked out perfectly—there were countless mistakes and mishaps. We got there by learning our way. This book shares the concrete steps, broken down into ten core principles, that we follow to achieve our dreams.

Our core principles demonstrate how we are changing the notion of what a restaurant can be as well as how to grow successful and committed teams in any industry. Now more than ever, these principles are what many industries, and particularly hospitality, need. In a world that so often feels upside down, the search for connection, significance, and belonging are front and center. Businesses that are able to recognize this and respond with authenticity not only grow their teams—they thrive.

There were sacrifices involved, but tremendous gifts came out of our commitment to each other as husband-and-wife co-founders, and to the business. Our experience shows what it takes to make a business partnership work, and still love each other at the end of the day. The lessons we learned are relevant not just for couples but for anyone committed to long-term partnership.

I share our story not as an expert on the restaurant industry but as a student of it. I hope to dispel some of the myths about the business of hospitality and reveal just how profoundly fun and rewarding it can be. We started with nothing and learned on the job by rolling up our sleeves and figuring it out. Our experience is reflective of how so many independent businesses get started—with a lot of grit, tenacity, and hands-on effort. And it's proof that you don't need deep pockets or degrees to follow a dream (although either might make things a little easier). Hard work, an outstanding team, and maybe some divine intervention, conspired to shape Chai Pani's story.

Our learnings offer guidance to other entrepreneurs with their own dreams, and leaders hoping to build a strong business culture. By re-examining what "care" means at work, we focused on making a positive impact for our teams, our guests, and our communities. The phrase

INTRODUCTION

"service ready" is used in the hospitality industry to describe the preparedness needed to open a business for service to begin. Every day we get our people and spaces service ready before we open the doors to welcome people in. The checklists are completed, pre-shift huddles are concluded, uniforms are on, personal items are tucked away, lighting is set, and the music is playing. But we've discovered that being *service ready* means so much more than just opening our doors to receive guests.

SECTION ONE

Why We Built It

Chapter 1

Finding Your Bliss, and Other Accidents of a Midlife Crisis

Our wake-up call came in the spring of 2009 when we found ourselves in the darkest months of the Great Recession. We had recently relocated from California's astronomically expensive Bay Area to Asheville, North Carolina, and were returning from a much-needed vacation near my childhood home on the coast of South Carolina. The break provided us with just enough time away from the bustle of jobs and school routines to realize that we were teetering on the brink of our own financial crisis.

After eighteen years in California, we had moved east in search of a place to build the life we envisioned for ourselves and our daughter. We chose Asheville because it's close to family, is rich with natural beauty and good food, and was affordable. This had been the right move. We paid off our debts, bought our first house, and had a plan to save enough so that one day we could reimagine our careers and be free from the nine-to-five doldrums. Meherwan had always fantasized about starting his own business. He studied management of information systems in an MBA program and kept a running list of techy entrepreneurial business ideas. But now we had to reimagine our lives much faster than we'd planned. Meherwan worked in high-end real estate—a market that was rapidly crumbling. Many of his colleagues were filing for bankruptcy. I was working part time as a professional organizer, not the most lucrative occupation in a small town.

In the post-vacation calm, we began to ponder the question, "What do we do now?" We plugged seven-year-old Aria into a movie. With Harry Potter casting spells in the backseat of the minivan, Meherwan quietly admitted that by fall of that year he'd need a new gig, or we'd be in trouble. I remember thinking five months was not a lot of time to reinvent ourselves. But that's all we had.

Up until that point, we had diligently slogged away at our jobs to pay the bills. We were living comfortably but were stuck in careers that held little meaning for us. I realized that we might be approaching our last chance to find something interesting to do with our work lives. It occurred to me that somewhere in the terrifying predicament before us lay an opportunity.

In what may have been a momentary lapse of sanity, I said, "If we're going to jump off a financial cliff so you can reimagine your career, it should be for something that you really love . . . you never got the chance to discover what you *really* want to do . . . now that there's no choice but to take a risk, THIS IS YOUR CHANCE to find the thing that really interests you, something that lights you up." It was easy advice to give someone else; I didn't know if I was ready to follow it myself. But it sounded good in the moment. My husband has always been a practical, hardworking man—what's the worst that could happen? With the last light of day fading into the mountains around us, we drove home quietly pondering the decision before us. Meherwan appeared to be lost in thought, as if something deep was stirring.

Late that night, after some time reading to turn off the chatter in my brain, I started to drift asleep. Meherwan had been silent, so I thought he was already sleeping. Suddenly he jolted up in bed and announced, "I've got it! I know what I want to do!" He was breathless with excitement. His eyes were lit up and wild as he declared, "I want to open an Indian street food restaurant here in Asheville!"

My mind instantly flooded with flashbacks of my childhood. My mother and stepfather had owned a restaurant that was the landscape of my youth. They loved their restaurant, as did our community, and it comfortably raised a family. It was wildly popular, but like so many successful independent restaurants, it required too much from them—leaving them burnt out without a retirement plan. I witnessed the endless labor they poured into the business and the toll it took on them. After years of backbreaking work, they got divorced, continued to run the restaurant as business partners, and then eventually sold it for just enough money to pay off the business's debts. I loved our family business, but their experience left me with no desire to own a restaurant.

Opening a restaurant had never entered any of our countless conversations over the years about what else we might do. I knew Meherwan missed the food he grew up with in India and had bemoaned its lack of authentic representation in the States. His eyes always lit up when experiencing the flavors of a perfect bite, one that would transport him back home. But never had he expressed *any* interest in the food business, so I was shocked. After catching my breath, I said something like, "ARE YOU OUT OF YOUR FUCKING MIND? Forget everything I said about finding your bliss! The restaurant business is insane!"

And so our adventure began.

We had to do a lot of soul searching. Despite my immediate fears, his excitement began to spark my curiosity, so we started imagining what it could be. Meherwan craved his mom's homestyle Indian cooking and the flavors of chaat (snack) shops and street food—the backdrop of his childhood. These two categories of Indian food were hard to find in the States at the time, so I could see the opportunity. I began working through the baggage I had about restaurants from my childhood and realized that embedded in all the difficulties were some qualities that interested me—and a truckload of experience and lessons already learned.

From the time I was ten, I had worked every station in my parents' restaurant, and that instilled in me a deep love of service and good food, and an appreciation for the unique bond that can form within a restaurant team. There's a special kind of magic that happens—not only for the guests but behind the scenes. In my family, chefs were like rock stars—admired for their creativity and wildness. The addictive thrill of service with its adrenaline-fueled ride had its hooks in me from a young age. But it also left me with a deep understanding of the difficulties of making a restaurant work.

Seared in my memory is the feeling of holding my breath in the backseat as I balanced a wedding cake on my narrow thirteen-year-old legs, while my mom drove faster and faster to reach a wedding site in time. I'll never forget the terror of helping her carry the cake (half my height), while praying I didn't trip. The cake was a breathtaking masterpiece, a labor of love that took her days to create. The idea that one misstep could ruin the whole thing (and someone's wedding!) stuck in my mind as a metaphor for the restaurant experience: always just one stumble away from falling on your face.

There are many gifts to glean from summers spent sweating in a professional kitchen and dodging tourists through a packed dining room. I had some good ideas about what *not* to do, but a lot to figure out about how we'd do things differently. My parents' restaurant ran them ragged. For years my mom was at work by 4 a.m., rolling out croissant dough, while my stepdad had been up all night trying to balance the books. They had little time or energy left over for family vacations or activities. They were engaged by the creativity of their business, but running it was grueling. They'd built a special place that produced phenomenal food, but like so many restaurants, the margins were razor-thin, the work overwhelming, and the business unpredictable, even when it was busy.

I didn't want to relive that story again. To get me fully on board, Meherwan had to sell me on the idea. He had to have a compelling pitch about how our story would be different. He began working on a business plan that was in part an exercise in convincing me of the concept, as well as a tool for raising money. He stayed up night after night like a mad artist, plastering our walls with charts and graphs of research. Then he'd put on his suit and resume his nine-to-five sales job. His business plan took shape and served its purpose on both levels—it was that good. He put his MBA background and his sales skills to excellent use. His elevator pitch was that running a successful restaurant takes a highly developed palate for great food, brilliant storytelling and branding, and solid business-management knowledge. He believed that his professional background in sales, along with growing up in India with a fabulous home cook for a mother, made him uniquely prepared for this venture.

Most importantly, he addressed my concern that we have an exit strategy. Not a way to exit the business, but a way to exit the phase that many restaurateurs spend their entire careers in: that phase of relentless work and doing everything yourself. Restaurant pacing is not typically conducive to traditional family life. The long hours don't naturally fit into parenting schedules, dinners at home, holidays, and the luxuries of togetherness to which we had become attached. To address this concern, the business plan incorporated a structure for growth and expansion that would (if the stars aligned) provide us with a more sustainable career that didn't conflict with how we wanted to exist as a family.

Seeing the idea take shape made me think we could build a different kind of restaurant—one that incorporated the best practices we'd learned from our upbringings and careers in other industries. I was also excited about the impact I believed I could make by bringing my own unique perspective on managing people to a work culture known for burnout and high turnover. I wanted to create out-of-the-box ideas for restaurant management and believed that together we could change the notion of what a restaurant can be. I realized we could create our own reality at work and build a community around what matters to us. The freedom to create our own work culture touched on what I most wanted to contribute to the business. After lots of hard, honest conversations about our hopes and fears, we realized we might just have found our calling.

Embarking on Meherwan's vision required a lot of faith. We had to have faith in ourselves in order to jump into the unknown and trust our ability to learn whatever would be needed on the job. We had to dig deep to navigate all that was to come, and to decide to work on this project together. My childhood informed my instinctive resistance, but it also prepared me for one of the most important roles I would take on. From our initial conversations, it was clear that part of my role would be to play devil's advocate to Meherwan's rosy notions. **A visionary needs a balancer, someone who will speak the truth and stress-test wild ideas that aren't fully formed.** A great partnership benefits from a yin/yang or optimist/pragmatist balance. Meherwan needed a sounding board and someone to point out the things he didn't see. Or, to challenge an idea until the "why" crystallized. I offered Meherwan's vision some practical grounding. Our different approaches provided an essential balance for our venture together.

After much deliberation, we decided to take the leap. We tossed around potential names for the restaurant and were struggling to land the right one. I asked Meherwan about the kind of food he was imagining and what it would be called in India. And then it hit him. He said, "Back home we call it 'chai pani.'" The literal translation means "tea and water," but he explained it's slang in India for going out for chai and snacks. It also has a funny double meaning used to refer to a small bribe. If you want to get something done quickly you might offer a little "chai pani" money to sweeten the deal. The name felt perfect. It conjured an image of the food he wanted to highlight, along with a nod to our goal of not taking ourselves too seriously. As the details came together, our shared excitement helped us muster the courage it took to jump into the unknown. Before we knew it, we discovered how deeply we both wanted this dream to happen.

Chapter 2

How to Start a Restaurant with $60K

As our business plan was taking shape, we set out to raise money. It was the peak of the Great Recession, and banks weren't lending. They definitely were not lending to newbie restaurateurs. President Obama had just promised to fund the SBA to get loans rolling again, but it would take time for the money to flow. Without a proven track record in restaurants, deep pockets, or major collateral, we were facing a seemingly impossible task.

After venting about the struggle to my friend Angi, she mentioned that our mutual friend, Isaac, had bemoaned the lack of good Indian food in Asheville and was fantasizing about opening a dosa cart. While traveling in India, Isaac got hooked on the crispy, savory crepes, buttery with ghee and tangy with fermentation. He was daydreaming about how to bring them to our town. Angi encouraged us to share our idea with him. That connection proved to be a pivotal moment in our restaurant story. Isaac and I grew up together. Being a decade older, I babysat for his family. He was one of the few old connections we had in our new town. At that time, he was in his late twenties, a high school teacher who spent his weekends gardening, skateboarding, and seeking out the best swimming holes in the surrounding mountains. While we were in different phases of life and didn't spend a lot of time together, he felt like family to me. I knew him to be a quietly intelligent, kind, and thoughtful person. Importantly, he shared our connection to India. Isaac had been leading study-abroad groups there, with a focus on cultural immersion. After seeking out the best street food stalls across India, he was eager to introduce this food to America.

He and Meherwan met to discuss the idea of an Indian street food restaurant. In India, street food is as vast and varied as the land itself. Each region has its own twists, and flavors differ city by city. The common denominator is an explosion of flavor. Crispy, crunchy, sweet, and savory—often all in one bite. From zesty spiced corn charred on an open flame, to newspaper cones filled with bhel puri: puffed rice tossed with peanuts, fresh onion, cilantro, spices, and tamarind chutney. The street food of India is its own category of delicious, but in 2009, it was not a well-known culinary category in the US.

Isaac loved the idea of introducing this food to Asheville, and he had some savings (pieced together from living frugally on his teacher's salary) that he was interested in investing. While processing the idea with his girlfriend (now wife), Jessica, he wondered if it was a smart investment. She told him, "It's not crazy if you believe in it." Isaac and Jessica's faith in us and in the concept was the first indication we got that the idea might just be viable. Not only did he provide us with some seed money that bolstered our ability to secure more funding, but he also believed in us when we needed it most.

Next, we needed a space. We were searching for an elusive thing—a second-generation restaurant (aka cheap) in an ideal location. Asheville has a charming, walkable downtown, and foot traffic is essential to making a new restaurant visible. Available commercial spaces downtown were very hard to find. We'd heard a rumor about an old greasy-spoon diner going out of business in a perfect location, so we begged Meherwan's real estate buddy to get us inside before it was listed.

Meherwan, Isaac, and I visited during lunch service the following Saturday. It was a beautiful spring day, and the sidewalk was hopping.

Approaching the entryway of the small 1920s building felt ominous. It seemed barricaded by multiple doors. To enter you had to walk through large wrought-iron gates, a door that opened into a dim foyer, and then another door that led into the restaurant. Walking inside was like stepping back in time to a dark and dingy joint from the '80s—one that probably hadn't been deep-cleaned since then. The dining room was covered in musty old carpet (dear god), generic light fixtures hung from an industrial gray drop ceiling, and a beige canvas awning hovered over a shellacked, clunky wood bar. If the carpet hadn't absorbed enough grease over the years, the awning caught the rest.

The sleepy diner was filled with decades-old furniture and fixtures. The space had been home to countless restaurants over the years—none that were recently successful. The grease and grime had gotten out of control and taken over everything, down to the handle on the bathroom door.

We stepped into the kitchen and chatted with the cook/owner who was singlehandedly managing the two customers there at peak lunch hour. He stood over the fryer in a stained white T-shirt, with a cigarette hanging out of his mouth. The place smelled like stale french fries and sadness. But the price was within the range we thought we could raise, the location was undeniable, and we had discovered it before it hit the open market. That gave us an edge: a chance to present our pitch before we got rapidly up-bid by more qualified candidates.

We had not yet raised all the funds we needed, so we had to trust we'd find the rest. The location was too good—the kind of opportunity that might not come along again. If we waited to get all our financial ducks in a row, we'd miss our chance. So, despite our lack of resources, we took Meherwan's business plan and made our novice pitch to the building owners. By the time we met them, the space had been on the market for a few days, which had produced a slew of competitive applicants. Our town was in the middle of a renaissance even amid the recession, and downtown properties were hot commodities. Our real estate agent told us that most of the other applicants had more financial backing and experience than we did.

Our meeting with the landlords took place in a conference room in the back of a real estate office. Walking into the meeting with Sammy and Laura Rawlins, I immediately felt steadied by Sammy's smile and sturdy handshake. It was clear that he was a true Southern gentleman. And his wife, Laura, was equally warm and gracious. They seemed genuinely interested in us and our concept. They listened attentively, asked detailed questions in a distinct drawl, and ultimately made us feel more confident in ourselves. It was apparent after that first meeting that they would be wonderful landlords. They'd recently bought the building and cared about maintaining its historic charm while also creating a vibrant business there.

We made our pitch. We were presenting an Indian street food concept in a small Appalachian city with a significant lack of cultural diversity. And we were presenting it to a darling couple from Atlanta who had no experience with Indian food. After that meeting, we wrote a thank-you letter, pouring our hearts out about how much we wanted this opportunity, and then waited what felt like an endless expanse of days for their answer. We knew that our plan and budget only worked if we found a fixer-upper cheap spot in a perfect location—the rarest combination. We waited and waited, and got all tied up in knots. The waiting revealed to us just how much we wanted this dream to come true.

Meherwan was at work in his real estate office selling (or trying to sell) properties for a mountaintop luxury gated community in the middle of a market that was in free fall. He was struggling to focus on work while wondering what was going to happen. He was so stressed about how much he wanted this restaurant that he searched for a way to ground himself. Calling on instinct informed by his upbringing in the spiritual traditions of India, he decided to pray. In the attempt to block out the environment, he stood in a corner of the office and prayed to the wall.

Facing the wall with his back to the open doorway, ignoring how he must appear to onlookers passing by, he decided to offer something in his prayer. It's an Indian custom to offer something to God when asking for something. People will "give something up" as an offering. Meherwan was holding a cup of coffee (probably his fourth of the morning), so that was the first thing to offer up that came to mind. And, he did! He gave up coffee as he asked God for something he deeply wanted—this restaurant.

I share what happened next with no exaggeration on the timeline. Within minutes of Meherwan offering up coffee, my Italian espresso machine—my most prized possession—died. I was at home, in the middle of making a cappuccino, when it hissed and moaned its last breath. I was devastated, knowing it would be impossible to fix and we were too broke to buy another. It had survived the cross-country journey to our home in Asheville, where I built a dedicated coffee corner (one might say altar) in its honor. That coffee machine was a sacred object to me.

In the precise moment that my cherished espresso machine died, Meherwan got a call from our realtor. He was still standing in the corner of his office on the mountain where cell reception was bad, but he heard enough to know that Sammy and Laura were offering us the restaurant space. Meherwan hadn't even had time to set down the cup of coffee that he had just given up, and immediately called me to give me the news.

I was standing in devastation next to the smoking carcass of my espresso machine when my phone rang. The call went something like this:

Meherwan: Honey, great news! [static]
Me: WHAT? I can't hear you!
Meherwan: We got . . . [static]

Me: I CAN'T HEAR YOU! And the coffee machine just died, so I can't talk right now!

Meherwan: It's ok babe, I just gave up coffee and we got the . . . [static]

Me: (dumbfounded) WHAT?! What do you mean you gave up coffee? I love that machine and know we can't afford another one, but I'M NOT GIVING UP COFFEE!

Meherwan: Babe, you're not hearing me . . . WE GOT THE . . . [static]

Me: (a bit inconsolable at the thought that he was suggesting I give up coffee just because the machine broke) I DON'T KNOW WHAT YOU'RE TRYING TO SAY!

Meherwan: Honey, it's all gonna be ok . . . WE GOT THE REST . . . [static]

And so, it began. My husband gave up coffee, and we were granted a restaurant. He turned in his resignation letter and hasn't had a sip of coffee since that day. One might call it superstition, magic, coincidence, or perhaps divine intervention. All I know is that we were grateful for the helping hand. Our personal spiritual beliefs lead us to call that helping hand Grace, which framed the entire restaurant journey for us.

The landlords saw something in us and appreciated our business plan. Sammy eventually shared that it was the line item for salt and pepper in our projected budget that gave him a hint of our attention to detail. Sammy and Laura were our first champions and over the years became dear friends and forever a part of our restaurant family. We still rent that restaurant space from them, as well as our corporate offices that we expanded into years later when they bought the building next door. Their trust in us, along with Isaac's initial partnership, were the fuel that helped light the spark of Chai Pani.

How to Start a Restaurant with $60K

In July of 2009, we signed the lease. Getting the right location was a crucial step toward our dream, but we had our work cut out for us. Without culinary degrees or professional training, we relied on ingenuity, the experience our lives had provided, and a ton of sweat labor. Some "signs" along the way (like the well-choreographed timing of a broken espresso machine) were the little nudges we needed to trust that we were headed in the right direction.

The day after we received the news from the landlords, we were making breakfast in our pajamas as we threw together a list of the most urgent priorities before us. The list was scribbled on the back of a piece of junk mail in the mad dash of getting Aria off to summer camp and Meherwan to his office. He had given a couple weeks' notice and had to hold down his job until we secured the rest of our funding. We'd emptied our savings account buying our house, so had no wiggle room financially.

URGENT TO DO:
1. Secure funding! Make appointments with all SBA options, small lenders, and our bank, and research other options.
2. Gather remaining amount needed for down payment on the lease.
3. Make a deal with Johnny's to buy their furniture and equipment.
4. Spread the word and assemble a team.
5. Learn how to run a restaurant!

Each one of these items could take years—especially the last one! But because we were so excited to get started, we didn't freeze in fear. Instead, we laughed at the ridiculousness of what we were trying to do. I learned in that moment one of the most important things needed to launch your own business: **lack of fear**. I packed Aria's lunchbox, Meherwan and I kissed each other goodbye, and we divvied up the list. Without knowing it at the time, we had stumbled upon a crucial business lesson: **Just start! If you wait around until you know how to do all the things needed to manifest your dreams, you'll never get anything done. It often requires a leap of faith to jump in and trust that you'll figure it out.**

That momentum and excitement set the tone for how we handled the daunting tasks on our list, and it steeled us for the hard road ahead. There wasn't time to learn how to raise money. The deadline for the deposit on the space was quickly approaching. We'd been granted a rare opportunity—so we had to just go for it.

Raising money to open a restaurant is never an easy task, given the track record of new restaurant failures. But opening a restaurant as two green restaurateurs in the middle of a nationwide financial collapse with banks on lockdown was seemingly impossible.

A few key turns made the whole thing attainable. The first was finagling a deal with the operator of the restaurant we were taking over. Getting them to agree to sell us everything helped make our plan achievable. We negotiated a package price of $40,000 for all existing restaurant fixtures, furniture, and equipment (FF&E). We didn't have the $40K yet, but luckily the owner of Johnny's Uptown Grill agreed to a payment plan. The equipment was old and filthy, and the furniture and fixtures were a mess, nothing like the aesthetic we envisioned. But, buying it all for that price on a payment plan allowed us to open with no financial backing. That deal made it all possible, but we had to trust that we could rely on our creativity and hard work to transform the space.

We were desperate to secure deposits for the lease and FF&E and were having no luck with traditional loans. So, we wrote a letter to friends and family asking for help with micro-loans and enclosed our business plan. Our crowdsourcing effort secured a collection of small loans ranging from $2,000 to $7,000 each. Five friends committed to low-interest terms on five-year loans. Another longtime family friend, Ann Edelman, heard about our plan and offered to come in as an investor. Combined with Isaac's and Ann's more substantial investments, the contributions added up to be enough to secure the lease and give Johnny's a deposit.

Since most of the money we raised was going to the deposit and lease payments, we had to get creative and think out of the box with the build-out, renovation, and opening. We began to spread the word in our community that we were looking for help. What happened next shaped not only our restaurant opening, but our entire business.

Johnny's Uptown Grill closed, leaving a major mess in its wake. Isaac volunteered to help us set up the restaurant on his summer break from teaching. The day the landlord gave us the keys, I was away working at a camp called the Youth Sahavas. It was hard not to be in Asheville the moment the restaurant space became ours, but I'd been helping run the camp most of my adult life and wanted to honor that commitment. As it happened, the Youth Sahavas turned out to be the best recruitment place for young adults who love a creative challenge. I returned home with a list of volunteers interested in helping us.

When Meherwan and Isaac got the keys, they rushed over to the space, unlocked the grease-smudged glass front door, and were hit with a tidal wave of rancid air that had built up since the business closed the week before. Gagging from the smell, they got to work. They pulled and scraped the carpet off the original terrazzo stone floor as it oozed a foul black sludge. They filled countless giant trash bags with the old carpeting. When they hauled them off to the dump, it looked like they were transporting body bags in the back of Meherwan's Jeep. It took days just to remove the disgusting carpet from the dining room.

When I arrived back in town, I drove straight to the new space. I felt overcome with emotion standing there for the first time as a restaurant owner, absorbing that it was actually ours. But there was little time to dwell as I immediately got busy organizing piles to donate and dump. The clock was ticking. The funds we had would barely cover the needed renovations, so to make rent we had to open within *two months*. Despite the seemingly impossible mountain of work ahead of us, the excitement was both palpable and energizing.

A handful of friends were in between school, work, or moves, and they jumped in to help. Some of my recruits from the Youth Sahavas started to arrive, crashing at friends' houses. Other local friends showed up on their days off. Before we knew it, we had assembled a small team to help deep-clean the space. We had no money to pay this crew, but in the summer of 2009, it was easy to live cheaply in Asheville. We could only afford to pay eight dollars an hour for the people who needed it most, along with a future food credit we called "Dosa Dollars." Some friends refused to accept any money, taking their whole "pay" in Dosa Dollars. We kept a tab of what we owed in a small index card file box that eventually lived under the cash register. It stayed there for years. Word spread fast, and more friends began to show up.

The community that gathered to help us was an essential ingredient in our success. While their remarkable generosity and talents were key factors, there are universal qualities learned from their example that I highlight throughout this book, which can be recreated in other businesses and environments.

We discovered that by utilizing the resources we had to work with, we had all we needed. Learning how to make a recipe shine with limited ingredients can become the foundation of something great. We worked with what we were given—a group of friends and learnings from our life experiences. As it turns out, our lives had been preparing us for what was to come.

Chapter 3

How We Got Here

Meherwan and I were born on the same day in the same year, and we have orbited around each other ever since. We grew up on opposite sides of the world, in different cultures, but are linked through a spiritual community. Literally from the beginning, our backgrounds informed the ethos of our restaurant adventure.

Meherwan was born in London. His parents, Dara and Amrit Irani, moved from India to England in 1969 after an arranged marriage. When Meherwan was three years old, just after his brother, Jamshed, was born, the Iranis returned to India, where Meherwan's parents still live. His father Dara had a genetic disorder that caused loss of vision. He began to lose his sight in his teenage years and went completely blind just after Meherwan was born. Their move back to India allowed Dara and Amrit to raise their family surrounded by a large and supportive community that anchored them.

Meherwan's great-uncle was a renowned spiritual leader known as Meher Baba. Born Merwan Sheriar Irani, he was given the moniker Meher Baba, meaning "compassionate father" (a sign of respect). He passed in 1969 and left behind a worldwide community of followers, several expansive properties in India and abroad, and a charitable trust based in Meherwan's hometown of Ahmednagar. These sites became places of pilgrimage for His[1] followers. In the early 1970s, Meherwan's grandmother, Viloo, turned their family home into a guesthouse known as Viloo Villa, for Meher Baba's followers visiting on spiritual pilgrimages.

Driving through the villa's lacquered green gates was like stepping back in time. The main house on the property was a large single-level bungalow with an expansive veranda that overlooked manicured grounds. A row of simple cottages curved behind the villa. One cottage housed the kitchen, a few were for long-term guests, and Meherwan, his brother, and his parents squeezed into another. Meherwan's parents devoted their lives to Meher Baba and helped care for the pilgrims who visited from all over the world. They lived among a community who moved there to be of service to Baba and the directives of His Trust, which include free medical clinics, schools, and community services for the impoverished area.

Meher Baba's centers don't follow the customary traditions one might find in ashrams in India, such as all-day meditation rituals. His centers are places to gather and learn about His message through stories, celebrations, and lots of good food and chai. His aim was not to form a religion, nor did He suggest that people abandon their cultural or other religious traditions to follow Him. Christmas is celebrated at Baba's home, along with Diwali. Meher Baba was known for his sense of humor and love of the arts and entertainment—from both Eastern and Western cultures. So plays, music, poetry readings, and joyful cultural celebrations continue at Baba's home to this day.

His teachings emphasize that at the core of all main world religions is the same message about supreme love: for each other and God, which He

---

1   In keeping with the Indian custom to demonstrate respect for spiritual teachers, Gods, and saints, I capitalize Meher Baba's descriptors throughout this book.

defined as one and the same. Thus, a philosophy of service to others was woven through Meherwan's upbringing. Everyone around him was there to be of service to God, to each other, to the community, and ultimately to their own inner spiritual lives. Looking back on Meherwan's childhood, it's easy to see how his life prepared him for what he would one day do.

From an early age, Meherwan was surrounded by powerful women running the show. A typical afternoon at the villa would find Viloo playing cards—trying to lure visitors into a competitive game of canasta—after spending the morning coordinating everyone's comings and goings. Meanwhile, Raju, the housekeeper, would be serving fresh lime sodas during cocktail hour in the sprawling sitting room adorned with antiques. At Viloo Villa, one could come on a spiritual pilgrimage *and* enjoy the finer things in life. It was a lively and hospitable environment that taught Meherwan the joy of gathering large groups around a table of delicious food. So much of his desire to care for people and feed them developed in these formative years.

Guests were treated like royalty. Gathering for mealtimes anchored everyone's days. Elaborate dishes were served around a long formal dining table laid with fine china. Meals ranged from full English breakfasts with toast, eggs, and tea, to Indian curries for dinner. Meherwan's mother supervised the kitchen, relying on both her culinary instincts and experience in England to guide the cooks on accommodating Western tastes. This not only formed Meherwan's palate around both Eastern and Western sensibilities, but the blending of cultures became familiar to him. Amrit's cooking inspired how Meherwan would forever think about the possibilities of Indian cuisine. He became accustomed to weaving stories through food and community—skills that we relied on when we started our restaurant.

Visitors came from all over the world, and many became close family friends. Pete Townshend (famed guitarist for The Who) visited on a pilgrimage, befriended Meherwan's family, and gave private concerts in the villa's front yard. It was an international parade, while Meherwan and his brother ran around, getting into trouble in the sun-scorched fields. Despite the relatively grand environment of Viloo Villa, his parents' resources were extremely modest. Their only vehicle was a scooter, so the family of four would squeeze onto it to get around town. Meherwan would stand on the footbed between his mother's arms while she steered, and behind her, Jamshed rode on his father's lap.

While helping run Viloo Villa, Meherwan's mother also developed a business selling Indian jewelry and gifts to the villa guests. She was a naturally brilliant salesperson with a sharp business mind, and steadily grew her boutique to generate a solid income. Her entrepreneurial spirit influenced Meherwan's later ability to dream up business ventures and bring them to fruition.

Throughout Meherwan's childhood, his parents modeled deep spiritual devotion and the tenacity to overcome life's challenges. His father never complained about going blind—he learned to cope and got on with life. Dara manages so well that people who meet him for the first time often don't know that he can't see. His charming personality is always the first thing people notice. Echoes of his father's infectious laughter can be heard in Meherwan's today. And his mother was a model of strength. She demonstrated how hard work and believing in yourself can manifest just about anything. Her independent nature formed the way that Meherwan viewed what's possible. Meherwan's parents modeled how commitment, purpose, and devotion can build a beautiful and meaningful life.

Meherwan spent his teenage years running around with friends on their motorbikes and interacting with the many guests who continued to visit his home. Uninspired by school, he often skipped class to sneak to the bazaar and indulge in the best savory samosas in town at Bansi Maharaj. But fortunately, his bright mind helped him pass tests. He went on to complete his undergraduate degree in India and then, at age twenty, made a fateful move to the States with a full scholarship to attend an MBA program at the University of South Carolina, a decision that would bring our orbits closer together.

My parents, Roslyn (Roz) Taubman and Rusty Prall, met in college, playing music in a rock band. Like many of their peers, they dropped out of traditional paths to be part of the 1960s counterculture movement. They got married young, and my mom was pregnant with me at Woodstock. They lived in a communal house where popular bands like the Velvet Underground would crash while on tour. When I was born we moved into our own little home. Around that time, my mom discovered the teachings of Meher Baba. She was yearning for a life of deeper meaning, felt aligned with Baba's teachings, and was inspired to reorient her life around a spiritual focus. My dad had deep respect for Meher Baba, but he wasn't sure if the life she wanted was true for him. They recognized that they were on irreconcilably different paths, so at twenty-one years old, with only fifty dollars in her pocket, Mom packed up her van with my baby crib set up in the back. She left my father and moved us to the coast of South Carolina, to live next to Meher Baba's Center in the US.

We moved into a small apartment complex full of other young people drawn to be near the Baba Center and His close mandali (disciples). The mandali who lived there were charming elderly women from wildly different backgrounds—an heiress, an accomplished ballet instructor, and a British piano teacher. Their warm personalities, deep spiritual commitment, and stories of Meher Baba drew people in. Those mandali became like grandparents to me, and the community support anchored us in an otherwise unsettled time. We scraped by with my mom making candles that she sold at tourist shops in town.

My father remained in the Northeast, so our time centered around vacations together—exploring the outdoors, camping, swimming, and surfing. He instilled in me a deep love of the ocean. I still remember the smell of sun-dried salt on his shoulders as we spent all our time riding waves until the last light tipped into the sea. Our relationship remained loving, although not integrated into my day-to-day life.

At a young age I learned that life could change rapidly, and everything you know one day can be totally different the next. But I recognized the courage it took for my mom to follow her truth (and for my dad to honor his), even though it disrupted our lives. She demonstrated to me that you can just get up and make a change when you need to. Their separation left me with some wounds to heal, but ultimately, it led all three of us to a good place. This left an imprint in me that influenced how I embraced making big life changes.

My mother married Marshall Hay when I was five years old. Marshall discovered Meher Baba's teachings while in college, and he moved to Myrtle Beach to be of service at Baba's Center. Marshall became one of my father figures and played an active and supportive role in my life. After they married, my brother Ben was born. Marshall and my mom were engaged in the nearby Baba community which provided my brother and I with a tight-knit, loving community that felt like a large extended family. My mom and Marshall separated when I was eighteen, but Marshall and I remained close. Marshall and Rusty both remarried, so my family grew over time with stepbrothers and sisters.

My childhood existed in two worlds.

When I was seven years old, my parents built the house that I grew up in. Positioned on a wooded acre lot near the beach, our family home is nestled in a neighborhood that borders the Meher Spiritual Center's five-hundred-acre nature preserve. The Center's neatly combed sand paths meander through dense woods beneath a canopy of old live oak trees dripping in Spanish moss, past rustic cabins where people stay on retreat. The land is anchored by a pristine lake with a small boat house, communal kitchens, and places to gather. The winding paths lead to a private beach that feels a million miles away from the spring-breakers who flock to Myrtle Beach. Preserved in its simplicity to this day, the Baba Center remains a peaceful retreat in stark contrast to the touristy beachwear stores, miniature golf courses, and super Walmart right outside its gates. I spent much of my childhood in the ocean or running around the Center's natural sanctuary, ensconced in its magical oasis.

The people who visited the Baba Center formed an engaging, albeit eclectic, community. The same people who were the backdrop of Meherwan's childhood in India visited Baba's Center in Myrtle Beach. People from all backgrounds, religions, and cultures came to the Center for "rest and renewal of the spirit," and to learn more about Meher Baba.

Then there was my life beyond the haven of the Center. School was miserable. In the academic desert of Myrtle Beach, I toggled between Christian private schools where I hid my spiritual life from friends and teachers, and public schools that looked (and felt) like prisons. My classmates were raised in conservative homes where the idea of an Indian spiritual teacher was unheard of. They ate Wonder Bread sandwiches and Twinkies for lunch and had never seen the likes of the sprouted wheat avocado concoctions my parents packed for me. To find friends, I learned how to navigate both worlds. Their company helped me survive school, but I hid much of my life from them (including the sandwiches from my lunchbox). Back at the Baba Center, I could be myself again.

When I was around ten years old, my mom opened Latif's Bakery & Café, a French-inspired patisserie. She had no formal training, but my mother loved to bake and was quite talented. Drawing from her artistry and determination, she made something unique that stood in contrast to the generic restaurant chains in the area.

SERVICE READY

With limited financial resources, she did everything herself, from laying the tile in the kitchen to baking everything from scratch. Eventually, Marshall joined the business and they ran it together. Latif's was a hit from day one and rapidly outgrew its small storefront. After a few years, they pulled together enough funding to expand to a bigger location across the street—transforming an old gas station into a beautiful bistro. This normalized for me the idea of building a business on limited funds by rolling up your sleeves and figuring it out on your own. I spent weekends and summers learning the ropes of the restaurant business by working every position. I loved the energy of the environment and found I excelled at hospitality. As a teenager, I relied on the feeling of disappearing into the fast-paced ride of service. My mother's ability to build a successful business by relying on tenacity and creativity would forever influence my belief in what's possible.

When I graduated high school, I fled Myrtle Beach. For my first two years of college, I attended Appalachian State University in the mountains of North Carolina. The class that piqued my interest was Psychology 101, and I began to wonder if helping people was my calling. I was particularly drawn to creative therapies for children like drama and art. Searching for a university where I could specialize my studies in these areas, I found a few programs in California. I'd spent summer vacations visiting my childhood best friend, Raina, who'd moved to Southern California, and I was entranced by its charms. I loved the coastline's natural beauty and the feeling of openness that I experienced there, so I hatched a plan to move to California.

To prepare for the move, I worked all summer at my parents' restaurant, saving up $1,200 to buy a 1969 VW camper van. I packed up my belongings and spent a few weeks driving across the country with my boyfriend, John, and our mutual friend, Holly. Tears streamed down my face as we pulled away from my childhood home. The trees along the Southern coast bend away from the ocean, their trunks twisted and arched from the persistent sea breeze. The way they remain anchored in place despite whatever comes at them represented strength to me. Their gnarled shapes reveal the passage of time. The trees lining our driveway felt like spectators witnessing my departure. I realized while driving away just how much this landscape had been a source of stability. I'd miss the way the thick summer nights smell of honeysuckle, and the murmur of ocean waves that were the soundtrack of my childhood. Ultimately, that grounding helped me grow wings. Through the tears, I steered my VW camper van west.

I moved to the stunningly beautiful Marin County, across the Golden Gate Bridge from San Francisco. The Baker family, friends from the Baba community, had offered me a room in their home and a nanny job caring for their darling five-year-old daughter. Such a soft landing was an incredible gift. The Bakers became like family, and being a nanny was second nature for me, solidifying my interest in working with children and studying psychology.

I went back to school to earn my degree in child psychology at Sonoma State University. I have utilized that education throughout my life, particularly as I learned to manage people. (It turns out that a degree in child psychology is quite useful in running restaurants!)

San Francisco had me immediately under its spell. It was the early '90s, right before the dot-com world exploded. The city had a rare and diverse culture and was a wonderland of natural beauty and activity. Live jazz echoed out of bars around foggy corners, dance clubs pulsed all night in the Castro, and I felt alive and free exploring it all. I ended my relationship with John, realizing that I needed to be on my own to figure out who I was. I was twenty years old and loving life in the Bay Area, getting lost in the shelves at City Lights bookstore, hiking the hills over the Pacific, and sipping cappuccinos in North Beach. I was getting to know myself and dreaming big about the life I wanted to build. I felt myself *becoming*.

Chapter 4

Our Paths Merge

Technically Meherwan and I first met as kids, but I don't remember it. I was nine years old, and my stepfather had taken me to India to visit Baba's home. Traveling to India at such a young age changed me. After being exposed to the complexities of that culture, it felt impossible to remain concerned about my worries at the time, like fitting in at school or having designer jeans. Visiting Meher Baba's samadhi (tomb) in India for the first time, the caretaker gently held my face in his weathered hands as he bellowed his customary greeting, "Welcome home!" His words felt true.

On that trip, I met Meher Baba's younger sister, Mani, whose charms with children (and people of all ages) were legendary. She sparkled more than anyone I'd ever met. She scooped me up in an embrace that felt like a reunion. I was utterly enchanted by her and wanted as much time with her as possible. She felt like my fairy godmother. Ultimately the relationship I formed with Mani sparked a longing in me that was the beginning of my own spiritual path.

Marshall and I stayed at Viloo Villa, the home where Meherwan grew up. While we were there, Meherwan was away at boarding school, but he returned right before we left. While I don't recall the meeting, I have vivid memories of everyone making a big fuss about it because we were born on the same day. People joked that we must be destined to be together. The comments saddled us with so much pressure that I'm told Meherwan and I ignored each other completely.

The time I really remember meeting Meherwan was when we were eighteen years old. I'd traveled to India that summer to volunteer in the free medical clinic run by Meher Baba's Trust in Ahmednagar. After visiting India throughout my childhood, I was there without a parent for the first time, and I loved it. I felt at home and deeply connected to the people and the culture. The consistent rhythms of the day, the genuine hospitality, and the spiritual focus moved me. I knew then that India would play an important role in my life.

One evening, I spotted Meherwan on the hill where people gather twice a day for arti (prayers and songs). He was playing guitar alone on a stone wall in the blue light of dusk. The sight of him gave me a shiver. He looked like an Indian rock star with his ripped jeans and halo of curly hair. He'd injured his leg in a motorcycle accident and was stuck in a big leg brace, unable to run around with his friends. I finally worked up the courage to introduce myself. We exchanged some awkward small talk and went our separate ways.

When Meherwan was twenty, he came to the US for graduate school. He needed to complete a few college credits before entering the MBA program at USC, so he registered to attend community college in Myrtle Beach. He'd been invited to stay with a family in the neighborhood where I grew up.

I was home from California on my last day of Thanksgiving break when the phone rang. A family friend called to let me know that a boy exactly my age was in town—Dara and Amrit's son, Meherwan. This friend thought it would be nice for Meherwan to meet other young people, so he encouraged me to reach out. I was busy packing, so even though I was intrigued, I didn't call him. But as I zipped up my suitcase, I had a spontaneous desire to run over to the Baba Center before heading to the airport. The impulse was weird because I didn't have any particular reason for wanting to visit right before my flight. But I felt such a strong calling that I followed it.

I ran the quarter mile of sandy paths from my house over to the Center, and up the stairs from the little boathouse that sits on the lake. I was in a full vintage 90s outfit: cowboy boots with a long hippie skirt and a floppy felt hat over the untamed curls that reached halfway down my back. In the distance, I spotted Meherwan outside the communal kitchen chatting with someone and drinking chai. He did a double take as we caught each other's eye. I recognized him right away, even though years had passed since we last saw each other. I flew over to him in a whirlwind, realizing two things: that I would be late for my flight, and that I knew now why I was drawn to make a last-minute dash to the Center. We chatted for a few minutes, and then I buzzed off with the distinct awareness of having just seen someone who would be very important in my life.

The following summer I returned to Myrtle Beach to work in my parents' restaurant and save money for a big adventure. I was taking a semester off to travel the world with my friend Brooke, and had designed a research project so I would get school credit. We had a thirty-dollar-per-day budget that we intended to make work by camping and being frugal. Our trip would take us across Western Europe, hiking through the Alps of France, Switzerland, and Italy, and then on to Nepal where we'd backpack in the Himalayas. The adventure would culminate in Ahmednagar, India, where we'd spend a few weeks at Baba's Center, recovering from our trek in the modest, quiet comfort of the pilgrim retreat.

Meherwan and I became good friends that summer, waiting tables in my family's restaurant, where he was working while in college. All the young people working at Latif's ended up hanging out together. We'd go out for drinks after work and take a nightly swim in the ocean to wash away the stress of the restaurant. Meherwan and I were shy with each other, but slowly we formed a sweet friendship. The summer flew by. Before I could figure out what I felt for him, my departure date arrived. Our goodbye felt charged and awkward in a way that neither of us understood. I promised to send him postcards from my adventure, and I took off.

I realized I was in love with Meherwan while walking hand in hand with a gorgeous man in Venice. Brooke and I were both enjoying the skilled flirtations of Italian men. We met two particularly charming ones who took us out to a fancy restaurant (our only luxurious meal that trip). I was having fun, and the guy was a perfect gentleman, but I was thinking about Meherwan the entire evening. I confessed this realization only to my journal—it felt too vulnerable to admit to anyone else. While Brooke and I continued to explore the world, I started telling men that I had a boyfriend back home, even though he existed only in my heart.

Meherwan realized he was in love with me a few days after I left when he got a stomachache for days on end. His manager at the restaurant (a wise Indian graduate student who'd taken Meherwan under her care like a younger brother) said, "You're obviously lovesick!" Stunned by this idea, Meherwan asked what she was talking about. She replied, "Don't you know that you're in love with Molly? It's totally obvious!" It struck him as being true, although he hadn't yet admitted this to himself, and he wasn't sure that love could actually make you sick.

After my travels, I returned home for Christmas. My mother realized that Meherwan was without family for the holidays and invited him to join us for Christmas dinner. It was my first time seeing him after I'd turned him into my imaginary boyfriend. I was nervous. He clearly was too. But I felt an unmistakable attraction to him, a magnetic pull. Our connection deepened, and we spent much of our time together, but he was terribly shy with me. I had to return to California in a few days, and time was running out.

One day we were hanging out alone at the house where he was staying. Lounging on the sofa, he played "The Lady in Red" on the guitar. His gentle voice made me swoon. I felt as though he was singing to me, but he wouldn't make eye contact. The air was electric between us, and it was clear that I would need to make the first move. I look back and laugh at my young self. Not knowing how to come right out and tell him how I felt, or how to interpret his shyness, I decided to break the ice by sharing what had been tumbling around my mind for months. I gasped in some air and announced that I needed his advice. He finally made eye contact as I rambled that I was confused about a guy who liked me. Sure that I had forgotten how to breathe, I continued, "And, I don't know what to do because I like someone else." Meherwan looked at me perplexed, and then I said, "That someone I'm talking about is you."

And then he kissed me.

The kiss was tender and sweet. An overwhelming feeling washed over me—*Meherwan felt like home*. It felt like the most natural thing in the world, as if we had always been together.

We fell fast in love and didn't leave each other's sides for the next few days. The shyness fell away, and our fleeting time together felt euphoric. We walked the beach and wandered on the Center hand in hand, sharing our hearts fully. Saying goodbye felt impossible, but we were flying high from the exhilaration of new love, so we promised each other that we'd make it work.

For the next year and a half, we spent all our money on long distance calling cards since this was life before cell phones. We talked for hours every night. I saved every penny I could to travel home on breaks, and Meherwan visited me a few times in California. The long-distance relationship was hard, but it allowed us to stay in the romance phase where our time together always felt blissful. We wrote love letters, I mailed him a bottle of rain (oh young love), and he sent me poetry.

Meherwan was in the last months of his graduate program when he came to visit me for spring break. During that trip, we hatched plans for him to move to California as soon as he finished school. As I drove him to the airport for the hard goodbye, "In Your Eyes" by Peter Gabriel started playing on the radio—it was our song. We both started to cry.

Waiting in line to check in for his fight, Meherwan suddenly sat down on the edge of his suitcase, crossed his arms, and announced, "I'm not leaving. I can't be away from you any longer. This is too hard." I knew with certainty in that moment that he was my person. I asked if he was serious, and he explained how he'd been thinking he could get the last credits he needed to graduate by doing a project remotely.

I fell into his arms.

We found a pay phone in the airport and called the Bakers, with whom I still lived in exchange for occasional childcare, to ask if they might consider allowing Meherwan to stay with me in their home for the couple of months I had left of school. They thought the whole thing was terribly romantic and agreed to let him stay. Meherwan never checked in for that flight, and we left the airport giddy.

We spent a magical couple of months exploring the Bay Area together. He fell for the city's culture and diversity, and relished finding Indian dives that served the food he'd been missing from home. We finally got to spend more time together, and it was glorious. We were beginning our relationship in real life—not just long-distance. We never looked back.

Building a Life Together

That summer, Meherwan flew east and then drove back across the country with his brother, Jamshed (who planned to attend college in the States), and my brother, Ben (starting film school in San Francisco). They packed Meherwan's hand-me-down sedan with their belongings, and it looked like they were driving a clown car across the country, with soccer balls and basketballs spilling out every time they opened a door.

After I graduated, Brooke and I moved into an apartment together. It was in a funky old 70s building, but there was a pool, it was in a beautiful neighborhood in Marin, and it was affordable. When Meherwan, Jamshed, and Ben arrived, they moved into an apartment in the same complex. *Friends* was the top TV show at the time, and it felt as though we were living in our own version of the sitcom. We spent our free time hiking and exploring the cultural abundance of the area, finding Indian food in the city, and having big cookouts on our ramshackle decks with our growing community of friends.

San Francisco was full of young college graduates looking for work as the peak of the early 1990s recession took hold. Finding a company willing to sponsor Meherwan's work permit was challenging with so much competition. As a British citizen, he was allowed to stay on a tourist visa, but he had to get creative to support himself. It became clear that Meherwan needed a green card to be able to have a career in the Bay Area.

We had been dating for a few years, and it was time to decide if we were going to build our futures together. I had some fears about marriage, but he had enough conviction for us both. Around that time, we got a letter from Mani, Meher Baba's sister (Meherwan's great-aunt). Mani was considered the figurehead of Meherwan's family, and she'd heard that we were in a relationship. She wanted us to know that she was happy about the news, and we had her blessing. And, by the way, it would make her very happy if we decided to get married while she was still alive. Her charming letter and expression of support meant the world to us. I had such deep respect for Mani, and trust in her, that it helped me feel ready to take the leap. After a late-night tearful discussion about my fears, he caught the moment I finally felt ready and proposed.

We went to India for our engagement ceremony, every detail of which was lovingly planned by Mani. The festivities were my first real introduction to becoming a part of an Indian family. Speaking in Hindi and Gujarati, teams of aunties wrapped me in beautiful silk saris as I held my arms in the air while they spun me into the colorful fabric and giggled about things I didn't understand. There were ceremonies and prayers, laying of garlands, presentations of gifts, and endless people to meet and photos to take. It was overwhelming, but the care Mani took planning the days of events carried me through, and deep in my soul I trusted my decision.

My mom came to India for the event and asked me if I had any concerns about marrying Meherwan. I told her we were different in so many ways, but not in the ways that really mattered. I also said that I felt in my gut that Meherwan could become one of the greatest men of all time. I still believe that, and at age fifty-five, he's proving me right.

Married Life

Once Meherwan and I made the commitment to each other, a lot of my fears about marriage fell away. I trusted that we would do whatever it took to make our relationship work. We planned a beautiful wedding for the spring of 1995.

We both have big families, and we didn't have the budget to host a large-scale event. We had to get inventive. Our friends and family rallied to help us pull off an extraordinary celebration on a minuscule budget. Our wedding was the first time that all the disjointed parts of my life came together in one room: my birth father's family, Jewish relatives on my mom's side, close friends in the Baba community, college friends and work colleagues, and Meherwan's family from India. The remarkable thing about us sharing the same spiritual community is that despite growing up on opposite sides of the world, we had many friends in common from our childhoods. So our wedding felt like a family reunion, bringing loved ones together from all around the world. Both of my fathers walked me down the aisle. It was a cross-cultural multireligious feast of love. We discovered that we knew how to throw a really good party—one that made people from all backgrounds feel comfortable and unified. We did it by relying on ingenuity instead of deep pockets and utilizing my mother's pro skills at designing an abundant meal on a budget. The belief that we could pull off something extraordinary with the help of our friends and family would circle back to us years later when we started Chai Pani.

Our Paths Merge

Married life was good for us, and after a few years we started planning for a family. At that time, I was working as a doula, supporting women and their partners through labor, delivery, and postpartum care. I felt deeply connected to children, and I was ready to be a mom. Fate had different plans, and we discovered that having a child wasn't going to come easily for us. We went through several challenging years that stretched us each to the brink. Those were dark times. We had different ways of coping with our stress and grief, creating a chasm in which we almost lost each other. How we made it through and became a family is a story for another book. But we made it. As hard as that time was, the challenges we went through strengthened our marriage. When our daughter was finally in our arms, our world was in balance again. We had undeniably and permanently fallen in love, and I was overcome with gratitude to finally be together.

We named her Aria, which means "an elaborate melody"—a perfect description of how I see her. Her beautiful dark-brown eyes would light up and shine like stars, and a huge smile would take over her whole body whenever she saw me. Our bond was deep and strong, and I savored every minute with her. She is the greatest gift of my life. I wanted as much time as possible with Aria and committed to find work that allowed her to be my primary organizing principal.

By then, I was working for Peter Coyote, a multi-talented actor, writer, and Buddhist priest who's well known for his masterful voice-over work, particularly with Ken Burns. I managed his complex life, and he trusted me to communicate on his behalf with everyone in his circle—from Hollywood megastars to old friends from his time as a leader with the "Diggers," a 1960s counterculture movement. My childhood of adapting to diverse environments left me with an understanding of how to make people comfortable and establish rapport with just about anyone. Years later when I was learning how to be a leader in my own company, the impact that Peter had on my development was clear. He modeled how to sustain a wildly busy and successful life while remaining true to himself and his spiritual core. I studied organizational systems to find the best ways to manage the multitudes he juggled. Over time I grew those skills into a job consulting for entrepreneurs and artists in need of systems to manage their lives. The organizational skills that were etched in my brain from that time were critical when starting our business.

Once he received his green card after we got married, the first job Meherwan could find was at a luxury car dealership. His plans of working in the IT sector were put on hold since those jobs were difficult to come by in the recession, and he needed a paycheck ASAP. He loved cars and was enticed by the lure of the sales bonuses. He thrived in the retail environment, becoming the top seller at every dealership he worked in, eventually moving into management. Working in sales turned this shy Indian boy into a gregarious extrovert when the situation required it. He earned a good living, but the schedule and unpredictability of sales were exhausting.

Supporting a family while facing the rapidly increasing costs of living in the Bay Area was daunting. And the area was changing. The tech boom had swept through the city, diluting some of the unique charm that originally drew me there. We found ourselves moving farther and farther north in search of affordable housing, and spending way too much time commuting to work or to see friends. We wanted to buy a home and began searching for other areas to raise our family.

We moved to Asheville in the summer of 2005 when Aria was three years old. We chose Asheville because of its strong sense of community, abundance of good food, and easy access to natural beauty. It's also close to family. I devoted myself to finding a home and building a life for us. A few weeks after the move, I woke up one day feeling completely different. There was a lightness in my shoulders, like a weight had been lifted. I felt like I was swimming in the current of a stream that was flowing in the direction I wanted to go. Asheville was the right fit for our family. We'd found our home.

SECTION TWO

How We Built It

Chapter 5

Leadership Lessons from Dancing Guy

There's a YouTube video made by Derek Sivers, popular with tech start-ups, about creating a movement. It's called "First Follower: Leadership Lessons from Dancing Guy." In the three-minute video, we watch a man dancing wildly, shirtless and alone in a field. The narrator explains that the leader is the person who had the courage to start dancing, but what happens next is crucial to a moment becoming a movement: someone starts dancing alongside him. Why is this crucial? That second dancer publicly demonstrates how to follow. Being a first follower is an underappreciated form of leadership: they're the one who calls friends to join in. The next follower is a turning point. It's no longer two people dancing together—three is a crowd, and proof that the leader has done well. The focus shifts from the leader to the collective. That attracts more followers . . . and now we have a movement! As the field fills with dancers, the narrator explains that "it was the first follower who transformed the lone nut into a leader. There's no movement without the first follower."

This brings us back to July 2009. Meherwan had a wild and wonderful idea, but he was dancing alone in a field. I was the second dancer—the first follower who helped transform him into a leader and called to my friends to join us. Isaac was the tipping point that set the stage for more people to join us, and that created a movement.

Isaac spent his summer helping us renovate the space, and friends offered to lend a hand. The way people came together around our project resembled what I imagine a barn raising might be like. The willingness of people to show up and work for either eight dollars an hour, or future food credit, or no pay at all, can best be understood in context of the Youth Sahavas and the bond it provided us.

That summer I had been working at the Youth Sahavas, a summer camp for teens in the Meher Baba community. "Sahavas" is a Sanskrit term meaning to dwell together or be in close companionship. In the context of the Youth Sahavas, it means to be together in the company of God and/or love (depending on how you define spirituality). Secluded in the nature preserve of the Meher Spiritual Center, teens spend five days without their families, leaving the pressures of the world behind, and come together in a loving and supportive environment. Being in the peace of that sanctuary, in a truly inclusive community, unplugged from social media and the noise of the world is transformative—for the teens and the volunteers who run the camp. After a few days, the walls we all build to survive out in the world begin to crumble. The days revolve around fun activities: music, art, dances, going to the beach, creative workshops, discussion groups, and amazing meals—miraculously cooked in a makeshift tent kitchen. The food service is run to this day by my mother and rotating volunteers that she transforms into a professional kitchen team, despite truly challenging conditions. From a young age, she imprinted in my imagination the possibility of creating magic out of thin air (actually, 100+ degree very humid air), without the needed supplies or infrastructure. Her devotion to this cooking challenge (as well as her approach to life in general) created a legacy for me about relying on one's own grit and inventiveness to manifest something truly special.

The Sahavas is where I learned that making and serving food with love can not only be a transformational experience, but addictive. It taught me how much freaking fun hard work can be if it's approached with the right frame of mind. The mindset is simple: Don't take yourself too seriously. Leave your worries outside, focus on the job of serving others, and have fun doing it. This kind of work can provide an unexpected reward in the form of a break from our internal chatter—relief from all that noise and overthinking. There's a gift in the doing. In my years of volunteering there, I've held many roles, but the one that I loved the most was the food service. The running of the rest of the camp felt like a beautiful classical composition—the kitchen felt like rock and roll. Irreverence and humor abound, along with 100 percent devotion to creating excellent meals that nourish much more than just our bellies.

My background with the Sahavas provided a model for how to organize teams that integrate a philosophy of service. It's gruelingly hard work that requires being of service in a way I haven't experienced anywhere else. And I've never laughed harder or had more fun. It is where I discovered what's possible when a community of people come together with a shared mission and focus on the love. My friend Matt Shepard describes it as a "blueprint for humanity of what's possible when we're working from our highest selves."

Bringing the restaurant buildout team together meant translating the work ethic I'd absorbed at the Sahavas into the real world. Meherwan and I were lucky to begin our project with people who already understood the atmosphere we wanted to create, since many of them had already experienced it through the Sahavas. This made it pretty easy for us to establish a fun and collaborative work environment. But this dynamic is possible for anyone bringing a group together. It helps if the focus is on the bigger picture: something that the team feels connected to and that matters to them. In our case, they believed in our vision and were excited about it. Leading the group that opened Chai Pani taught us that **building a team with a high level of commitment, collective excitement, and solid work ethic requires inspirational**

leadership. We weren't always perfect at this. But we were inspired by the people we'd assembled, and showing up for them helped us develop our leadership muscles.

Opening on such a tight budget and timeline meant doing everything ourselves. There was an impossible number of things to do. I held on to my sense of humor as best I could and tried to stay positive, but it took a lot of intention to avoid getting frazzled. We got the keys to the space in mid-July and needed to open by mid-September (at the latest), or we'd run out of money. This is an insanely short period of time to renovate a space, design a menu, hire and train a team, build a brand, and market an opening. As newbie restaurateurs, we didn't know what we didn't know, and that probably kept us optimistic (or naïve) enough to attempt this ridiculous task. On the outside, I was rolling with it: directing the team, trying to stay organized, motivated, and energetic. Internally, I was walking a tightrope. If I maintained my balance, I'd be ok, but the accumulating challenges would make me feel wobbly, threatening to tip me into overwhelm.

The buildout of Chai Pani looked like pandemonium, but most days it felt like a really fun dance. Peaks of tumult flowed into something beautiful. What got me through that phase is what still makes me excited to go to work every day. Working in an environment where you can be yourself and people have your back is energizing, even when the work is demanding beyond description. The simplest of gestures of support can save us—someone on your team noticing when you need help and stepping in at just the right moment is game-changing.

Being aware of how others are feeling, noticing when support is needed, and remaining flexible enough to respond are touchstones that can shift chaos into art. When team leaders have each other's backs, it sets the tone for everyone else. It becomes contagious. This one dynamic can define a company's culture.

It was clear from the beginning that having Isaac help manage the buildout was key. His frugal instincts perfectly fit the challenge we faced with our budget. It was during this time that his nickname, "The Island of Calm," took hold. His tall, grounded presence paradoxically takes up very little energetic space. With a quiet nature, not from shyness but from taking everything in with careful intention, Isaac remains unflappable to this day.

I remember sitting on the restaurant patio one sweltering summer afternoon, with tourists passing on the sidewalk. I was trying to tackle forms we needed to submit for permits. Tears that I'd held back for weeks began to trickle down my cheeks. These forms were full of questions that I couldn't answer. That was a constant state of existence for me—being asked questions I had no answers for. "Does the outdoor lighting meet the Night Sky Ordinance for the City of Asheville?" "How big of a dispenser do we need for chai?" "How do we enter daily sales into Quickbooks?" I had no idea how to answer any of them.

Isaac sauntered over and peeked at the tear-stained papers. He gently asked if he could help with one of those "stupid forms." I felt like he was offering me his oxygen mask on a plane about to plummet from the sky. Without any further discussion, I passed him the form. He tucked it in his back pocket and went back to hauling junk, giving me a much-needed moment to pull myself together. This is how Isaac rolls.

Isaac continues to balance Meherwan's fiery founder energy and steady my mind if it's spinning. He trusted us from day one, instinctively and beyond reason. That's just his nature. He trusts people and has high expectations of them. He leads by example and inspires people to want to do a good job. His work ethic, combined with his enthusiasm to share Indian street food with our community, was infectious. Showing up every day that summer didn't feel like work to him—and that helped set the tone.

In 2009, there was not a single Indian restaurant in the United States (that we were aware of) representing the culture and food in the way we wanted to. There were fine dining establishments with regionally specific Indian cuisine, and plenty of great funky dives with authentic Indian food. But no one had elevated Indian *street* food and served it in a welcoming environment, where we hoped people from any background or culture would feel comfortable. Pairing that with the kind of craveworthy comfort food served in homes across India had not yet been done in a restaurant. We were banking that offering both of these genres together would give us a competitive advantage, but we were entering unknown territory.

Our goal was to introduce the food of Meherwan's childhood to America. We intended to change how people in the West thought about Indian food. Many of the friends who showed up to help us had been to India, so they understood what we were aiming for and that we were creating something radical. They knew firsthand how underrepresented Indian food was in the US at that time, and they were motivated to help us change that. We'd assembled a team who not only understood the mission, but also instinctively knew how to help us set the right tone in the work environment.

Years later as our business grew, we looked back on that opening phase to analyze the magic of our success. This beginning taught us how impactful it is when a team feels linked to a bigger mission—and **how important it is for the work to offer the promise of connection and belonging**. We identified these two key ingredients as qualities to replicate—and as essential components in the execution of our vision. This provided us a solid foundation upon which to build.

I stood in the dining room surveying what we'd inherited from the previous restaurant. Surrounded by burgundy cracked vinyl booths, metal chairs with ripped padding, and stacks of white square outdated ceramic plateware, I got to work figuring out what could be salvaged. The equipment was dilapidated. The walls of the walk-in cooler were patched with duct tape, and instead of a proper compressor (standard for restaurant walk-in refrigerators), a window AC unit hung from its ceiling. Somehow, miraculously, it managed to hold the right temperature (or at least it did until we put it to full use).

As the team hauled away truckloads of junk, I redesigned the space. We had no budget for new things, so the goal was to open without buying anything that we could repurpose. The $40,000 buyout we negotiated with Johnny's included everything in the building—all furniture, fixtures, and equipment, right down to the chipped beige coffee cups.

We faced a gargantuan challenge transforming Johnny's into the aesthetic we wanted. But as the project crystallized, the process felt familiar and surprisingly comforting to me. Memories from my childhood came back, scenes of watching my parents building their restaurant, and my mom coming home speckled with paint after standing on a ladder all day. I felt at home in the broken-down restaurant mess that surrounded me, and inspired by the process of transforming it.

We organized the redesign around color, since painting was the most affordable way to revamp the space. I was desperate to find someone who could help me achieve the look we wanted. We couldn't just throw a lot of color on the walls; we wanted to be intentional with placement and selection to curate the right look. The goal was to capture the cacophony of color and energy that explodes on the streets in India, and the exuberance of enjoying snacks from the chaat stalls. We wanted to transport our guests from Chai Pani to India by engaging all the senses—without overwhelming them. The challenge was to hit the right notes inside a narrow thousand-square-foot dining room in a 1920s building in Asheville. Enter, Michael (Mikey) Files.

Mikey and I grew up together. Being a decade younger than me, he was close with Isaac and was one of the neighborhood kids I babysat. We'd worked together at the Youth Sahavas, where that year I hired him to provide comedic relief in the kitchen. The role was necessary because it's hard to create a functional team of volunteers to work sixteen-hour days cooking in a nature preserve, where the heat index under the cook tent tips over 120 degrees. That year I took over the kitchen from my mother (who was in the middle of opening her own restaurant). I needed the right people alongside me to pull it off. I knew Mikey could bring a lighthearted party atmosphere to work. So, despite his lack of cooking experience, I recruited him for the Sahavas kitchen team with the sole job of making us laugh.

We hadn't spent much time together since we were kids, but that summer we got to know each other as adults. While I was at the Sahavas, Meherwan and Isaac were back in Asheville scraping up the old carpet from the restaurant. I shared our restaurant vision with Mikey, and he was excited about the idea. He was planning a move to New York City but offered to swing through Asheville on his way. He was going to spend a few weeks helping us out and be Isaac's right hand with painting.

As he settled into the renovation work, he quickly became the person I went to with design questions. Mikey had recently lived in India, spending a year working in an art gallery in Mumbai. Importantly, he understood the feeling of joyful, carefully crafted chaos that we wanted to bring to the restaurant. Mikey was the only person who would spend hours with me analyzing the nuances of the color blue, to find just the right hue reminiscent of weathered Indian street art and how to utilize white space to bring balance.

We were a couple weeks into the renovation when Mikey found me in the tiny office, hunched over a pile of potential logos. I didn't like any of the designs, but in the rush of our impossible timeline, I had convinced myself to stop trying out different designers and just go with the least horrible version in front of me. Mikey gasped from the doorway, "You CAN'T choose that awful font! No! It looks like a yoga studio logo. And don't even get me started on the one that tries to look like Sanskrit. Is this the best they came up with?"

Leadership Lessons from Dancing Guy

While Mikey stood in the office doorway covered in paint, I asked him to stay and help me design the brand. Seeing a spark of intrigue in his eyes, I said, "When will you ever get another chance to redefine how America understands Indian food while working with your friends?"

Mikey never moved to New York and became another essential ingredient in the success of Chai Pani. Utilizing his artistic talents and background, he fearlessly jumped in and, like the rest of us, began to learn on the job (while also hauling junk to the dump). He relied on his art degree and deep understanding of Indian aesthetics to help us pull together the design. His particular genius lies in his untamed imagination. He can interpret the images in Meherwan's mind and manifest them in real life better than anyone. He understands how important the details are in good storytelling, and he cares about the story we set out to tell. He was as lit up as we were about disrupting the notion of what a restaurant could be.

As word spread, people continued to offer help. Jeremy, a friend from the West Coast, had recently relocated to Asheville and was just starting out as a contractor. He took on aspects of the remodel that went beyond our DIY abilities, accepting a payment plan we could manage. All these years later, Jeremy is still our preferred contractor and his team leads all our restaurant buildouts.

Longtime family friend Peter Nordeen, a highly skilled and brilliantly frugal builder and contractor, heard what we were up to and showed up one day. While surveying the state of the restaurant and the ragtag group of friends on the job, he announced without provocation, "I can start work tomorrow." Peter refused to accept a penny in payment, agreeing only to be gifted Dosa Dollars. He helped us decode the many mysteries of the eccentric old building. After a few days of assessing the scope of plumbing issues we were facing, he proclaimed, "This won't work. There's over ninety years of bad plumbing layouts layered on top of each other—you will have constant drainage issues."

SERVICE READY

Without further discussion, in quintessential Peter style, he marched into the kitchen with a sledgehammer (while the crew was just finishing days of deep cleaning all the kitchen equipment) and proceeded to demolish a wall. This revealed a maze of old pipes, still wrapped in the crumbling original newspaper used for insulation in the early 1920s. After covering the entire kitchen (and freshly cleaned equipment) in a layer of drywall dust, he singlehandedly redesigned the plumbing to be more functional for a restaurant's needs. I saw the look on Isaac's face as he mentally tallied the days that had been wasted cleaning the kitchen. But when an expert is volunteering their time, you don't complain about what kind of mess they make. You simply hug them with gratitude and clean up after them.

The full buildout team came together with the addition of Jonathan Ramsden visiting from California, Matt Shepard to assist with the painting and graphic design, Will West on college break, and a host of other friends who rolled up their sleeves and jumped in.

I showed up for work one day to find my longtime friend Angi scraping the old vinyl sign off the front window, Matt and Jessica up on ladders painting, Mikey setting up a video camera in the middle of the dining room to capture the magic (oh how I wish we could find those recordings), Meherwan in the kitchen with Peter sorting through yet another plumbing issue, and Isaac scraping the old carpet glue off the floor with Will, while Jeremy and crew tore down the iron gates that blocked the entrance. The sight of this team at work stopped me in my tracks. Music was blasting, dust was flying, and excitement permeated the air. In the comfort and support of that company, I believed we could accomplish anything.

When I say it took a village, I mean it. Friends wove Aria into their summer activities so she was well cared for, allowing me to spend long August days in the restaurant space as we raced toward opening. I missed spending our summer days together picking blueberries in the mountains and swimming in creeks. But I had to keep my eye on the prize. I was building this business in great part so that I could have control over my work schedule, in order to spend more time with Aria. I wanted to pick her up from school every day and be there to make dinner and help with homework. We wanted to avoid having two parents wrapped up in full-time careers. The goal was for one of us to be more flexible and able to work around her schedule. I knew I would be overstretched in the beginning, but the hope was that owning this restaurant would allow me to shape my work schedule around Aria's life.

Mikey and I were struggling to finalize the wall color and were going around in circles. We'd taken down all the light fixtures, and the new ones weren't in yet, so we were viewing paint swatches (isolating each color by looking through paper towel rolls) in the dark while shining flashlights on the wall. We were getting close but couldn't decide.

Desperate, I reached out to Katie, a family friend who happens to be a fantastic designer. She'd just wrapped up an interior design job for a billionaire's home in Mumbai. After a lifetime of travel in India, she understood what we were going for. We couldn't afford to hire her, but out of absolute kindness, she agreed to help us select a color palette that would work with the old burgundy booths and outdated furniture. She laughed as I gave her a tour with my phone camera, while stepping over cleaning crews and piles of sawdust. Upon seeing the space, she declared, "I don't think you could have found a place further away from the aesthetic you want!" And yet, she knew we could pull it off and helped us get there.

As Meherwan, Mikey, and I finalized the décor, we decided that a way to bring the feeling of the streets of India into the restaurant was through the faces of the people. My close friend Mehera was living in India at the time and working as a photographer. Her work truly captures the spirit of India. We didn't want polished photos of the Taj Mahal; we wanted actual street scenes. Mehera has a special talent for making people feel comfortable, and that allows her to capture someone's character in a single shot. She caught the twinkle in the eye of a chai seller, the warmth in the namaste of an old farmer, the contagious joy of a young child cuddling a goat. The background of her photos is a snapshot of the daily scenes that unfold across India. But what you see conveyed in her photography is love. She captures the inexplicable joy that you witness in the most unexpected places in India.

Mehera gifted us a collection of photos taken in Meherwan's hometown. Her art brought just the feeling we were looking for. Initially we couldn't afford high-quality printing, so we had poster-size prints made at Sam's Club, mounted on foam board. One of the first things we did when we finally got more financially stable was reprint the same photos in a higher quality and larger size and hang them in handmade rustic wood frames. Those prints survived multiple renovations, wall color changes, and a move, and they still grace the walls of Chai Pani.

We were workshopping the right logo when I remembered a T-shirt my buddy Nick had created. It was screen-printed with a cool design reminiscent of the art found on the lavishly painted Tata trucks of India. I called Nick and asked if I could use his shirt design to adapt to a restaurant logo. He graciously offered it to us, and as an added major bonus, that conversation led to his partner, Rochelle, designing our website. They were about to depart on an adventure driving to South America, but Rochelle still volunteered to help, building our first website from internet cafés along their camping route.

The number of friends offering their incredible talent and time blew our minds. Mehera, Nick, and Rochelle joined the group accepting Dosa Dollars as payment. They all have more credit than they could ever use. These love offerings served as a sort of blessing of the space, and the brand. The collaboration was given freely to help support our dream. It set our profound experience of gratitude that continues to this day.

Working within our frugal budget taught us to micromanage every penny. If you aren't religious about smart spending, building a restaurant can quickly become so expensive that it sets a business up for failure. We had no choice but to work with the scarce funds we had. While that seemed like our biggest challenge at the time, it turned out to be one of our greatest blessings. It forced us to learn an important lesson that influenced how we built everything that followed. **You don't need deep pockets to create a beautiful space. Frugality doesn't hinder creativity—it can amplify it.** Telling a clear and compelling story is far more meaningful to a restaurant's success than having expensive furniture. Now that we're able to secure whatever funding we need, we still hold on to those early lessons, which helped our restaurants survive many ups and downs.

What started out feeling like a challenge to pull off without "professional" help, ended up being one of our greatest strengths. Our business was enhanced by the collection of friends who helped us execute the vision. Receiving the graciousness of others was key to manifesting our dream.

Over time we discovered how impactful our work climate was on new hires and the people who joined us. Collectively, we'd set a high bar for how the environment should feel, and new people were enticed by that—and leveled up to meet it. Because we all held lofty notions about a positive work atmosphere, we had to keep our shit together. Meherwan and I couldn't fall into fatigue-induced reactions of bossing people around, or allow the stress of a situation to affect our mood or management style. Overwhelm would sometimes slip out, but the team would dispel disruptions quickly.

Somewhere in the frantic buildout days leading up to the opening, we stumbled upon a surprising discovery. Amid all the pressure and impossible deadlines, we were having the time of our lives. This had to do with the environment we'd created. I set the tone to be one of gratitude for each other, grace under pressure, and acceptance of imperfections. This created lightness and fun despite the crazy hard work. Meherwan brought fearlessness, determination, and a vision that kept us moving forward.

The nature of the restaurant industry, and the bootstrap way most of us come to it, involves a belief that **everything is figure-out-able. This requires that we have a "get it done" attitude and do not allow fear to guide decisions.** We had everything on the line and every penny to our name wrapped up in opening this restaurant. Fear of failure is a natural response to that level of vulnerability, but Meherwan and I tried our best to not be afraid—or, at least not at the same time.

Meherwan was pretty adept at managing fear. He had quiet moments of panic but worked them out inside his head. I needed to process my fears out loud with him in order to release them. At times our different coping mechanisms were maddening, but usually they saved us, providing balance. Not wanting to freak out our team with my moments of fear, I learned how to manage it. It was like inviting my fear over for a cup of tea, telling it where to sit, and then just getting on with my business while it rattled on. I learned not to repress it or allow it to build up (and later explode), but I did not give it my full attention. I suspect this is a practice for many first-time entrepreneurs.

We loved finding solutions to the impossible and being immersed in the creation of something special alongside a team of remarkable people. It was invigorating—a feeling that carried us through the backbreaking work leading up to Chai Pani's opening day.

Chapter 6

Moms (and Craigslist) to the Rescue

As we approached the end of August, we placed our first help-wanted ads on Craigslist. Asheville is a small enough city that word of mouth plays a significant role for service industry workers. But we were new to the Asheville restaurant scene, and the idea of Indian street food was unfamiliar. Also, we were not able to pay the most competitive rates at the time, so applications arrived in a slow trickle.

Lucky for us, my dearest old friend Raina offered to be our first manager. Raina and I met when we were eleven years old at the Baba Center. Her friendship had been a lifeline for me. She was the first friend I had with whom I could be fully myself. We were joined at the hip until she moved to California in high school. Our connection was the beginning of my understanding of the importance of finding your people—the ones who love and accept you just as you are. Raina had recently moved to Asheville from LA and had worked in multiple restaurants throughout her life. She brought a level of experience that we needed. We didn't have clear systems in place yet, or training protocols, or any kind of HR. We needed people we trusted to maintain the hospitality environment we wanted both for our guests as well as with our team. And we needed someone willing to figure out all the details alongside us in real time.

Isaac went back to his full-time teaching job at the start of the school year. But he was invested in Chai Pani's success and offered to work part time in the evenings and on weekends. I planned to run all the front-of-house lunch shifts during the week while Aria was at school. So, between Isaac, Raina, and myself, we had the front-of-house management covered.

The back of house was harder. Meherwan wasn't planning on becoming a chef when we started Chai Pani. He wanted to run the business and set the menu, but he didn't have the training or experience to manage the operations of a professional kitchen. The challenge was finding a chef who had the culinary skill and palate we wanted, the high level of professionalism we expected, *and* the willingness to work for a low salary. Needless to say, we were not attracting top talent, and the résumés we received were pretty bleak.

The best fit we could find was an experienced chef who'd moved to the area from New Orleans. I'll call him Frank to protect his privacy. We were down to the wire, and Frank claimed to be eager and willing to manage the chaos of a new concept opening. With our kitchen manager in place, we began to slowly fill out the rest of the crew.

I grabbed every résumé with any sign of potential and called the applicants in for back-to-back interviews. I met each person at a café table on the restaurant patio while the renovation work inside continued. I planned to ask anyone interesting to stay on for a second interview. There was no time to wait a day for them to return for follow-ups. We went through some real duds—burned-out line cooks clearly just hopping around to the next thing, not investing much energy or care in their work.

Then James Adam Grogan sat down across from me. Well dressed in an ironed button-down shirt, with neatly combed hair, he exuded professionalism. He was soft-spoken and intelligent. James had some decent cooking experience—but I was sold by his earnest, sweet smile and bright eyes. I had a strong feeling that he had a golden heart and was someone we could trust. That initial instinct turned out to be more prophetic than I could have imagined. James has a calming charm, and he instantly felt like someone I'd known forever. He emphasized how much he cared about quality and that he was eager to learn Indian cuisine. Success! I ran inside, screaming through the front of house to anyone listening, "We found someone great!" One down, the rest of the staff to go.

The remaining interviews were pretty rough, but the last person I met that day redeemed my hope. Daniel Peach, a nineteen-year-old, blond-haired, blue-eyed Carolina boy, was looking to relocate to Asheville from Charleston. Daniel was mature for his age, with a polite and engaging personality. He'd worked in a restaurant kitchen so had some basic experience and wanted more. But he was really drawn to us because of his fascination with India. We spent most of the interview talking about Indian culture and Eastern philosophy. He'd recently picked up a book on Hindi, hoping to teach himself the language. I grabbed Meherwan for an immediate second interview, sure that we'd found another gem. Meeting Meherwan, Daniel commented that he'd heard about an Indian saint who had the same name. When Meherwan explained that Meher Baba was his great-uncle, Daniel was flabbergasted. It felt like there was serendipity at play. That instinct was confirmed when I got an email from Daniel that night with a courteous thank-you note. As a hint of the role that Daniel would end up playing in the business and in our lives, he signed the letter "Chai Pani Ki Jai!" Ki Jai is a traditional Indian refrain that offers a blessing—the equivalent of saying "all hail" or "cheers" to Chai Pani.

After we'd run through all the applications, we were still short in the kitchen. We were getting close to just enough people to fill the front of house, but the back of house still needed help. To maximize our time and efforts in the hiring process, we planned an open house, hoping to generate some buzz.

Raina and I spread the word around town, set up two stations on the patio, and spent the afternoon interviewing everyone who showed up. This approach proved to be a good strategy to attract non-native

English speakers. Showing up in person worked better for people who didn't have résumés or anyone who felt more comfortable applying face-to-face. After a day of screenings, we slowly added to the kitchen crew.

Toward the end of our open house, I noticed a jovial, solidly built Hispanic guy putting his name down on the interview list. His pronounced dimples and the twinkle in his eyes drew me over from across the patio. I introduced myself, and he explained in broken English that he'd heard the open house was the best way to apply. I grabbed him out of the line and fast-tracked him to my table. His presence was so warm and gracious that I immediately knew he would be a good fit. We chatted for a few minutes about the dishwasher role. I asked if he felt he could handle that kind of intensity. He replied with a smirk, "Mrs. Molly, I can work hard and fast, you don't need to worry." Ladies and gentlemen, meet Gustavo. To this day, I've never met someone who works harder or faster.

Meeting James, Daniel, and Gustavo gave me hope that we could build on the unique atmosphere we'd created during the buildout, and that together we could make something special.

James, Daniel, and Gustavo survived the chaos of the opening that was about to descend on us, and they did it with grace. Over time they worked up to management positions, and to lead entire divisions in our growing company. The best part is that they became family. Not bad, Craigslist.

As the team took shape, it was clear that an essential role was missing: No one in the kitchen knew how to cook Indian food! With Frank in place as the kitchen manager, the expectation was that he would lead operations. Since Frank didn't have experience with Indian cuisine, Meherwan planned to head up the menu design and training. It was evident that this was an overly ambitious idea within the short period of time we had to finish our punch list of remaining tasks. It was time to call in the big guns.

Meherwan's mother flew in from India, and having Amrit's support and culinary skill was a turning point in the execution of our vision. The day after she arrived, she was up at dawn and off to Chai Pani with Meherwan to help teach the team how to cook Indian food.

The newly assembled kitchen crew showed up for basic training with Amrit. Three tall, lean, blond, handsome young Southern love bugs, and one short, older, slightly cranky Italian guy. By the end of her first day, Amrit had the whole crew calling her "Mom." She and Meherwan worked together to recreate and scale the recipes she'd made for him throughout his life, along with the street food of his childhood. They adapted traditional Indian dishes into lighter versions that appeal to Western palates while also conjuring deep-rooted nostalgia for Indians.

I could hear her voice bellowing from the kitchen over the construction clamor, "Pay attention!" "The onions have to be browned longer—this isn't French cuisine!" "Wash your hands for God's sake!" "Taste this . . . smell this . . . see the color of those roasted spices. . . ." The cooks respected her authority and happily accepted her guidance, along with some loving snaps of a kitchen towel if they were goofing off. She gave them a crash course on the fundamentals of Indian cuisine. In the process, she unschooled whatever they'd learned in other kitchens. Essentially, she handed down her culinary wisdom to a line of white boys—and they received it graciously.

The next thing we knew, fragrant spices were wafting out of the kitchen, filling the dining room (still a construction zone) with deliciousness. Sticking to the ritual she maintains at home in India, she served lunch to everyone in the building at 1 p.m. She'd arrange the tables in a long line in the middle of the room, sometimes snaking them around construction debris and painting ladders with people still standing on them. Proclaiming that the "babies in the kitchen" needed practice, she oversaw the preparation of multiple-course meals and then insisted that we all pause work to come together and eat. I'm certain that if Amrit hadn't arrived, I would have lived off cereal for weeks.

The food was sustenance that we all needed—but something else was happening with those family meals. Amrit helped set the tone for the culture we were building. One day I approached the packed table with an overwhelming feeling of gratitude upon seeing the scene before me. Daniel, wearing a hippie bandana, was talking with Amrit about Eastern philosophy. Our new landlords, visiting from Atlanta, listened in politely while enjoying lunch. The rest of the long family table was involved in conversation—including the postman, a random passerby that Amrit pulled in off the sidewalk, and a collection of dust-covered workers. Everyone was invited to the table. Work was paused no matter how urgent it felt at the time. We ate together, laughed, shared stories, and filled ourselves with food that nourished much more than just our bodies.

Out of necessity, we lived by the Silicon Valley start-up motto "move fast and break things." It functioned as a reminder not to waste time worrying. We had to just keep moving and not get bogged down about decisions, or stress about things being just right. The bonds that formed in the building of Chai Pani were the fuel that got me out of bed every day. But tired to the bone, I wondered if things would get any easier once we actually opened. We lived in the in-between: existing between our previous life with familiar routines, and the unknown of whatever was about to happen. The buildout phase felt like being suspended in time.

With the large iron gates removed, we had opened the foyer to an entryway we hoped to transform into a beautiful work of art. Mikey headed up the creation of a mural around the front door reminiscent of the traditional art that adorns trucks in India. Working with a crew around the clock, they tried their best not to drop paint on the food suppliers and delivery people who came and went around their ladders all day. Spotlights lit up the mural into the night while passersby lingered on the sidewalk, trying to figure out what all the commotion was about in this spot that had been sleepy for years. One night as Meherwan drove past the storefront after leaving at 1 a.m., he spotted Mikey and Matt lying on their bellies across the sidewalk, painting their masterpiece on the door frame. This moved Meherwan to tears.

On breaks from the kitchen, Amrit set up a sewing machine in the dining room and made colorful curtains out of Indian saris to hang over the hallway entrance and to cover the bar back shelves. The way that she tackled the intensity of the work was inspiring. This capacity to embrace work wholeheartedly was a legacy we inherited from both of our mothers. My mom was running her own brand-new restaurant at the time, which kept her too busy to be with us in person, but she was an invaluable source of guidance and fielded my endless questions. We were able to exchange resources and compare notes about the ridiculous challenges and adventures of the restaurant world. This sense of camaraderie was a big support for us.

The way our mothers modeled steadfastness was sealed in our developing young psyches. Both women were entirely self-made. Without college degrees or formal training, they built successful entrepreneurial businesses that supported their families. They were twenty years old when they had us, and they are each fiery, strong women who made their way in a man's world. Not only do they both embody strength, they are two world-class cooks!

They offered much advice through the restaurant opening, which we (for the most part) received gratefully. There were times when we needed to make our own mistakes and carve our own path. I remember my mom looking at our proposed menu and proclaiming it had way too many items on it for counter service. We got a little prickly at the idea of changing the menu at that late stage, but it turned out she was absolutely right. It just took us some time to realize it. Amrit read over some of the names of the dishes Meherwan wanted to use and scoffed. While she loved his idea of demystifying dishes by renaming them in more familiar Western terms, she helped us avoid any confusing cultural mash-ups. Merging American food culture with Indian was complicated enough. She nixed the "fish taco" term, and we settled on "fish wrap" instead. Kheema pav (a traditional Indian street food sandwich) became "sloppy Jai"—something that Americans would recognize, without adding a third culture to the mix. Our moms chimed in with advice, but they both understood from their own life experiences the importance of us figuring things out on our own.

Our mothers both overcame insurmountable obstacles to start their businesses. Their example taught us a critical lesson: **Fear is the greatest obstacle for any entrepreneur. Overcoming it is a requirement. Committing to a vision means having the dedication to move ahead despite fears or insecurities.**

In the final few days before opening, there wasn't time to sit down. Meherwan slept in the hall of the restaurant on a ratty old cushion, and the team took naps in booths in order to work through the night on the final punch list. We needed months longer to be able to open with a fully trained staff and clear systems, but the money was all used up; every credit card was maxed out. We had to open our doors and sell some food, or we wouldn't be able to keep the lights on.

Meherwan and I relied on an unspoken understanding that we needed to hold it together through the final stretch, which felt like an Ironman triathlon. For the sake of the team, we knew we had to stay the course and not melt from exhaustion. We'd been married for fifteen years, so we knew how to work through challenges together. That strong partnership, bolstered by a remarkably dedicated team, made it possible to survive the grueling race to opening.

Most restaurants start with a "soft opening," an event that gives the team practice while also serving as a marketing tool to spread the word and alert the press. When I suggested we plan a soft opening, Meherwan looked at me with bleary eyes that spoke the hard truth. There was no time or money for soft openings. We didn't have the luxury of waiting for training to be complete, or for the recipes to be ironed out, or for the paint to dry—we had to just say a prayer, hold our breath, and open the doors. We had to **just start**.

If we couldn't do a soft opening, then I insisted we pull together a small party for the team to give the staff a round of practice with systems and plating, and as a gesture of gratitude for everyone's hard work. We'd keep costs down by only serving what (we thought) we had extra supplies of. The night before opening day, we fumbled through that party and fed the construction team, workers, and friends who had carried us to that point.

Aria was the photographer, and she captured the chaotic scene with her delicate seven-year-old hands, barely able to hold up my old-fashioned camera. The register wasn't programmed yet, so I handwrote people's orders on a dusty ticket pad left over from Johnny's. Meherwan worked with the team in the kitchen, using a long piece of painter's tape to hold all the incoming order tickets (since we hadn't yet bought a ticket rail). The dinner service was hectic and disorganized but full of cheer and celebration. Most of all, it honored the people who made the whole thing possible. I helped clean up from the party and then headed home with Amrit and Aria while Meherwan stayed to program the cash register. This was the final item on the checklist that absolutely had to happen before opening day. Little did we know that our cash register had other plans.

Chapter 7

Opening Day: The Art of Jugaad

On the morning of September 23, I arrived at Chai Pani a little after 8 a.m. to get ready for the opening scheduled for 11:30 a.m. Meherwan never made it home that night, so I assumed there were some major issues going on. Butterflies were swing dancing in my belly when I walked up to the door and saw Mikey *still* up on the ladder, *still* painting the mural. I stepped around the ladder and entered the restaurant. Meherwan stumbled out from behind the freshly hung sari curtain looking like he'd taken a ride in a tornado. He was a total mess. With bloodshot eyes he said, "I've tried everything; the register won't print tickets in the kitchen. It won't print tickets any fucking place at all."

Since we couldn't afford a POS (point of sale) system, we'd bought an old school digital cash register from Sam's Club that was supposed to be able to print in two places. We began Chai Pani as a counter-service model where people ordered at the bar, took a number, and had food delivered to their table. Given the distance from the register (where customers would order) to the kitchen in the back, having tickets print in the kitchen seemed an essential component for service to function.

Meherwan had stayed up all night trying to get the register to print. He climbed through the dusty cobweb-filled ceiling crawl space to install wiring, tested, retested, and reprogrammed it all night long, but the damn thing just wouldn't print. It turns out there's no service support line for cash registers bought at Sam's Club.

Meherwan seemed ready to fall apart. One thing I discovered early on about a strong partnership is knowing when the other person has reached their point of overwhelm. A gift that our long, shared history brought our business partnership is the ability to read the signs and know each other's tipping points so that we can step in when help is most needed. We relied on not falling apart at the same time. Initially, we did this from instinct, but over time, we learned to practice it intentionally. This helped our marriage as well as our business, and it prevented our staff from seeing us fight. There were countless times that we missed the mark, but we always tried to catch each other.

Staring at the cash register, I quickly realized we had no choice but to jugaad it.

"Jugaad" is a term used throughout India to describe the reliance on ingenuity to make something happen with what you have, instead of waiting to have all the right parts or pieces. Sometimes it means bending the rules, or getting inventive with your resources. Meherwan says it's like figuring out how to make chai with a Zamboni (the ice-resurfacing vehicles at skating rinks) because that's all you have, and why waste a perfectly good machine?

Meherwan gave his best salesman pitch: "We can figure out a plan B. We have to open today. People are going to show up. Can we find a way to make this happen?"

By "we" he meant "me." I put on a brave face to reassure him, even though I felt I might crumble. These are the things we do for love.

The only option I could think of was to beg our beloved band of friends-turned-painting-crew (some of whom were running on forty-eight hours of pretty much no sleep) to put on clean Chai Pani T-shirts and spend the day carrying tickets from the register to the kitchen. I didn't think our brand-new food runners would be capable of getting the food to tables (and clearing them) as well as the tickets delivered to the kitchen—we needed more hands to pull it off. Being the rock-star human beings that they are, Matt, Mikey, and Jonathan agreed to help run tickets. They were tired to the core, unshaven, unbathed, and spattered in paint—but they did it. If I'd had time I would have cried with gratitude.

I gave Meherwan the green light, and we scrambled to set up for our first service. I had five minutes to learn how to work the ludicrous-non-printing register, we gathered the freshly hired, barely trained employees, and before we could blink there were fifteen minutes left until opening.

A line had begun to form outside as we buzzed around like bees on speed. Last-minute issues were resolved at breakneck speed. Ruby called from behind the bar, "Does anyone know how to make a lime rickey? It's on the menu, but I don't have a recipe." James, ever calm, emerged from the kitchen (optimistically) wearing a crisp white chef's coat and said, "None of us know how to make an uttapam. Can anyone help?" Angi realized we didn't have any change for the register. Food runners looked like deer in the headlights trying to identify the endless array of dishes they didn't know how to pronounce correctly. The "sound system" (Pandora played off my cell phone) wouldn't play. Daniel discovered that the corn bhel menu item was supposed to have a dressing. I recalled a page from Oprah's magazine that I'd saved to show Mikey a particular shade of blue and remembered that the issue had a similar recipe in it. I found the magazine in the office and threw it at Meherwan as he passed by. They adapted it on the fly into "cumin-lime dressing" and made a quick batch for service. A version of that tasty dressing is still on our menu today.

And then in the middle of the mayhem, Meherwan's mother announced that we couldn't open without having a Pooja ceremony. A Pooja is an Indian ceremonial tradition that marks important events. The tradition differs in detail depending on family background, but the practice stretches across all Indian religions and cultures. The common threads woven through most Poojas are: making an offering to God, blessing the space and/or people, and taking a moment for gratitude and prayer. I had no idea how to stop the frantic last-minute preparations for a prayer ceremony with customers staring at us from the other side of the door, but I wasn't about to argue with my mother-in-law.

At 11:45 a.m. (fifteen minutes past the planned opening time) we gathered our crew into the front of the house. The already exhausted cooks, the increasingly terrified young food runners, the whole team paused the last moments of preparation and came together for a Pooja ceremony to bless the space. Meherwan's mother assembled the ceremonial items; I'm pretty sure a coconut was cracked, a sacred photo was placed in a spot of honor, a bell was rung, and we held hands in a big circle, closed our eyes, and had a moment of silence—while the line of customers watched from the sidewalk.

This moment would never come again, and my mother-in-law knew it. She made us stop and give thanks, and ask God, or Grace, or each other for help. I'm deeply grateful for her guidance in that moment. The pause for centering that she made happen that day helped set us on a course that is uniquely our own and became an essential part of the scaffolding behind Chai Pani's success. It helped us focus on what really matters. I'm sure some new employees were deeply moved, while others wondered what the hell they'd gotten themselves into—but together we took a collective breath and opened the doors to a line up the block. That line never went away.

That first day began with me behind the register that I hadn't had time to learn. Meherwan was our kitchen expediter, a position that sets the pace and ensures dishes are made correctly and directed to the right tables. This was his first time ever running expo in a restaurant. Bollywood music boomed, our customers were forgiving of our fumbles, everyone had fun,

Opening Day: The Art of Jugaad

and miraculously we pulled off a couple of hours of chaotic lunch service and brought in way more business than we were prepared for.

We'd quietly announced our opening, imagining that some strategic social media posts and a simple sign on the door would spread the word over time and give us a gentle start while we figured things out. Without us realizing it, the news had spread rapidly—totally catching us off guard. I learned later that in a moment of panic the day before opening, Meherwan had doubts about our quiet campaign and threw together a press release that he emailed to the local media. Clearly, they got the message.

I ran the register, handwriting two copies of every guest's order on the old ticket pad I'd found, sending one copy to be hand-delivered to the kitchen and using the other to ring up the customer and then give to the bar for drink orders. It was an insane system, but we made it work.

It was a struggle to learn an unfamiliar register and move the lunch line through this cumbersome ordering process, but eventually I found a rhythm. I loved welcoming people into the space and felt joyful despite the pandemonium. Every job I'd had up to that point helped me remain calm under pressure and project a warm and hospitable environment for our guests. My life had prepared me to be a gracious host—even though my legs were wobbly from fatigue. I loved the energy of that crazy opening day, and the excitement I felt from the guests was like a shot of adrenaline.

After a couple of hours, my fingers had gone numb from writing so many tickets. I hadn't eaten or even had a sip of water, and my brain was starting to get scrambled. At the expo station, Meherwan had two long rows of tickets lined up along the counter after abandoning the painter's tape that had been holding them in place. Matt came flying around the corner, and the wind in his wake blew all the tickets into the air. Things were beginning to fray. The small pan of okra they'd prepped the night before ran out in fifteen minutes. The single blender of green chutney they made lasted less than an hour. The kitchen line was set up with a ridiculous system that required each plate to go through five separate steps in different locations before eventually landing at a station where it got cold waiting for someone to add the finishing garnishes. The cooks were drowning, and dishes were taking forty-five minutes to get to guests.

We had no system in place to communicate with the kitchen, so there was no real-time way for me to know what we were out of. The food runners, their arms full of plates, had to yell in my direction that certain items had been eighty-sixed. By the time I got the message I'd already taken new orders for those items. We had no warning system to know the count left of each item—we would just run out. Since no one else knew how to run the register, I was trapped with the non-stop line of guests. I'd yell to Ruby, who was working the bar, "Go to table 8 and tell them we're out of what they ordered." She was covered in sticky raspberry syrup and lime juice from hand-juicing all the drinks, but she would run to the table and then bring their new order back to me. As lunch progressed, we were rapidly running out of items, and by the time Ruby gave me the table's new order we were often out of it. My nervous system felt like It was about to rocket out of the top of my head.

In that moment of recognizing that we were fully in the weeds, I looked up and saw a news crew standing in the middle of the restaurant with TV cameras. I stood frozen, thinking, "What the hell are they *doing* here?" And, "This will surely be the straw that breaks me." I was in absolutely NO state to give an interview—especially not on camera—and no one else could cover the register. Meherwan was buried in the kitchen trying to reorder the tumble of tickets, his mom was manning the uttapam station—we were all in a frenzy.

I thought I was going to fall apart right there at the register when I caught Matt's eye from across the room. He saw the panic on my face, connected the news crew as the source of it, and did the most thoughtful thing for me. It felt like he caught me while I was falling. He mouthed from across the room, "It's ok, I've got this." And right there in the middle of the lunch chaos, he gave a fantastic, spontaneous interview—unshaven, with paint splattered over his thick black curly hair tied back in a ponytail. His interview made the evening news. I guess in our little town in 2009, a new Indian street food restaurant with a line out the door was newsworthy. We were grateful for their acknowledgment and forever indebted to Matt for his graceful and quick rescue. It was one of the countless times that I thought I must be the luckiest person in the world to have such good friends.

And then, halfway through lunch service, *we totally ran out of food.*

At the time it seemed inconceivably disappointing to have to close our doors early, send away a line of customers, and not be able to open for dinner, but we had no choice—there was no food left!

After turning away the disappointed customers at the door and serving the remaining guests inside, Meherwan and I collapsed in a booth to assess what to do. My mother showed up for lunch to discover that we had closed. I'll never forget her coming over to comfort me as I lay in the booth in a puddle of exhaustion. At the time, it seemed horrible to have to close after just a few hours, but my seasoned restaurateur mom said, "This is absolutely the best kind of problem to have! It will just create even more buzz. And it'll buy you guys some time to get your shit together." Her wisdom was spot-on. Since our bank accounts were empty, we took the money from the register that we'd made that day and went out to buy supplies to cook more food for the next day. We spent the rest of the day prepping and training and beginning to iron out the countless problems.

That night we crawled home. Thankfully, we'd planned for a friend to pick up Aria from school and feed her dinner, bringing her home just before bedtime. I stumbled upstairs, cuddled Aria in bed until she was asleep, then closed our bedroom door and fell into Meherwan's arms. We both broke down in heaving sobs of tears while we held each other.

They were tears of exhaustion, but mostly they were tears of gratitude. Meherwan's idea had worked, and as madcap as the day (and past two months) had been, our town showed up and welcomed us. The idea had clearly captured people's attention.

On day two we ran out of food again, only this time we managed to stay open until 2 p.m. We struggled through one more day closing early and then closed for the entire weekend to get it together. It was scary to slow the momentum of the buzz and excitement, but we had to press pause to recalibrate. We put a sign on the door that read:

> *Thank you, Asheville, for your overwhelming*
> *support and excitement!*
> *We're closed to adjust our systems and hire more*
> *team members. (Anyone want a job?) We promise to be*
> *back open with gusto and samosas flying in three days!*

We took the weekend to reassess everything—the menu, supplies, training, and every system that broke down in those first few days. The kitchen team recalibrated. The instantly famous okra fries would need to be prepped hours before service to make enough, and the curries reminiscent of nightly dinner in Meherwan's home growing up would need pots three times the size. We redesigned the kitchen line, bought a ticket track, began the process of doubling our staff, and started their training. We hired everyone we could find, including friends we happened to pass on the sidewalk. We ordered up on our food supply and mapped out what it was going to take to produce quadruple the food we had anticipated needing. And then, after the nuttiest week of our lives, we opened back up again to an even longer line down the block. That time we finally made it through the day without running out of food. We stayed open for lunch *and* dinner, and all the way straight through the busy fall season.

Opening Day: The Art of Jugaad

It became second nature for us to use the term "jugaad" when directing our team. When someone would say, "But we don't have x, y, z," our answer was, "Jugaad it." This was our code for "get creative, figure it out, work with what we have." It became part of the DNA of Chai Pani and informed how we did just about everything in those early years. We started out relying on jugaad because of our limited time and resources, but we continued with the practice because we discovered that it makes a better product—one that reflects the unique personality of a business. When we utilized jugaad well, we found better answers, and the results had more soul.

Jugaad is about more than making do with less. It has to do with ingenuity and thinking outside the box. Now, as we grow our restaurant group, we have established the jugaad way of doing things as a core fundamental principle. Even if we could afford to spend millions on a restaurant buildout, we believe that money is better spent on other things—like maximizing what we can pay our team. We don't have to have lighting designers who cost tens of thousands of dollars tell us what we can figure out ourselves if we take the time, do the research, and pay attention to what works. While I'm sure lighting designers are wonderful to have, we've managed to figure out lighting that works for us. And after countless hours spent learning our way through it, we believe this effort creates a product that's more aligned with the story we want our unconventional spaces to tell.

The solution to the broken register printer that got us through opening day ended up being the ticket system Chai Pani used for years. If anyone had told me that we would rely on runners to physically walk order tickets back into the kitchen FOR THREE YEARS, I'd have thought our business was sure to fail. It seemed impossible (and stupid) to do it that way. But once we perfected the old-school handwritten ticket system, it worked well enough that we didn't change it until we could afford the POS we wanted. We didn't have extra money or credit to rescue us. We thought outside of the box, relentlessly. Opening the way we did taught us essential skills that we needed as we learned how to make a restaurant function well. Now, the art of jugaad is woven into everything we do. It helped us start the business, and it ensured we survived the Covid pandemic. It's one of the essential bricks in the foundation that our company is built upon.

As we recovered our energy after the opening, we began to analyze the gold we could mine from all the mistakes made. Two lessons emerged from the chaos that we wanted to hold on to. **The art of jugaad is a foundational strategy for success. And we discovered that running a restaurant in our own unapologetically unique way, Pooja ceremonies included, would become a pillar of our business ethos.**

Chapter 8

Year One: Finding Our Roles

The first year of Chai Pani was a process of figuring everything out on the job. We remained super busy, so we continued to scramble as we hired up and kept dialing in our systems. We didn't fully understand how to appropriately set our menu pricing, so we were undercharging relative to the cost of product and labor. Even though the volume of guests remained high, without having a good revenue model in place, we were underwater financially. Extreme frugality remained a primary focus.

In the kitchen we had rags under the fryers to catch leaking oil, an oven that wouldn't light dependably or close fully, recycled ice cream containers holding all the spices, orange buckets from Home Depot for supply storage, and a head chef who wasn't embracing the nuances of Indian cuisine quite the way we'd hoped. In the front of house, the fifteen-dollar folding chairs I'd bought from Ikea were already falling apart. Isaac kept a pile of broken chairs downstairs where he'd salvage parts to Frankenstein them back together. We were still hand-delivering tickets to the kitchen, and I struggled to get all the new hires trained effectively before they were thrown into the hustle of service.

We continued to micromanage every expense as we figured out the complexities of restaurant cash flow. We couldn't afford the rates that food distributors charged, so we did most of the weekly shopping ourselves at Sam's Club, except for product bought from local farms. Since the city only picked up trash one day a week and we couldn't pay for private services, we hired a local character who needed work. Mike looked like the love child of Jerry Garcia and Santa Claus. "Trash Can Mike" came by every day to empty the trash and take it to the dump in his van, which sometimes doubled as his home. After a polite but firm call from a local church, we discovered that Mike was pocketing the dump fees we gave him and tossing the trash in the church dumpster and other spots around town. Isaac, being the good neighbor that he is, asked Mike to drive him to his dumping spots, and together they dumpster-dove to retrieve our trash. Mike sheepishly apologized and, surprised we were giving him a second chance, promised to never do that again.

We couldn't afford a liquor license, so we only served wine and beer. The staff created sake cocktails to expand our offerings—which, despite their best intentions, were pretty sad. We continued to jugaad it.

It was clear that we had a hit on our hands, but learning how to manage the business was a process—excellence wasn't reached until farther down the road. In those early days, the food was hit or miss. Some dishes were great, but they weren't consistent. Guests weren't necessarily responding to a masterful execution of Indian food (yet) but more to the idea itself, the energy of the space, and the sweetness of the team.

Our early reviews were all over the place. Despite some criticism and disappointment with our inconsistent execution, our community was remarkably supportive. We navigated some drama from a competitor who relentlessly left fake bad reviews and tried multiple ways of undermining us. Meherwan would get spun out by each bad review, Isaac felt gut-punched by them, and we were all frustrated. We eventually got word through the grapevine about who was behind this campaign. We realized that we felt sorry for the guy—he sucked, so we decided to rise above it and not give him any more energy or even a response. We made a commitment from then on to only look for patterns in bad reviews so that we could address them. Outlier bad reviews are usually just that: outliers. Often when a guest cares enough to let us know about a disappointment, they will call or email us—a much more effective way to be heard. And we pay attention. I made Meherwan promise that he'd stop reading reviews. Someone else from the team could respond accordingly without him boarding the emotional rollercoaster.

A few months after opening, Daniel Peach came to Meherwan red-faced and announced, "I'm pretty sure I'm about to lose my job." He described the scene that had just unfolded in the kitchen. He was barreling down the cook line carrying a heavy pot of hot chai while yelling, "Behind you" (customary in a professional kitchen), as he tried to pass safely. Frank refused to budge and got bumped as Daniel struggled past him. Frank snapped at Daniel not to "bulldog him," to which Daniel had responded, "You're an asshole." Daniel found Meherwan in the office to apologize and share his side of the story. Daniel knew he'd lost his temper and acted unprofessionally. Meherwan made it clear that under no circumstances could he call someone a name. Reassuring Daniel that he wasn't about to lose his job (but did need to apologize to Frank), they had a good conversation about managing reactivity in the heat of the moment.

Minutes later Frank came to Meherwan complaining about Daniel. As Meherwan recalls it, Frank, puffed up in righteousness, explained that we had to keep these "young punks" in line so they would learn who's in control. He went off about the need for more discipline. New to kitchen slang, Meherwan wasn't sure what the term "bulldogging" meant, but he got the gist. He acknowledged the inappropriateness of Daniel calling Frank an asshole and then reviewed our expectations regarding managing the team. In our view, Frank was missing some key leadership qualities that we expected from him. We didn't want to rely on the standard restaurant militaristic brigade system. We're aiming for a more humanistic way to manage a team. Frank, the restaurant veteran, looked at Meherwan like he was speaking another language. In fairness, he was exhausted. He'd put in an enormous amount of work. He was doing his best, but it became painfully evident that Frank was not the right fit.

Soon after that exchange, we made the difficult decision to let Frank go. It was our first firing, and we tried our best to handle it kindly and with care. He was of course upset. I'm sure he felt underappreciated for the work he'd put in. He left convinced that we would eventually learn that strict, aggressive control was the only way to run a kitchen.

His departure created a leadership gap in the kitchen team. This led to a fateful turn in Meherwan's career, and for Chai Pani. He had to jump in and take the reins. In the process of learning how to manage a kitchen and cook at a professional level, Meherwan uncovered a passion that had been inside him all along. He discovered his talent as a chef. This firing also confirmed our suspicion regarding the importance of protecting the work atmosphere from personalities or behaviors that bring it down.

Sometimes the biggest challenges become our greatest opportunities. I witnessed a change in Meherwan. It was like watching his true nature reveal itself as layers of other roles he'd played his whole life began to peel away. It was beautiful to see him transform before my eyes as he did the hard work of learning the craft. In his taking over the kitchen, "Mad Chef Irani" was born. He grew out his beard, gave away his business suits, and came fully to life. Most days he resembled the character Animal from the Muppets—wild, a bit crazy, and free. Despite the eighty-hour work weeks and utter exhaustion, he seemed totally happy.

Literally on the job, he taught himself every station and how to manage the operations of a professional kitchen—*and* lead the team. Being in the kitchen and working alongside the cooks allowed him to create the culture in his own unique way. He had vivid memories of how dishes should taste but didn't yet have the skill to recreate them. Alongside Daniel and James, he'd watch YouTube videos of street food being made in India, then they'd scale up and adjust recipes and test until the flavor hit on Meherwan's memories. They figured it out together. The new structure was liberating and allowed the cooks to contribute and rapidly grow their skill sets. By eliminating the traditional kitchen hierarchies, Meherwan managed the team by defining zones of responsibility. He was in charge, but everyone was treated with equal respect—no matter their role. Contributions and ideas were welcome. Without any previous indoctrination into traditional kitchen-management structures, he invented his own. In doing so, he created a more inclusive and dynamic environment. He loved it and never looked back.

The personalities of the team began to infuse the space. Camaraderie carried them through backbreaking shifts. In the first month after Frank left, Daniel and James recorded their hours on the wall of the downstairs storage room (aptly nicknamed "the dungeon" due to its dingy, damp darkness). In one pay period of that intense phase, they collectively recorded eighty hours of *overtime*. There's a delirium that ensues when you arrive at work before the sun comes up and leave long after dark for days on end. Because of the remarkable natures of these young cooks, they bonded and laughed their way through it—instead of falling apart or walking out. They carried us, and each other, through that time.

Humor was key. Michael Goode, a seasoned line cook, joined the team during our hiring frenzy in the first months after opening. Along with his punk rock persona, he brought with him a dry wit and infectious laugh that could turn around any bad mood. He coined my favorite nickname in the restaurant. There was a long dark nook sandwiched between the side of the walk-in cooler and the wall, just wide enough to hang some brooms and cleaning supplies. It was a place where things were known to disappear and then reappear without explanation. Michael called the nook "Narnia," convinced there was some "spooky magic shit" happening back there. The kitchen team made up nicknames for all the dishes to keep everyone laughing. The vegetarian thali became "tree hugger," uttapam was "Uma Thurman," and chicken pakoras were "pachyderms." The cooks were abundantly entertained watching the perplexed looks on food runners' faces hearing them call out, "Can I get three tree huggers with a cheesy Uma Thurman and four sides of pachyderms?"

People were given nicknames as well, most of them meant in good humor. In the front of house there was "Frodo" for his lost Hobbit look, "Maria" from *The Sound of Music* for her tendency to wander around in circles with her arms outstretched wide when looking for something, and "the Riddler" for her relentless habit of using way too many words to ask questions.

Kipper, an old friend who'd just moved to Asheville from San Diego, joined the front-of-house team after I ran into him on the sidewalk. His exuberant, larger-than-life personality kept us all in good cheer. He was a uniter who helped us stay bonded as a team—both front and back of houses. His enthusiasm also ensured that our customers got the same level of attention that I wanted them to have when I wasn't the one taking their orders. He would get so excited explaining the menu to new guests, he'd high-five them with such intensity that people would lose their footing.

Meherwan's hair had grown into an unruly helmet of curls that shook in response to his frantic ringing of the "order up" bell. It would echo over the patrons dining in the space, infusing the air with alarming urgency—making us jump in response. We began to assess Meherwan's stress level based on the pace of the bell ringing. He managed the intensity of the work fairly well, but sometimes the exhaustion would seep out in momentary bursts of frustration. The staff took those flashes in stride. They seemed to understand that he was working himself to the bone, so they forgave his moments of intensity. This wasn't always the case, but their patience with the ridiculous pace we were all working was remarkable.

Kipper's girlfriend at the time, Sara, was dining in Chai Pani one particularly busy lunch when Meherwan was ringing that bell like a madman. Realizing that we had to get more runners into the mix to get the food out faster, I hired her on the spot, in the middle of her lunch. Sara fit right in. After learning the ropes, she started keeping a little book behind the bar entitled "Crazy Shit Meherwan Says." In it she recorded the litany of ridiculous jokes and (sometimes) inappropriate, hilariously out-of-context, good-humored things he'd say during a busy shift. When levity was needed, she'd read them aloud to lighten the mood and entertain the staff. Thanks to that team, showing up for work was like going to a party with great friends.

I was undergoing my own transformation as we settled into our new restaurant life. By leaning into my natural instincts, I was becoming the "Caregiver in Chief." I tried to ensure that everyone, no matter their role, felt valued and seen. The team started calling me "Chai Pani Mom," and it stuck. I'm comfortable in the role of mother and see it as a place of strength. It's not appropriate to expect that all women leaders should want that role—or that all businesses need a mother figure in order to thrive. It's just what came naturally to ours and was what we needed at the time.

I was significantly older than most of the people I was working with, so I wasn't trying to be their buddy or fit in with them socially. I was comfortable just being myself. This led me into a style of management that worked for me. I attempted to lift everyone up into success instead of managing down with relentless direction. I believed in them and tried to help them believe in themselves. I relied on this management strategy to soften the impact of the chaos of our beginning. I also became the counterpart to Meherwan's more directive style of managing. We balanced each other, and that helped us all get through the opening year.

The first year of Chai Pani continued at the same breakneck speed with which it began. We learned by trial and error, made countless mistakes, and worked harder than ever before. But the exhilaration we felt in finding work that we loved fueled us.

Meherwan becoming head chef had a significant impact on our personal life. With his new role in the kitchen, we had even less time together. It took some effort and time to figure out how to manage our workflow and home life as we tumbled through.

We still did *everything* ourselves. The restaurant couldn't afford a laundry service, so at the end of my shifts running the register, I would double-park in front of Chai Pani and load the day's dirty kitchen rags into the back of my minivan. Each bag weighed about eighty pounds and reeked beyond description. Most days I made it to the laundromat with enough time to throw the rags into the high capacity washing machines before rushing to pick Aria up from school. Then I'd drag her with me to transfer them to the dryer.

One day, Aria's friend was coming home with us from school, and I didn't have time to get to the laundromat before picking them up. Aria and her friend climbed into the backseat and shrieked, "Oh my god! What is that smell?" I had become so used to the stench of dirty rags that I'd blocked it out. Anyone who's worked in a professional kitchen will tell you that the used rag bin gives off a foul smell unlike any other—one that's pretty impossible to ignore. It's shocking what we become too tired to notice. In the first year of running Chai Pani, I was that tired all the time.

I bribed the girls with ice cream on the way to the laundromat, and that distracted them for a few minutes. This is the reality of running a restaurant on a tight budget. **Learning how and when to be frugal is an essential skill in restaurant management, and it's reflected in a million small details—down to the kitchen rags.**

I promised Aria that I'd never pick her up with friends again with those rags in the car. As challenging as it was, I kept my promise. She never knew what it took for me to honor that commitment, or how I shaped my days around picking her up from school on time. I didn't share these things with her because I didn't want her to feel burdened by my choices. Even though it was a lot to juggle, I recognized that owning my own business allowed me the privilege to make my own schedule, and I was grateful for it. The flexibility allowed me more time with my daughter, and that's what mattered most to me.

Managing the conflicting responsibilities of parenting and running a restaurant is no small feat. Balancing home and work life is difficult because the hours are demanding and don't easily fit into traditional routines of family life. When everyone else is on vacation, restaurant workers have to show up. Meherwan and I made it work (only occasionally losing our minds) by having clearly defined roles. I made Aria my number one priority and organized my days around her schedule. I wanted (and needed) to work at the restaurant, but I held on to simple routines like picking her up from school as a way to remain consistent for her. In order for me to leave my shift in time to pick her up, another manager had to come in early. The scheduling was complicated but made it possible for me to be there for Aria in the ways she was accustomed to.

I anchored around the commitment to my time with Aria. When work conflicted with school pickup, I simply said, "Sorry, I'm not available then," rather than putting myself through mental gymnastics every time. The process of wondering if I could be available, or if Meherwan should step in—or worse, how to make myself available every time and place I was needed—would have made us all crazy. Having clear boundaries freed me from evaluating the pros and cons with every decision. From that place, we eliminated daily tension around the logistics of life, and we could relax into our chosen roles.

There were many times when this impacted what work I was available to take on. But the way I saw it, we were a stronger family unit if I hired out the things I could delegate at work instead of delegating away my time with my child. I savored being Aria's mom and didn't want to miss her childhood. This worked well for us because we chose roles that came naturally to both of us. While Meherwan craved more time with Aria too, we were committed to providing her with financial stability as well as time with us both, and we were more effective in parenting and in our business if we each prioritized our respective responsibilities. Being truly honest was key—even if it necessitated many hard conversations over the years.

Our delegation of responsibilities required Meherwan to be all in at work—the captain who couldn't take his hand off the wheel or his eyes off where the business was headed. We couldn't both steer at the same time; that would have been a disaster. The buildout needed us both behind the wheel to pull off such a challenging timeline and budget. But once Chai Pani was open and we were running the business together, we tried to stick to clearly defined roles.

Running a business as a couple is complicated, and there's no one-size-fits-all solution. It's possible there are couples who effectively co-lead and co-steer a business, but if they do exist, I think they have some explaining to do. The rest of us mere mortals benefit from assigning one person to make the final decisions and keep their hands on the wheel. Many couples I know who co-led businesses together ended up separating either romantically or professionally. It's that complicated. And it's not the best choice for all relationships or businesses. Meherwan and I landed in a place where we collaborate on the map and decide together where we want the business to go, but I let him drive.

In our business, our personal strengths defined the shape of our most impactful roles. Meherwan is a natural decision-maker and was able to manage the relentless pace and work demands in a way that would have done me in. He could travel to food events where he'd feed and chat with thousands of people all day, go out and network with restaurateurs all night, and then wake up the next morning and slog his way through emails and back-to-back meetings. His stamina as a CEO is a gift he gave our growing company. Mine was my ability to be focused on our people in a dependable way that created a consistent culture at work. I did this while holding all the pieces of our life together in a calm(ish) and cozy container: the birthday parties and holidays, playdates and sick days, meal trains, carpools, homework support, grocery shopping, etc. Tracking the threads of family life while staying on top of responsibilities at work would have made my husband's head explode. For me that came naturally. I could turn work off to be fully present in Aria's life. I did this with a lot of multitasking, as well as working fewer restaurant hours than him and using that time to take care of home life. This freed Meherwan to be more present with Aria when he was home, instead of dealing with never-ending domestic chores.

Our business benefited from Meherwan's ability to hold deep and relentless focus on one thing at a time. And our work teams and home life benefited from my ability to manage running back and forth between two worlds and still be fully present wherever I was. The way we divvied up our roles placed Meherwan as the face of the business when his reputation as a chef grew. This spotlight was an incredible opportunity to elevate our culinary acclaim and helped to set our restaurant apart. So, we ran with it. In the public eye, our origin story as a husband-and-wife duo gradually morphed into the story of a self-taught chef. He started getting invited to "chef-y" events all over and discovered that he was very comfortable in front of the camera and on stage. Placing Meherwan front and center was an intentional strategy that worked for our business and for the phase of life we were in.

For the most part I was happy working behind the curtain. When his mini-celebrity-chef status took off, I was never clearer that one of us needed to be anchored at home to keep things stable. During those years, I tended the nest at home and at work so that he had a solid launching pad to support his ascension.

Being a co-founder is not a role, it's a title. It's a statement of what happened in the founding of our business, not what we do day-to-day. Our roles had to be clear, and when we arranged them thoughtfully, we managed to not stomp on each other's toes . . . sometimes we stepped on them, but we tried not to stomp.

The reality is that sometimes it requires a huge amount of trust when you are partnered with the same person in life and in business. Meherwan ultimately trusted my calls within my zone of the business and with our homelife, and ceded to me when we disagreed in those realms. We argue, we help each other see things we're missing, we both make good cases for our ideas—but we attempt to gauge how far we should push the other person relative to the potential outcome of the decision. For example, if we have faith that a potential mistake won't make a significant impact, we'll try to let it go and set the other free to move quickly. But if a potential mistake feels like something that could break us, we'll put up more of a fight. We learned over time to choose our battles wisely. But in the end, it's an act of courage to trust your partner to make a good call—and know that they will take your input into careful consideration.

Sometimes we made a mess of things. I couldn't always keep my hands off the business wheel, and Meherwan wasn't always clear how to balance his role as a father when so much of his time was spent at work. We continually reshaped and reconfigured our roles. That process is what I refer to as the "messy middle" stage of our growth. We had to keep reinventing how to run the business together, and we didn't always know *how* to juggle parenting and being restaurateurs. There were plenty of missteps and hurt feelings. But we stuck it out and learned what worked for us and, most importantly, what didn't.

One of the goals I had in starting a business was to create a professional culture that allowed some flexibility, not just for myself but for the whole team. If we were going to be a business that prioritized people, we had to create schedules that reflected that priority. Society's tangled and contradictory expectations lead women to believe that we can do *everything all at once*. Many juggle a full-time career while also being full-time caregivers. It's important to acknowledge that it is very hard to do both things with the highest level of your attention *at the same time*. There are impossibly conflicting priorities pulling us in too many directions.

Like many women, I had internalized the narrative that I can and should be able to excel at both simultaneously with 100 percent focus. Attempting that crushed me, leaving me feeling like I was failing both my family and my career. When we settled into running our business, I was able to structure my work with clarity about where and when I *could* give my focus. That freed me to experience a radically more balanced life. I don't view it as a choice between work and family, I view it as a yes/and (if you want or need both), with careful planning around how/when. Women do not need more pressure to be in ten places at once. In order to be able to thrive in my career as well as in my role as primary caregiver, I needed honest conversations and equal participation from my partner in designing sustainable plans for how we would balance it all. All the single parents out there managing it alone should be seen as the superheroes you are—and deserve *radical* support from your workplaces and communities.

Co-founding a business with my life partner was motivated in part by the hope of creating some flexibility with how we prioritized our roles. It freed me to continually reshape my career and adjust the level of focus I could give it based on how much Aria and our homelife needed me. The roles that Meherwan and I chose happened to fall along traditional gender normative stereotypes, but I do not believe there is any right or wrong way to divide up the responsibilities. Plenty of men love being the primary caregiver, do it beautifully, and make that their organizing principle.

When things got confusing (which they did), we would reassess. Sometimes it required a deeper analysis of our skills to adjust our responsibilities. Over time we learned to ask ourselves a pivotal question: **What is our highest, greatest contribution to the business?** This is a way of focusing on where our individual strengths and interests fit with what the business needs most from us. This evaluation helps us discover where our personal superpowers most benefit our work. It's very easy as a restaurant operator to spend all your time dealing with to-do lists that could be delegated to someone else. If we delegate wisely, we free ourselves to make the most impact—and focus where we are truly needed. **Asking ourselves this question regularly also has a major side benefit: It leads us toward the work we love. It keeps us connected to the aspects of our careers that energize and light us up.** We got better at this process over time. As our company grew, we learned to go through this exercise not just with ourselves, but with our core team as well.

Growing up, I loved dance. I took dance lessons most of my life and worked my way up to join a dance company that required dedication. Reaching the level of en pointe in my ballet toe shoes was one of the most exhilarating days of my childhood. Wearing those glorious pink satin slippers with silky ties that wrap up and around the ankle felt magical.

The day I received my first pair of toe shoes, I ran over to show them

Year One: Finding Our Roles

to Margaret Craske. Margaret was in her nineties at the time, an accomplished British dancer and teacher at New York's American Ballet Theatre and the Metropolitan Ballet. "Miss Craske," as we called her, was a close family friend, one of Meher Baba's closest disciples. I loved her stories of the time she spent with Baba because they demonstrated his remarkable sense of humor. Margaret Craske, well known for her incomparable wit, was one of my most cherished people, and our shared love of dance only enhanced my adoration of her.

I flew up the stairs of her front porch waving my toe shoes in the air. She shuffled out with a shawl draped over her frail frame, wearing a grin that stretched across her face. She knew what a triumph this was. She insisted that I put the toe shoes on, as she watched carefully, studying the fit to be sure it was just right. Her tender, wrinkled hands held my foot as she showed me how to wrap the pink ties the way the professionals do. I'll never forget the earthy smell of the lambswool that she stuffed in the tip of the toe as she looked up at me with a knowing twinkle in her eyes. She was reliving her own first moment of wearing toe shoes and generously shared in my excitement.

Then came the hard part of learning how to actually dance en pointe. It was excruciating. My feet blistered and bled from the endless hours of practice; after six months my foot arches fell, and my body (not the ideal dancer petite) struggled against my unhealthy attempts to change it. Reaching the goal of going en pointe was thrilling, but it ended up pushing me past my enjoyment of dance. I was in my early teens by then, and the reality of practice taking all my free time became too intense. After a year, I dropped out of the dance company. I didn't want to spend my whole life in a state of pain. I didn't want to lose what I loved most about it, so I settled into dancing as a hobby. There was sadness in letting go of the dream of dancing professionally, but my teenage brain was ready to focus on other things.

In college I joined the dance company as a stage manager. My background in dance made me a fantastic stage manager, and I loved the thrill of being behind the scenes watching performances through the heavy velvet curtains. There were moments when I'd watch the dancers and feel a pang of sadness that I wasn't out there under the bright lights. But then I'd remember how much I hated performing. That was never the fun part for me. I loved the process of creation—the way the body becomes an instrument to communicate feelings, and with just the right arc of an arm you tell a story, making the music come to life.

This theme of staying behind the curtain became a regularly occurring thread throughout my life. I was good behind the scenes, helping the people on stage to shine. In my twenties I was a doula, supporting women and their partners through childbirth. In my thirties I worked as an executive assistant managing the fabulous life of a celebrity. I did a stint as a professional organizer, setting up systems for artists to support their careers. And then, I helped my husband birth a restaurant. I was effective and strong in the supporting role. But somewhere along the way, I discovered that I wasn't telling myself the whole story.

As our business evolved, I changed along with it. I started to feel some resentment that I was still doing the same job years later, playing the ever-familiar support role, while Meherwan was off learning so many new things. I began to feel constricted by my role in the business. But I kept at it, recognizing the importance of continuity. I was focused on building a strong ethos for our business and changing the notion of what a restaurant could be from the inside out. That was what I wanted and what the business needed. But as time went on, I could feel something nagging at me. If you are invested in the endless learning opportunities involved in running a business well, it can change you.

SECTION THREE

What We Built

Chapter 9

Our Core Principles

A year after we opened, *The New York Times* published "36 Hours in Asheville," an article that featured Chai Pani as one of the places not to miss. Along with a highlight reel of things to do in town, it read, "Asheville residents love their Indian food, and they are particularly taken with a bright, year-old café called Chai Pani." This article landed right before the peak leaf tourist season.

We had just gotten our legs under us after a year of deep learning on the job. A "snowpocalypse" that hit Asheville in 2010 left us relying on our cost-saving strategies while we struggled to recover from a hard winter. We finally upgraded the banner we'd been using for a year with a real sign, handmade by a local metalsmith and lit up from inside for extra visibility. It brought me immense joy to see that sign glowing into the night sky. That simple change felt like major progress. But we were still hand-delivering tickets to the kitchen, washing our own rags, and making do with funky equipment and furniture.

Isaac decided not to renew his teaching contract. He was excited to join us full time, becoming our first general manager. He spent the first few weeks on the job learning every station, including dishwashing. This allowed him to cover any shift when needed, instead of paying someone hourly to come in. His instinctive talents with the art of jugaad were essential as we budgeted our way through that year.

We knew the *Times* article would increase our visibility and business, but we had no idea how much. In those days we didn't have much time for strategic marketing—or really anything beyond the hands-on running of service. Meherwan ran the kitchen along with all the business of the business. Isaac and I handled the hiring and training and when we were on duty managing, we'd also run the host station or register to save on payroll. The three of us juggled the finances, billing, tech management, equipment repairs, ordering, and PR (basically just us posting on social media). We'd had no time for the big-picture strategic considerations the business needed. The *Times* article seemed the perfect opportunity to press pause and come together as a team before things got even busier.

Meherwan and I planned a "staycation"—which for us meant still working but not going into the restaurant. In lieu of getting away, we took a couple of days to do some much-needed deep work. Although we couldn't really afford to, we closed the restaurant for a day and squeezed our team into a hotel room for a brainstorm session.

We started the day with the group piled up on the two beds in the little room. We acknowledged that it felt like Chai Pani was lightning in a bottle from day one, and that was, in great part, due to everyone in the room. It was time to reflect, and for us to put our heads together and get some better systems in place. We asked the group, "What's working well? What's unique about our restaurant? What's broken/needs attention? What needs to change? Where do we want to go from here?" We scribbled out everyone's thoughts on giant post its. The first year of running Chai Pani had required so much from all of us, it was satisfying to spend some time reflecting.

After the team went home, Meherwan and I lay in bed alone in the hotel room staring at the notes taped to the walls. There was so much to digest, endless things that needed our attention, and very long lists of things to improve. But despite all the work reflected in the notes staring back at us, what began to emerge was a definition of what we'd built. In the scramble of learning how to run the restaurant, we had done what came naturally to us. We were hands-on in every decision that first year. Pausing for a day to ask the team, "What is special here?" was crucial in defining what we built. After the experience of firing the first head chef, we realized that we needed a clearer articulation of our company ethos, as well as our leadership goals and expectations. That was the first step toward more effectively teaching our team. Defining these principles would allow us to delegate and find a path for ourselves out of the weeds.

Scribbled across the poster paper, the outline of our core principles was beginning to take shape. "Team culture, warm and genuine hospitality, connection with community, FUN!, nourishing our guests with awesome food made with love, celebrating the vibrancy of the streets of India, introducing Indian street food as a cuisine—a whole new way of thinking about Indian food in the West, treating people with respect . . ." the list went on.

We held hands in silence, enjoyed the quiet, and took it all in. That day would be one of the most important steps toward making our business successful—and the work more sustainable. It wasn't just that we took time as owners to stop and think, we included the team of people who had been in the trenches with us from day one—and we listened to them.

We'd hit on something special, but we had been too busy to see the forest for the trees. For the whole first year of business, we were stuck in a reactive mode and not yet able to be proactive, set goals, and think big-picture. Most of the first year we were running around putting out fires (figuratively and sometimes literally), scrambling to learn how to run the restaurant, and just keeping our heads above water. This is the mode that many restaurateurs spend their entire careers in. **There's always a crisis waiting around the corner that can get in the way of**

doing the deeper work—the work that leads to effective, proactive planning. Learning how to avoid this trap is key to reaching excellence and unhooking from doing everything yourself.

What was reflected in those notes was confirmation that the dream we'd set out to build had come true. Taking one day and night away from the daily grind of running service felt like a week off. The time to reflect felt indulgent (but necessary) after the year of relentless work. It was so impactful that it became a turning point in how we functioned. We removed the notes from the wall and used them to write our mission statement and define our core principles. Those pages captured the things we hold most dear—what we want to make sure never changes. Defining them allowed us to begin the process of effective training so that we could pass the leadership torch to others without fear of losing what was most important.

Our core principles evolved over time, and we got better at articulating and perfecting them. We've matured as an organization and have much better systems in place now. But essentially, at our core, who we are today is pretty close to who we were in year one. We are still an innovative, scrappy organization trying to make a positive impact on the world.

Much of what we discussed that day was considered radical for restaurant management in 2010. At the time of this writing, our industry is evolving. Some of these concepts are now being recognized as "the new normal," which is promising. Implementing them effectively is the challenge, and that learning is at the core of our success.

I've organized the rest of this book around our ten core principles. As our story continued, we were provided endless opportunities for deep practice with each of these ideas.

OUR CORE PRINCIPLES

1. "Mindblasting" Hospitality
2. Being a people company
3. Meaningful growth
4. "Mastery in Servitude"
5. Fostering connection, inclusion, and belonging
6. Finding the elegant solution
7. Designing our own systems
8. What to do when things fall apart
9. Finding where the love lies
10. Storytelling with food and culture

Chapter 10

"Mindblasting" Hospitality

"It seems to me that our three basic needs, for food and security and love, are so mixed and mingled and entwined that we cannot straightly think of one without the others. So it happens that when I write of hunger, I am really writing about love and the hunger for it."

—M. F. K. Fisher, *The Gastronomical Me*

For the first couple of years, I continued working the register at Chai Pani during lunch. We had shifted to table service for dinner, but kept counter service at lunch. At our staycation retreat, it became clear that our roles needed to evolve in order to shift out of survival mode. My role had expanded into director of hospitality, which included identifying *what and how* to teach others in order to maintain the environment we wanted for our guests and team. But I kept working the register position so I could be intimately involved in shaping our service environment.

One day a sweet elderly lady approached me at the register. She explained that she was on a limited diet from her doctor and couldn't find anything on the menu that she could eat. She was there with a group of twelve friends, most of whom had already ordered and were seated at a large table in the middle of the dining room. I looked at her list of restrictions and struggled to find anything on our menu that worked for her. Finally, I asked, "Can you eat a scrambled egg?" It was the only thing I could think of. She exhaled with relief as she thanked me.

It's a phenomenon of restaurant life that curveballs always happen when you're busiest—ask any restaurant operator, and they will have a story to tell. That day was no exception. I got someone to take over helping the long line of people waiting to order while I made my way to talk to "Mad-Eye Meherwan" (one of his many nicknames in those early days), who was running the kitchen. During this phase he was overextended in every direction, and it showed.

Because he was my husband, and it was our restaurant, I wasn't intimidated by whatever reaction he might have to my asking for something special in the kitchen at the peak of lunch rush. I saw he was in the weeds with a full ticket board, so I came prepared. I helped myself to some eggs and butter from the walk-in and a small frying pan from the rack before I approached. I said, "I need to make two scrambled eggs for a guest." He looked at me as if I asked him to bake a French soufflé while flying to the moon. The kitchen went quiet while he glared in my direction. "A scrambled egg? What are we a freakin' brunch diner now?" I smiled calmly and firmly said, "No, but there's a sweet older lady who's here with friends, and she can't eat anything on our menu." He rolled his eyes. But because I was getting in the way, standing there with the eggs and frying pan, he assessed that the fastest way to get me to move was to just make the damn eggs. A line cook took the supplies from my hands and made the eggs before Meherwan had time to say no.

Since I had bypassed a queue of orders, the eggs came out before the rest of the table's dishes. Being the well-mannered lady that she was, she sat there not eating, waiting for everyone else's food to arrive. Of course, the eggs turned cold, so she left them untouched. As much as it pained me to do this to the kitchen crew, I knew what I had to do. I went back with another pan and two eggs in hand. The whole line of tattooed cooks looked up at me in unison as if to collectively say, "What the fuck?" But they were a bunch of big-hearted softies who didn't match their hard-core personas. I said, "Can you spare a burner? It'll only take two minutes." They didn't have a burner to spare, and they definitely did not want me in the way making eggs, even for two minutes. So, they made *another* round of scrambled eggs.

When I presented the hot eggs to the guest, she looked up at me with gratitude and in a deep Southern drawl said, "Well, I never! Thank you, dear. I thought I'd have to give up eating today!" She enjoyed her hot eggs while the rest of her party finished their lunch. That lady became a customer for life—once her special diet was over and she could finally enjoy the menu.

After the scrambled egg incident, I realized that we needed a faster and clearer way of communicating with the kitchen when challenges came up. And we needed an established protocol for everyone to follow to manage curveballs. There isn't time in a busy restaurant to explain the whole story about why you need something special, not to mention that chefs organize their walk-ins with intricate systems that would be a mess if everyone started rummaging around looking for supplies. We needed a way to ensure that the whole staff would go the extra mile to care for our guests, even if it meant making a scrambled egg in the middle of a busy lunch—and even when the owner wasn't there to push it through.

The Way of the Mindblast

Later that week, Meherwan and I were watching stand-up comedy to decompress after a long day. One of our favorites, Russell Peters (a Canadian-Indian comedian), was doing a bit about a comment from an Indian man who attended one of his shows. After the performance the gentleman approached Russell and said that the show was "mindblasting." Russell said, "Don't you mean 'mind-blowing'?" And the guy responded, "No no, anyone can blow your mind . . . you BLASTED my mind!" It is such an over-the-top, classic Indian way to describe something, and we latched on to it. "Mindblasting Hospitality" was born!

"Mindblasting" is the term we use to describe our goal of going above and beyond in taking care of our guests, our community, and each other. The intent is to be surprising and creative in service, and to pay such close attention to what's communicated that we know what to do to demonstrate how much we care. We aim to take people's breath away, and this requires collective creativity—especially in a fast casual restaurant where there is little time or extra hands. It's paying attention to a million details—while remaining focused on the big-picture goals. It's everything we do *to be of service*.

Fine Dining Attention in a Fast-Paced, Fun Atmosphere

Our number one hospitality goal is to help people feel loved—through the food, the people, and the environment. People dine out for many reasons. Conscious or not, they are craving something when they go out to eat. That could be a great meal, human connection, entertainment, nourishment, or even a general feeling of care. Our mission is to fulfill the customers' wishes—even the ones they didn't consciously know they had. We do that by creating a warm and welcoming environment where people feel seen, relaxed, and cared for. To pull this off, our team must collaboratively work together to be on the customer's side, while caring for themselves, each other, and the environment. Mindblasting Hospitality is *how* we approach this goal.

Acclaimed restaurateur Will Guidara describes the goal of creating a "legend" as shooting for an experience that people will remember—one that is surprising, or even "unreasonable." I love this idea, and it inspires our team every day. Our challenge is that we are not a fine dining

"Mindblasting" Hospitality

establishment but a casual, lower price point, high volume environment without the extra support available in fine dining. As Isaac, Raina, and I ran the front of house, we began stretching the boundaries that typically define service. We focused on the unexpected. If a guest was curious about our chaat masala spice blend, we'd bring it to the table in a small bowl for them to smell rather than just explaining its elements. We'd write down our chai recipe for guests who wanted to pick up the ingredients at the store on their way home. A regular customer who always asked for a specific modification on his uttapam got his own personalized key on our register that printed a receipt for him that read "Chris's special." We ensured the mailman and delivery drivers left with an iced chai or mango lassi on hot days. We fished keys out of locked cars for guests (something that always seems to happen on the busiest shifts). And we would walk a guest to their car in a downpour with our own umbrella when they forgot one. **Mindblasting Hospitality is about noticing the details of the needs each guest communicates, verbally or otherwise.**

Restaurants run best with shorthand. Finding the fastest way to communicate what you need while using the fewest words possible is the goal. Over time the term "Mindblast" became a code—a shorthand way to save a lot of words and cut to the chase in our communication. It not only defines our hospitality goal, but it also became a strategy for implementation.

For example, if a cook overfires a dish and ends up with an extra one, he can put it up on the pass and tell the expediter that it's for a Mindblast. Meanwhile, if a server has a guest who's waited too long for their table, or has tipped into the "hangry" zone, they can go to the kitchen and say, "I need a Mindblast." That's code for the expediter to connect the extra dish with that server. No further communication or justification needed. Food was saved from going to waste, and a guest's experience was salvaged by a free snack—all with just one funny word.

Our hospitality goals are lofty: We aim to provide fine-dining attention and care in a casual environment. We broke free from the traditional molds of formal service versus fast casual to occupy the space between. Executing with consistency comes down to translating our grand notions into practical strategies. We rely on our team's ingenuity along with in-depth training to implement a higher level of care without the infrastructure of extra staffing, slower pacing, and budgets that fine dining affords. Utilizing creative ways to engage our staff in the process is key, as is teaching them the craft from the ground up.

When I lived in San Francisco, I dined out regularly and enjoyed phenomenal food—from cheap dives to elegant fine dining on special occasions. But during my time there, I realized that something was missing for me in the dining experience. It didn't matter what kind of restaurant it was, the focus seemed to be primarily on efficiency. It felt transactional. I rarely got the feeling that any of the places, even the ones I visited often, cared that *I* was there. They cared that customers were there—but not about who those customers were. This left me feeling cold. I discovered (to my surprise) that I missed the touchstones of Southern hospitality.

In our restaurant, I set out to create an environment that feels relaxed, welcoming, and warm. One where people of all ages, and from all backgrounds and socioeconomic levels, feel like they belong. Everyone is invited to a seat at our table. Many years later, Chai Pani was named by *Southern Living* magazine as "One of the friendliest places in the South." This recognition reflected years of our team focusing on the details of hospitality. It's those little details that add up to a collective experience.

When I walk into any of our restaurants, I see a room full of all kinds of people. From young college students rushing to grab food between classes to elderly people experiencing Indian food for the first time. People from all backgrounds and cultures post up next to each other at the bar. We created the exact kind of space we set out to achieve.

In order to help each employee understand their role in creating

"Mindblasting" Hospitality

the atmosphere we want, I broke things down to the most basic fundamentals. We teach the foundation first by training every new hire in beginner-level etiquette. The goal is not to stifle anyone's unique personality. To the contrary, if everyone on the team follows these basic practices, we create a consistently warm and welcoming atmosphere—within which everyone's individuality can then shine. Effective training comes down to the details, and the basic "manners" we teach are no exception. Focusing on the microdetails is particularly helpful when working with younger generations who are sometimes more comfortable communicating through devices instead of face-to-face. You can't just say, "Be welcoming." You must show them *how*. It also allows us to hire people without any service background, because we're going to teach them the fundamentals. Every employee is trained to follow these guidelines:

ETIQUETTE 101 OF MINDBLASTING HOSPITALITY

Eye contact
- » This is a great way to communicate that you care and are paying attention to the guest. It also helps people know you see they need help and are on your way. Guests instantly relax when eye contact is paired with some kind of acknowledgment that you see them—best paired with a smile!

Posture
- » Our body language demonstrates that we care to be of service. When we slump over the counter, the guest feels bad about being there, like they are the source of our exhaustion.

Smile!
- » This is quite simply the most direct way to demonstrate care. A warm, genuine, welcoming smile is the fastest way to help someone feel at ease. It matters that the smile is

genuine—a plastered fake smile does not communicate care. If you don't like smiling at guests during service, a customer-facing role might not be the best fit f
or you.

Welcome guests as if it's your own home

» If you were hosting a party and a friend of a friend you didn't know arrived, you would never rush past them without making eye contact, smiling, saying hi, or welcoming them. Take this kind of initiative with our guests. See them, acknowledge them, and help them feel at home.

Stop, drop, focus

» When a guest approaches to ask a question or engage in conversation, stop whatever task you're involved in and pause for a minute to look up, make eye contact, and give the guest your full focus. The human being in front of you takes priority over other tasks. If you get a talker who's going on and on and you have too much work to do, continue with the work while you keep the conversation going (within reason), continuing to look up and make eye contact while working.

Help direct traffic

» Guests get lost in restaurants, and no matter how perfectly placed the signs are, people don't read them. When you see someone wandering around, ask if you can be of assistance. If they ask where the bathrooms are (etc.), if you have time, escort them. If you can't, then point them in the right direction.

Give way to the guest

» A wonderful way to demonstrate respect to the guest is to give them the right of way. Step to the side and gesture

"Mindblasting" Hospitality

for them to move forward. It makes people feel special. It's also the most efficient, safest (especially when carrying trays of food or drinks), and often fastest way to get where you're going, because you avoid getting tangled up in groups and dancing around who should go first.

Maintain calm—even when it's bonkers

» Take an extra second to slow down, take a deep breath (or three!), and get centered when you feel frazzled. No matter what (except 911 emergencies), never run through the front of house. If you work in a busy restaurant, there will likely come a moment when primal instinct urges you to run in an attempt to save time. Don't do it! Do not allow any amount of mayhem to influence your own pacing—it will only make you feel more frantic. Slow down, take a beat (and a deep breath), and move calmly. This helps keep your nervous system regulated and makes your guests and coworkers feel calm.

Make it easy to be a customer

» Approach service from the customer's point of view and be on their side. View the service experience through the lens that the guest experiences it. This is the only way to understand how it feels to them.

Instead of saying no, offer alternatives

» To be very clear: This does not include tolerating abusive or cruel behavior—that is a firm no. This is about what to do when we can't accommodate a guest's reasonable request. The goal is to figure out what we *can* do. The attempt to offer them something shows that we care, even if we can't accommodate what they wanted.

With this training for our team, we set them up with the tools they need to create the *quality* of care we aim for. There are weeks of training on all the operational aspects, but every employee gets oriented to the 101 of Mindblasting Hospitality. The accomplished restaurateur Danny Meyer emphasized in his book *Setting the Table*, that the distinction between service and hospitality is important: "Service is the technical delivery of a product. Hospitality is how the delivery of that product makes its recipient *feel*." We create great hospitality by hiring people who care about other people, then train them to the best of our ability to be set up for success.

Next, we create great service with fine-tuned organizational systems, so the team has what they need where and when they need it. Our workspaces are set up like a kindergarten classroom—everything has a home, is labeled, and fits the container and space where it lives. We utilize checklists that are well-thought-out and regularly updated to guide setup and breakdown for all stations on every shift, and maintain sidework checklists during service. We cannot achieve Mindblasting Hospitality if we're running around looking for paper bags because they aren't stocked where they should be. While this seems like an obvious tool, it's surprising how easily checklists can fall apart, letting the practice slip away. Many factors can make a checklist dysfunctional or obsolete: a management transition, a seasonal change that impacts service, role changes, a wave of new employees, etc. These can lead to a checklist needing to be updated, or taught in detail, for it to be effective. This sounds simple but is way too often overlooked. **Good checklists, if managed well and kept current, set the team up to execute excellent service. Importantly, the team needs to understand why they exist and why they matter. If they are just mindlessly checking boxes without attention to detail, the whole system falls apart. Checklists are an example of how the simplest of organizational tools, if used accurately and consistently, can change the game.**

"Mindblasting" Hospitality

Mindblast the Mistakes

No matter how well trained and organized the team is, mistakes happen. I don't believe there is ever really a perfect service—there's always something that can be improved. But we're not striving for perfection. Instead, we aim to perfect how we handle whatever mistakes occur, and utilize those opportunities to go the extra mile to demonstrate care. Learning how to gracefully manage the mistakes in service is an art form. Comping a meal that didn't meet expectations is the least we can do, but it isn't enough to blast someone's mind with how much we care. It's more meaningful to offer a gift or another dish that the customer might prefer. When we make a mistake, it's on us to give the guest a reason to return.

The team sets out to Mindblast our guests with a fantastic experience, and we encourage them to rely on their own agency to do this well. It's essential that they are empowered to handle mistakes by utilizing their own creative ideas. Communicating mistakes and problems with the manager on duty is important, so that patterns can be caught and fixed in real time. However, getting approval from a manager is not the goal. We don't want the staff to get bogged down waiting for approval from a supervisor to be able to blast someone's mind. This requires trust in the team. We give them some parameters, but then we set them free. **We closely manage the systems, the checklists, and the organizational setup—but we do not micromanage people. Let them be themselves, and they will shine.**

I can't count how many letters I've received like this one from a server at Chai Pani Asheville:

> *I just wanted to send a quick message of gratitude today.*
> *I had a customer this morning who revealed that he had been in the hospital for the last few days after a traumatic health scare, and the first thing he did upon release was come to lunch at Chai Pani.*

SERVICE READY

> He said it was his favorite restaurant and was the first thing he wanted after eating hospital food for a week.
> I Mindblasted him and comped his meal without question and let him know that we were happy he was still here and healthy enough to come see us. This sweet man was so touched he nearly cried.
> I was reflecting afterwards and was just so grateful that I work for a company that allows me to do something like that without worry that I'll get in trouble for giving someone a free lunch. I just wanted to extend my gratitude to you and Meherwan for promoting/supporting this level of care for people.

We have a bank of Mindblast stories collected over the years—examples of what's possible when a team member takes the mission seriously and goes above and beyond to take care of our guests, and each other. One of my favorites was executed by Josh, a Chai Pani manager in Atlanta. A customer called in a to-go order, and Josh noticed that the order had been sitting for a while and realized it was getting cold. He called the number on the order and reached a gentleman who explained that his car had broken down and he was stuck there waiting for the tow truck. The customer apologized for abandoning the order and offered to pay for it next time he was in. They chatted a bit, and Josh determined the guy's location. He then had the dish made again so it would be fresh and hot. Remembering the customer's favorite drink (he was a regular), he bagged it up with the food, wrote on the outside of the bag "Don't worry, be happy," and then delivered it to the guy on the side of the road. Josh refused to take any payment for the meal. Needless to say, he not only made the guy's day, but he also made a very devoted customer.

That guy went on social media to proclaim how great Chai Pani is and how cared for he felt. This kind of experience is the best advertising money can buy. However, that's not why we do it. That sort of goodwill

"Mindblasting" Hospitality

word-of-mouth advertising is a wonderful outcome of providing amazing care. **But, our reason for making the effort is that *it's what makes this business fun!***

Making people happy is satisfying. It even has been proven to change our brain chemistry for the better. A cocktail of endorphins floods our body when we deliver happiness—even by performing simple gestures like holding the door for someone. Great hospitality brings joy not just to those receiving it but to those who provide it. And it applies to how we can lift each other up to make service fun for our team.

Communication Strategies That Unite

In most restaurants, the front and back of houses operate in different worlds. They have different pacing, communication styles, and needs. They speak different languages. It's like they exist on two planets that orbit around each other during service. They work toward the same goal, but with entirely divergent processes. This is often the case in other industries as well: The sales team lives on a different planet from the factory line, or the tech department speaks a different language than the management team.

In the restaurant world, chefs rely on a collective rhythm. In the kitchen on a busy shift, their brains are maxed out—full of counts on dishes, ingredient build lists, pacing, and timing. They're absorbed in the muscle memory of what they're making and the tempo of the environment. Restaurant kitchens are like fire: hot, intense, dynamic, all-encompassing, and dangerous if out of control. When someone asks a cook a question it interrupts their deep concentration and flow. To prevent this, they use code words and simple call-and-response to communicate with each other: "heard," "on the fly," "behind," "hands." Try conversing with any busy line cook in the middle of service, and they will likely stare blankly in your direction as if they don't recognize what language you're speaking and it hurts their brain to try.

The staff in the front of house are also maxed out, but in a different way. They function in the realm of communication, using *oh so many* words to engage with people and field everyone's issues, personalities, and moods. They do this while tracking the needs and orders of every customer they're serving—all while trying to be engaging, kind, and attentive (noticing the expressions on everyone's faces), and managing every point of service. They are fully engaged mentally, physically, and psychologically—while also being on stage. Front of house is like a theater performance—the curtain goes up, the show begins, and they are *on* until the last guest leaves. An effective front of house looks like well-choreographed musical theater: The cast is engaging, fun, creative, alert, and happy—while internally they hold deep concentration remembering rehearsed lines, orders, pronunciations, names, and regulars' favorites. Being the front line for all guest interactions also puts them in the position of representing the guests' needs to the kitchen.

Two different planets using their own languages to achieve a collective goal creates tension. This is why a natural rub exists in most restaurants—a point of friction between front and back of house. Old-school styles of restaurant management allow this tension point to create communication breakdowns and cranky interactions that leave both teams feeling misunderstood. If a server communicates with a cook and gets a one-word abrupt response (normal on planet kitchen), it's easy for that server to misinterpret the exchange as dismissive or offensive. The cook doesn't necessarily intend to be rude—they are just communicating in the same way they do with the kitchen crew. But they might not realize that the server in that moment could be dealing with a difficult customer who's pushing them to the brink. The cook's response can be the thing that tips the server into overload—and often is. But the kitchen is left dumbfounded about what happened. However, a better way is possible, and that's the goal we reach for in our restaurants.

If front and back of house learn each other's languages and respect their different needs, we can approach these high-stakes service interactions from a place of understanding and support. Treating each other with this level of respect creates a supportive work environment that inspires Mindblasting Hospitality for the team as well as the guests. The server representing the guest's needs can communicate with the chef and walk away feeling supported instead of flooded. And if the communication was efficient, the chef won't feel like the exchange broke their focus. This level of understanding requires training. With that in mind, we teach our front- and back-of-house teams to respect each other's unique work environments—and understand each other's languages.

The front-of-house team is taught to:
- » Move through the kitchen thoughtfully and with respect.
- » Call out your presence loud and clear: "behind you," "on your left," etc. *Do not sneak up on people!* Cooks move at rapid speed and need to be able to get around their workstation without obstruction. They have sharp knives, hot oil, flames, and slippery surfaces to navigate, and they don't need surprises popping up that sabotage anyone's safety.
- » Think carefully about what is *most* necessary to communicate to the kitchen team and *use the fewest number of words possible in that communication.*
- » Only communicate special requests to the person on the line designated to receive them. Typically, this is the expediter, since they are specially trained to be fluent in both back- and front-of-house languages (a rare talent).

SERVICE READY

The back-of-house team is taught to:
- » Be respectful in their communications and remember that front-of-house staff are representing the guests, not themselves, during service.
- » Take a breath before responding to any request in order to speak with intention and respect instead of reactivity. Remember that the front-of-house representative is a human being who in that moment is navigating all the personalities and needs of our guests. Simple words of support like "I've got you," or a smile, go a long way.
- » Aim to be on the side of the customer. Do what you can (within reason) to find the *yes*. We can't break the functioning and flow of the entire kitchen by accommodating every special request, but we can stretch ourselves to ask, "What *can* we do?"

When these interactions go smoothly, from a place of mutual understanding, it's spectacular. That experience fuels excellence in service. The two planets can then function with flow—breaking down the barriers that often cause divisions and tension between the dining room and kitchen. From that place of support, we can accomplish anything together. The atmosphere is energizing and fun. We then find the humor about our different planets and celebrate our collective achievements. We become high-functioning teams that embody respect.

The Joy of High-Functioning Hospitality

The hospitality industry is about *being of service*. Achieving this goal and delivering great hospitality does not need to conflict with taking care of ourselves. If we build teams that are loving, well trained, organized, and supportive, we can experience the profound fun that's available to us in

"Mindblasting" Hospitality

this business without feeling smashed to smithereens. If we show up in a way that cares for our guests *and* each other, we receive tenfold back in the form of gratitude and connection.

It's indescribably rewarding to have an elderly Indian man stop you in the middle of the dining room and hold your shoulders while tears fill his eyes as he proclaims, "It's not just the flavors of this food, it's the *authenticity*. Thank you for bringing me back home." Or, when you see a note like this one scribbled in the Chai Pani guest book: "The food is so good, but the service is better than the food. . . . Everyone has been so kind. It's so busy and colorful and dynamic . . . and . . . amidst it all everyone is calm and present. I want to work here." These are the rewards that come back to us when we make and serve food with love and care.

One day I was dashing through Chai Pani right before service to deliver milk the kitchen needed. The front-of-house staff was seated in a silent circle, everyone diligently writing on a piece of paper. I had no idea what they were up to, but Matt Shepard, who was a manager then, was leading the group and gave me a wink, indicating they were in deep concentration, so I didn't interrupt. What I'd witnessed was what a server later declared "the best pre-service huddle ever." Matt, sensing some service fatigue in the group, began huddle by giving everyone a piece of paper. They each wrote their name at the top and passed it to the person next to them. Everyone then wrote an appreciation for each person as the papers made their way around the circle. They all left huddle that day with a collection of sweet notes about them. From something simple like, "Your shoes are cool," to deeper observations like, "Your smile lights up the room," the love notes completely shifted how that team was feeling.

Using a pre-service huddle for group bonding is an example of *how* we built a culture that nurtures our team—making service fun for them. The other important nuts and bolts about specials and eighty-sixed items can be sped up to reserve time for what's most needed.

Over time, we honed our strategies on how to execute this higher level of service and change the experience of *being in service*.

- » We focus on **context over control**.[2] We hire intelligent, empathetic, and passionate people and help them thrive by giving them the freedom to take care of our guests creatively. We provide tools, parameters, and resources but allow them to Mindblast guests in their own inventive ways. That freedom gives our team a sense of ownership over the process and engages them.
- » **Metrics and accountability** are how we track success. We envision what success looks and feels like and then work *together* to get there. We systemize the process, so we can humanize the experience.
- » **We say NO to "no-no lists."** You will not see a line on our menu saying we can't make substitutions or take requests about special diets. We strive to find the "yes" that also works for our team. This is particularly hard in a lower-price-point, fast-paced environment, but this is our creative challenge, and we do our best to meet it.
- » **It takes a village** to execute great hospitality, so "the Mindblast" is a team effort. We break down the divide that exists in many restaurants between the front and back of house by understanding each other. We collaborate in the hospitality mission—and have each other's backs.
- » **Reimagined service traditions.** We reinvent service structures to meet our unique goals. Rituals like the pre-shift huddle can be a chance to bond as a team, instead of just reviewing food specials. With very little extra time during service, we reclaim the time we have and reinvent

---

2 Adapted from Netflix culture deck, jobs.netflix.com/culture.

"Mindblasting" Hospitality

it. Tools like gratitude sheets, bonding games, and videos showing how our food is served on the streets of India are standard practice for pre-shift huddles.

» **Making people happy does not need to conflict with our own well-being.** It's one thing to say this, but our job is to teach people *how* to do it. Service can be a wild ride, one that creates stress responses in the body. Learning to identify our body's signals is an important part of preventing burnout. This is how we foster work environments that support people's mental health.

We provide a basic training to help our teams understand how their nervous system functions. In the rush of service, it's easy to interpret the body's stress signals as something negative. Our fight/flight response can get triggered, leading us into a stress cycle that's hard to stop. Understanding it helps us learn how to ride the waves of service without sacrificing our well-being. This training begins with recognizing the difference between a *stressor* and a *stress response* so we better understand our reactions and can learn to isolate what caused them. Then we can utilize simple but effective regulating exercises to return to balance—strategies that help us take care of ourselves so we *can* show up for others.

The idea that working in the hospitality industry requires repressing our own well-being and plastering on a "service mask" to push through toxic environments is an archaic way of functioning that needs to be left in the past. The old management strategies of repress, command, and control do not work for young people today—and none of us should have to experience them.

Supporting and being there for each other so that we can show up fully for our guests creates a kind of magic in service that is electric, and addictive in the best way. *That* is how we accomplish the goal of helping our guests (and each other) feel the love. *That* is Mindblasting Hospitality.

The world can feel pretty dark at times. We not only want to make some ripples that disrupt the darkness, we aim to drop a freaking boulder of love in the pond—impacting the whole thing. That is how we shift darkness toward light. It's how we make a difference through our work and how we can be a company that makes a positive impact on our communities, and in the world.

Chapter 11

Building a People Company

"If you see Buddha in the lane, feed him the ball."
—Phil Jackson, *Sacred Hoops*

We were driving to work one day in the second year of Chai Pani and found ourselves in a familiar disagreement. I was talking about an employee's feelings, and Meherwan was complaining that the person was being whiny. Meherwan was still new in the role of chef, alongside his other full-time job running the business. He was exhausted—we both were. We were working crazy hours and stacking up too many sleepless nights solving problems. The conflicting demands that most restaurateurs encounter were front and center.

Our team was growing, but we were in a big learning curve with how and what to delegate, and how to manage people effectively. All the questions about *how* to build the kind of work culture we wanted were bubbling to the surface. How do you hold on to young people? How do you teach them the job, inspire them to stay in it, and still get your own work done? There was never enough time in the day for us to do all that was needed of us.

Back to our disagreement... Meherwan was getting cranky with me for trying to address the employee's feelings, and he snapped, "I don't have effin' time for this person's feelings," to which I said, "Pull the car over." We'd had versions of this argument countless times. He was right that he didn't have time to deal with that employee's issue. But we couldn't stay stuck in the same loop. I told him that he had a decision to make. "You can be this mad chef covered in pakora batter, losing it and feeling like no one is meeting your expectations. OR you can start to work smarter. You have the ability to do this differently. You could be the Phil Jackson of restaurateurs! But right now, you're behaving like every other frustrated chef owner, getting increasingly irritated at everyone's incompetence, and digging your own grave on that kitchen line. I agreed to do this with you because you convinced me that we would build a different kind of restaurant culture *and* that we would not get stuck working this way forever. If you think you don't have time for our employee's feelings, then we are not running the business we set out to build. You don't have to figure this out all on your own, but you have *to try* to be the leader you have the potential to be if you want to keep me along for the ride." I sensed I should wrap up this monologue but was excited about my newfound Phil Jackson analogy. Realizing I may have landed on just the right hook to hold Meherwan's attention, I said, "What would Phil Jackson do? What would *you* do if you were looking at this from a distance and not all tangled up in the weeds?"

Meherwan absorbed what I said. I could see the wariness in his eyes, but he was intrigued by my comparing him to his favorite basketball coach, and his wheels were turning. "What would Phil Jackson do?" became part of our ongoing conversation about how to do things differently.

Why Phil Jackson? Nicknamed the "Zen-master," he was the basketball coach in the 90s and early 2000s of the legendary Chicago Bulls and then the LA Lakers, known for against-the-grain management strategies and for bringing out-of-the-box practices like Eastern philosophy and meditation to the world of men's basketball. He also was the coach of my husband's favorite players (Michael Jordan, Kobe Bryant, among others) and was a huge success. He was a maverick—someone who challenged the status quo of what it meant to be a coach at that time. I truly believed that Meherwan had everything in him to be that kind of leader. I could see it, but he was too exhausted from the work to dig deep. I had to push him until he believed it himself.

When we opened Chai Pani in 2009, restaurants relied on toxic, militaristic management strategies that were borderline (and sometimes overtly) abusive. The industry was known for burnout, high levels of addiction, and low retention rates. And it was predominantly a boys' club. There were revolutionaries forging paths toward more enlightened models, but they were the outliers. The average restaurant relied on dysfunctional strategies—some still do. Intimidation, inordinate pressure, and top-down power control was normalized. We set out to bring more humanistic management practices into our space. The realities of the day-to-day challenges made that aspiration hard to live up to.

Prioritizing Our People

In the early days when we didn't have the money to offer competitive pay or benefits, we relied on creating a supportive and happy work environment to attract and retain people. It doesn't cost a penny to listen to your employees and show them that they are valued—it takes time. We understood this conceptually but hadn't fully wrapped our brains around how to make the time to manage the process. Right around when I posed the question, "What would Phil Jackson do?" Meherwan came across a quote written by Howard Schultz, former CEO of Starbucks, that read, "We are not in the coffee business serving people, but in the people business serving coffee." The clarity of that statement helped us reorient how we worked. We began to reorganize our priorities so that we *did* have time to hear from our employees, and if that meant that we didn't get something else done on our to-do list, so be it. **We organized our time around the idea that we are a people business that happens to serve awesome food—not a food business that happens to employ people. This has to be reflected in everything we do.**

We begin with an assumption that everyone has something to contribute. We challenge our managers to think about that when they interact with every single person on our team. From the seemingly whiny employee with so many feelings, to the dishwasher who can't manage to show up on time, we stretch ourselves as leaders to find everyone's strengths. This helps them find it within themselves. **Learning how to lift people up into their roles instead of managing down with constant criticism is key.** I ask the team to think of each employee as if they are their own child—how would you want them treated? Probably with clear direction, honest feedback, respect, and kindness—right? Once we started practicing this, we discovered that everyone *can* make their own unique contributions once they feel seen, respected, and encouraged. The seemingly dysfunctional dishwasher is also a pro-level saxophone player who can't get to work on time because he's playing music all night. Is it worth coming up with a special schedule that fits his other job if the solution also works well for the restaurant? If it means he will stick around and be a productive team member, then yes!

Over the years we lost people who jumped ship for a dollar an hour more at another restaurant. A line cook quit for a higher rate of pay somewhere else. He lasted one day there and then asked for his job back. One shift at the other place helped him discover how much he valued the work environment in Chai Pani. We welcomed him. This happened on many occasions, and the people who stayed (or returned to us) were the ones who cared more about the quality of the work environment than the extra pay. That dynamic is contagious, and like attracts like. This led to us being able to build teams with solid retention and happiness levels. **Happy teams can execute excellence in hospitality with authenticity.**

This creates a cycle of success for the business once the critical mass of employees are there for similar reasons. When that tipping point is reached, it becomes more self-sustaining.

It took time for us to get there (and is always a work in progress), but our strategy led to the business being so busy and successful that down the road we *could* pay more competitive wages and offer benefits and health insurance—along with a healthy and happy work environment. What we discovered is that **the quality of the work environment hooks people above benefits and pay. A dollar an hour more doesn't prevent burnout, but a supportive and positive work environment can.** Anyone can offer benefits (or should), and a well-run business maximizes what they can pay their teams—but that is not enough to hold on to or grow people. We aim to create a work environment that people look forward to being in.

A People Culture

We made kindness cool—and rewarded it. Looking out for each other became a cultural norm. In the early days, I modeled the level of care I wanted our leaders to embody. If we wanted a work culture that prioritizes our people, we had to walk the walk. If an employee was sick, I drove them to the doctor. Someone was struggling with addiction, so I found a subsidized rehab program for them. When a tragic accident or loss happened in our team, I brought in trauma counselors to lend support. Isaac bailed someone out of jail for a traffic violation and picked team members up at all hours of the night when their cars broke down.

Workplaces often segregate the personal from the professional with a strict line in the sand, and when that happens an opportunity is lost. Professional boundaries are important, but they can be applied in a more nuanced way. We create an environment where people can ask for help when they need it and feel comfortable bringing their authentic selves to work. When people can be themselves, it creates a real community—and that strengthens the organization. That quality of care for our people came naturally to us because it's what we set out to create from the beginning. This set the tone for others to follow. Over time, I discovered that we didn't need the "mom" in the room to model it, we just had to teach it.

We established a monthly "Amblastador" award that highlighted a team member who'd gone above and beyond to take care of a guest or someone on the team. People could anonymously recommend someone by dropping their name and a description of why they were nominating them into a slotted box (bedazzled, of course). One manager won the monthly award because a team member nominated them for consistently taking the time to greet every staff member in the building when they arrived. Another person won because they noticed the kitchen getting slammed on a particularly busy shift, and with their own money, they ran over to the ice cream shop next door and bought a round of milkshakes for the whole kitchen crew.

We supported the team in every way we could, but I learned the importance of having clear boundaries, and how to avoid being a therapist. The need for this became crystal clear one day as I was meeting with an employee who was going through a difficult crisis. I realized I was in over my head as he asked me very personal advice on what to do. My brain scrambled to find answers that I wasn't trained to provide. I fumbled the interaction, and the dynamic with that employee got overly complicated. Over time I learned to say, "I care about you. And, I'm not qualified to offer advice in this area. Can I connect you with some good recourses for more support?" We now train managers to communicate this boundary when needed and we keep a vetted list of professionals to refer people to.

We started building our people culture by onboarding people we liked. Those people became managers and then hired people they liked, and that sustained the quality of the work environment as we grew. It wasn't about creating homogenous teams of people who were all the same. It was about finding different kinds of people who had one thing in common: They cared. The impact of that one strategy led to teams of people who enjoyed working together.

In hiring, we prioritize empathy and kindness over restaurant experience. This requires us to do a lot of training. But we believe it's worth it, because we struggle when we hire people based only on their experience level, not culture fit or personality. The number one reason we let people go is for being mean or disrespectful. They are given clear feedback first and opportunities to change, but ultimately **you can teach all the technical parts of a job, but it's much harder to teach someone to care about others.**

During that busy time around *The New York Times* article, a young woman named Charlotte moved to Asheville. We'd met a few times when she was a teenager at the Youth Sahavas. I knew her to have a bright presence and warm personality, and I wanted to get to know her better. I leaped at the chance to bring her on board, but (like myself at her age) she was convinced she'd already had enough of restaurant work. Charlotte was twenty-one years old and had moved to Asheville to be near friends. She was crashing with her close friend Ruby until she figured out her next steps. Ruby had worked with us since our opening and was one of the brave souls thrown into a management role (with very little training) during our tumultuous early days. Sleeping on Ruby's floor, Charlotte listened every night when Ruby came home and vented about how crazy things were, how we didn't have a POS system, and every shift was bananas busy. But eventually she realized that everyone she loved in town was working at Chai Pani—so she gave in and joined us. She quickly became one of our top performers. From her first day on the job, she fearlessly tackled whatever challenges she faced and immediately emerged as a leader.

I knew Charlotte was going to be a keeper after her interaction with one particular employee. To manage the influx of business from the *Times* article, we rapidly hired up. In the rush to get more support, we hired a few people who were not great culture fits. I found one of them extra challenging. For the sake of this story, I'll call her Tammy. Tammy seemed to be indoctrinated in old-school restaurant behavior, where people look out solely for themselves and gossip is normalized. I've worked in plenty of restaurants like that and hate that kind of high school environment.

I started to get increasingly agitated whenever I had to work with Tammy. It was difficult for me to manage her effectively. She'd get defensive and roll her eyes, spinning off in a huff like a teenager whenever I provided feedback or redirection. But she wasn't a teenager; she was a grown woman with a ton of restaurant experience. When she did engage with me, she always had an excuse or reason that justified her behavior. She might blame our setup, management style, or lack of this or that. Part of me would get jumbled each time we talked because, on the one hand, she made some valid points. Working at Chai Pani in those days *was* chaotic—she wasn't wrong. We were doing our best but couldn't fix all the things that needed attention. We were barely managing the increased volume, so I kept trying to work with her on adopting a more collaborative attitude. But whatever I tried didn't seem to be working.

Then during one busy shift, Charlotte stepped in. Her usual easy-going demeanor had been pushed too far, and she was done tolerating nonsense. She stood elegantly tall as she took Tammy aside right in the middle of the kitchen and said, "You can't be mean to people if you want to work here. It's a deal-breaker." Tammy appeared flummoxed at being scolded by a young server, but it was clear that Charlotte meant business. The direct peer pressure seemed to help Tammy "get it" and led to some concerted efforts on her part to adapt to our culture of taking care of one another. While we appreciated Tammy's efforts, the best of intentions do not always pan out, and in the end we had to part ways with her. But what we learned from the experience helped us.

A few important things happened when Charlotte took it upon herself to confront what she rightfully perceived as unacceptable behavior.

1. It clarified how important it is for everyone on our team to carefully protect the work atmosphere from being skunked by people who don't value it.
2. It helped me realize that a highly effective team is one that feels safe to speak up and is empowered to take action to protect their environment when needed.
3. I saw the potential in this remarkable young woman and knew that I wanted to grow Charlotte into a leadership position. When someone elevates the environment just with their presence, and backs it up with their actions, you fight to hold on to them.
4. Her actions helped me recognize the power of simple directness, something that I needed to work on in myself.

Individual professional development is key to preventing burnout in high-pressure jobs. That's a reality that can't be ignored. Washing dishes will always be a tough job. But if you can *master* being a rock-star dishwasher, there's very little you can't accomplish with the right support and training. In our industry we often employ young people working their first jobs, so we introduce them to the notion of *mastering* your zone of responsibility. Working in a restaurant orients them to the idea of a work ethic, and then we teach them how to reach excellence in their role. I wish that working in a restaurant was mandatory for everyone, because there really is nothing like the education it provides.

A "people culture" is fostered by mentorship and working with every employee on their personal growth plans. Providing opportunities for people to grow their skills and knowledge keeps them interested in the work. We think of growth not like a ladder but like a rock-climbing wall, where your next move could be one of several and might feel more diagonal than straight up.[3] This helps them stay engaged, looking forward, and inspired to try new things they find interesting. It's not about promising a specific position if they do x, y, or z, it's about education and inspiration. Our commitment to grow as a company stems from our desire to hold on to our people and provide engaging careers for them. This requires proactive mentorship beyond what is considered typical for our industry.

The Impact of Check-Ins

Since the early days, we've had a practice of check-ins with all employees. When Meherwan and I were hands-on running the restaurant, one of us personally spent time with every employee. Initially I started this practice from a reactive place. Whenever there were issues or some kind of interpersonal drama, I met with each person involved to individually hear their perspective. This worked wonders to unwind the little things that can spiral out of control and take over the dynamic of a team. What started as my instinctive reaction to conflict grew into an important practice that shifted from reactive to proactive. This helped us develop mentorships with every employee. It became a way to get to know everyone, provide strategic advice for their career trajectory, hear how they're doing, and help resolve conflicts when needed.

Check-ins are a valuable management strategy because:
1. Getting one-on-one time with people is important—for them as well as for us. They feel seen and heard, and it shows their perspective matters, strengthening connection.

---

[3] Inspired by the book *Help Them Grow or Watch Them Go* by Beverly Kaye and Julie Winkle Giulioni.

2. They provide us with essential information we need to keep improving how we do things.
3. They create a mentoring relationship and foster trust. When trust is established, mentees seek you out for advice on how to improve in their work—they ask for feedback. They understand that you are there to help them succeed, which allows space for dialogue and refinement.
4. Communication goes both ways and is not just about giving feedback. This is particularly important in restaurants, because the time we spend working alongside each other is wrapped up in the speedy swirl of service.

In the early days, I had not established clear guidelines for check-ins, so Meherwan and I had our own versions. Sometimes Meherwan's check-ins became feedback sessions where the whole time was spent giving the employee direction. Feedback sessions are important, but that wasn't my goal for check-ins. I also had not communicated clearly with the staff what to expect in these meetings. I realized after seeing some deer-in-the-headlights looks that people were afraid they were about to be fired! One cook, upon hearing that he needed to set up a check-in with Meherwan, took me aside with trembly hands to ask, "What the f is a *check-in*?" Additionally, we needed a more strategic and organized way to schedule check-ins. The reality of finding the time to do them consistently was a challenge.

I had work to do to execute my vision more successfully. Enter, my friend Annie (who also happens to be the mother of the fabulous Charlotte). Annie teaches management strategies to organizations and offered to train Meherwan in "active listening." She convinced me that it is one of the most effective tools for managing people. And, she smartly recognized that the best way to get this happening consistently was to sell Meherwan on its efficacy.

Active Listening as a Management Tool

The idea of having to spend time practicing something called "active listening" practically made Meherwan want to bolt. He was up to his eyeballs with problems, and the last thing he wanted to do was devote more of his time to making space for people to complain. Annie sold him on the idea by demonstrating that it was a highly effective way to resolve conflicts and issues, get "buy-in" from the team, and foster the kind of work culture we want along with giving people the feedback they need. To close her pitch, she added, "It's also the best way to get your kid to listen to you when she becomes a teenager." He agreed to give it a try.

We hired Annie to do some one-on-one active listening trainings with Meherwan. And by "hired" I mean she offered her time freely, knowing we had no money to pay her. Much later down the road I was able to officially hire Annie (and pay her!) to train our managers in the practice. Her guidance is now woven into our manager training program.

Learning the art of active listening singlehandedly changed how Meherwan manages people. Looking back on those early restaurant years, it's easy for me to see how it also helped our relationship. Our management struggles in those early days boiled down to two personal themes:

1. To be more effective with his feedback, Meherwan needed to soften his communication style to avoid overwhelming people. Deeper listening, less directing.
2. I needed to learn to be more direct and proactive with my feedback. More clear-cut guidance, less coddling.

When we didn't actively work on these things, we'd butt heads. It's not great for a married couple to be in a constant loop of critiquing each other's imperfections at work. Learning the art of active listening helped us change that dynamic. It's a tool that helped both of us become more effective leaders.

Meherwan began to rely on this practice, and it was a game changer. He loved the shift it made in his interpersonal dynamics and how effective it was in resolving conflicts—as well as getting a team to want to hear what you have to say. The idea of active listening is simple, but the *art* of it is nuanced.

THE KEYS TO ACTIVE LISTENING[4]

Physical Attention
- » Face the person who is talking.
- » Notice the speaker's body language; does it match what they are saying?
- » Try not to do anything else while you are listening.

Paraphrasing
- » Restate basic ideas and facts to show you are listening and understanding what is being said.
- » Check their meaning and your interpretation.
- » Check to make sure your understanding is accurate by saying: "It sounds like what you mean is . . . Is that right?" or "So what happened was . . . Is that correct?"

Reflecting
- » Show that you understand how the person feels.
- » Help the person evaluate their feelings after hearing them expressed by someone else.
- » Reflect the speaker's feelings by saying: "Are you saying that you're angry/disappointed/glad because . . . ?" or "It sounds like you feel . . ."

Clarifying
- » Get more information.

---

4   Adapted from the Global Peacebuilding Center, United States Institute of Peace. www.buildingpeace.org.

- » Use a tone of voice that conveys interest.
- » Ask open-ended questions, as opposed to yes/no questions, to elicit more information.

Encouraging
- » Show interest by saying: "Can you tell me more about that?" "Really?"

With this practice in place, we approached our staff check-ins with a clear process to follow. Just having a process provided a surprising level of clarity with how to tackle sticky team dynamics and issues that came up. We discovered that simply learning how to *listen* well resolved much of people's frustrations. They felt heard and respected. When you repeat back to someone what you hear them say, it helps them realize what they feel. That experience is validating. Through that process you get to the core truth. Not only do people feel heard, they become clearer about what's really bothering them. Since so many issues get resolved through the process of active listening, we had fewer "problems" to solve. The problems we did need to resolve were more straightforward and easier to manage.

We learned the hard way that one-on-one check-ins are much more effective for resolving conflict than larger group listening sessions. During one unusually bumpy patch with Chai Pani's team, our GM called the staff together. His intention was to do some active listening with the group so their concerns could be heard in hopes of resolving tension that was brewing. Throughout the meeting, a few upset people dominated the conversation. Their intensity whipped the whole group into a frenzy, and the GM was left feeling defensive. He confessed to me later that it was the hardest meeting he'd ever facilitated. The large group dynamics had inadvertently created an "us versus them" dynamic—the opposite of his goal. Over the years we attempted different versions of group meetings to address concerns or conflicts. These almost always ended in disaster. That kind of complex group listening session would likely be more successful with a professional facilitator. However, when we sat down one-on-one with each individual, we could get to the bottom of the problem and move forward.

Getting the full team together is important—but in our experience, that group time is best reserved for staff meetings, announcements, trainings, and celebrations.

Active listening helped us become the people company we want to be—not just in theory, but in practice. It's not that problems don't arise—conflicts are part of life, especially when working with teams. People are messy and complicated. We can't expect to have zero challenges. **Our goal is to create a work environment where those conflicts can be resolved, not repressed.** This is how we grow highly functioning teams that are not afraid to tackle challenges and are able to work through things that might otherwise bog us down.

Somewhere in our second year, check-ins became official, not just something we did in response to problems. We schedule them a couple times a year, and every person on the team meets privately with their supervisor.

During that time, they are asked about:
1. Strengths: What has been going well in the last six months? What is something you feel proud of accomplishing?
2. Challenges: What has felt needlessly difficult? Is there anything that you set out to do but encountered roadblocks or other issues that prevented you from meeting your goals?
3. Goals: What would you like to accomplish or work on in the next six months? What do you hope the next six months will look like for you?

4. Support: What can your managers or coworkers do to help you reach these goals?
5. General Comments: Is there anything you would like to share?

Managers track their notes on a form along with action items to fill out, specifying "what" and "by when." This provides them with a tool to manage plans for any needed changes and follow them through to completion. This is how we track progress and make sure any action that's needed has been taken. And when hard things come up during the check-ins, instead of being reactive or defensive, we actively listen.

It's a huge investment of time to implement a practice like this across a company. Time is a resource. But we consider the investment of this resource a way of honoring our commitment to being a people company. Through the years we learned to carry that goal into every decision we make, into all aspects of the business—from the quality of our work environment to our budgeting. It's how we created a culture that people want to be a part of.

There's a lot of buzz about putting people first as a business retention strategy. Learning *how* to do that practically and authentically was fundamental to our growth and success. **Prioritizing our people means keeping that concept front and center in everything we do—including our own growth planning.** For our team to continue to grow with us, we needed to grow the business in order to provide opportunities for them. We were just starting to get our legs under us after the first couple of years, but the desire to hold on to our people tumbled us headfirst into conversations about expansion.

Chapter 12

Meaningful Growth

"The only way a company can grow, stay true to its soul, and remain consistently successful is to attract, hire, and keep great people."
—Danny Meyer, *Setting the Table*

After a few years of running Chai Pani, we'd mentored a team that we trusted, and they were ready for bigger roles. It was time to grow.

Our first step was building a downstairs bar and lounge. When the small bookstore on the lower level of the Chai Pani building moved out, the landlords offered us the space, and we jumped. We had finally gotten our full liquor license for Chai Pani, and since the spaces were connected, we could utilize the same license for both spots. Continuing to jugaad our way through, we transformed the old bookstore into a cool cocktail lounge. We once again relied on ingenuity to create a beautiful space on a tiny budget. The design was inspired by the vibe of Indian streets at night—with twinkly lights and distinctly darker jewel tones in contrast to the bright upstairs restaurant. Mikey handmade dioramas filled with funky memorabilia and collectibles from around India. I found a stunning piece of handmade wrapping paper with a gold paisley design laid over a regal sapphire-blue background, which Mikey turned into wallpaper by "modpodging" it to the bathroom walls. His brother,

Daniel Files, did much of the work by plastering the small squares of fibrous paper onto the walls with craft glue—and then shellacking the whole thing with a washable finish. It was an insane project (and would be impossible to ever remove), but the dramatic impact of that wallpaper was worth the ridiculous undertaking. Mehera, whose photos decorate the walls of Chai Pani, did a nighttime photo shoot of streetscapes in India, bringing our walls to life with scenes that unfold around food carts at sundown.

We named the place MG Road Bar and Lounge in honor of the main street in most Indian cities that becomes the central hub of activity. We wanted to create a neighborhood gathering place, as well as a spot for people to hang out while waiting for a table upstairs. MG Road Bar and Lounge became exactly that. It went through many evolutions, adapting its look and story with the changing tides of our city. At the time MG Road opened, Asheville had only a couple of high-quality cocktail bars. MG Road filled a needed niche and leveled up the bar scene in town, making a mark by being an approachable and welcoming environment serving elevated cocktails.

With our confidence boosted from that success, we began to strategize opening a second restaurant. In late 2012, Isaac's brother-in-law, Joey, found a great spot for a potential Chai Pani in Atlanta. It was the perfect (hard to find) combination of a funky old restaurant space (i.e., affordable) in a great location. We made a quick trip to Atlanta to scope it out.

Housed in an expansive renovated industrial garage, the former restaurant owners had left behind all their outdated furniture, fixtures, and equipment. They'd closed it up with everything left in place—from the mussel shells littering the kitchen floor to supplies still in the storeroom. A new concept would require a thorough deep cleaning and full redesign, but the space checked all our boxes. Good location, walkability, activated nearby community, *and* a presence in Decatur, a large suburb of Atlanta—a major metro market. This would give our growing brand much more reach and visibility—an important next step after opening our first location in our small hometown. On paper everything looked right, but something about the expansion was making me uneasy.

As we talked it through, I started to feel worse. Meherwan was convinced that it was the right time to take this step. Chai Pani's popularity had surpassed all our projections. We had a loyal fan base, we'd already expanded with a successful bar, and importantly, our team was ready for growth. I understood all of this. But then Meherwan said, "If we don't open in a bigger market, we will not be able to make a profit." Even though I knew he was right, he was touching on the core of my concern.

We were up against the volatility that all restaurants face, where a bad winter (we'd just experienced Asheville's two worst winters in thirty years) or an increase in cost of goods would put us in the red. We had no savings, were still paying off our original investment in the first Chai Pani, and had no credit to leverage. To survive those rough winters, we'd had to borrow emergency funds from one of our original investors, and Isaac had leveraged his own personal credit to secure the business a credit card because Meherwan and I were still maxed out from the first buildout. The business was thriving in popularity, but we were losing money annually. We were still operating on a shoestring with no safety net and were barely paying ourselves. When cash flow was really tight, Meherwan, Isaac, and I wouldn't take paychecks so we could cover payroll. Financial crunch times are inevitable, especially in an industry with such small margins, and we still had work to do to dial in our revenue model. I knew that growth was one potential path out of the cycle. But I also knew that building a Chai Pani in another city would personally stretch us beyond what our family was ready for.

We managed the first few years by living off adrenaline. The excitement of the popularity of our first place gave us the energy to run on fumes. We'd made some progress in delegating and setting up better systems, but we were still juggling too much because we couldn't afford more support. It felt like we were standing on top of a mountain that took everything to climb, and were just starting to catch our breath. I could see another mountain in the distance—a beautiful one with meadows full of sunshine and flowers, a land where we could afford to expand a fabulous support team—but there was a deep valley between where we stood and that vision.

I was worried we didn't have enough fuel in our tanks to make it across that valley and up another mountain. We had no energy saved up. I admitted to Meherwan, "I'm scared about what will happen when we run out of gas. I'm worried about the impact on our relationship if we continue sacrificing all our free time to the business, and I'm concerned about having enough time with Aria. If we open another restaurant the same way we opened the first one, it could break us." I continued, "You might feel like you have it in *you*, but it requires too much from us as a family." I knew my concerns would disrupt Meherwan's momentum. As my husband, I trusted he wanted to hear them, but as my business partner, I knew he was frustrated that I wasn't 100 percent on board, even though I understood it would be good for the business.

Meherwan challenged each of my concerns like he was swatting flies. His energy was frenetic—similar to the energy that had sparked the first Chai Pani, but this time it was laced with fear. I sensed that fear was driving the decision, and that was the heart of my concern. I wasn't questioning the decision to expand, I was challenging how we could do it more strategically and get fear out of the driver's seat. The conversation lasted most of the trip back to Asheville, and my body felt tense as we pulled into our driveway nestled in the woods. We hadn't resolved the debate but agreed that we needed to shelve the conversation in order to show up for Aria. After tucking her in, we went to bed too exhausted to discuss anything further.

The next morning, I woke up with a fiery rash covering my body. I found someone to take my shift at Chai Pani and called my doctor. The on-call nurse suggested that I was having some kind of allergic reaction, or bedbugs from the hotel in Atlanta. This didn't seem right to me, so I called Evan, my acupuncturist friend. He asked, "Have you been experiencing anything particularly stressful lately?" I laughed. He then said, "I think you have hives." After protesting that I'd never had hives before, Evan asked, "Have you ever been this stressed out before?"

My body was confirming that we could not build our second restaurant the way we built the first. It would tip the balance of our marriage and family life. And we could not use the idea "we must grow to survive" as our primary reason for growth. That would be coming from a place of fear. **Fear clouds vision and our ability to make clear decisions. Doing anything out of fear of losing what you have is not a great reason to grow.** Or, at least it shouldn't be the *only* reason. Meherwan shared my concerns about the balance of our family life, but they didn't dominate his attention as they did mine, and he remained optimistic that we'd just figure it out. My radar was more acutely dialed in to the undercurrents of our family dynamics—just as his was focused more around the needs of our business. My body was screaming for my attention. It worked.

Creating Rules of Engagement

Identifying and voicing deep, nagging concerns became one of our rules of engagement. Over the years we came to understand the value of pausing at important inflection points. This was always my instinct (and often what I personally needed), but it took Meherwan some time to get on board with the benefits of pausing for reflection. After seeing how powerful it can be, we standardized this practice.

Meherwan was right that expansion would insulate us from the financial volatility that existed with our business, especially in a small market with a seasonal economy. Having more than one place would also allow us to pay ourselves from two stores and thus take less money out of each business. This would help us climb out of the cycle of using any profit to pay off debt, only to rack up more debt to get through the next bad winter. Our situation needed to change—but *how* was the question on my mind. As if right on cue, the day that I was home with hives, a tax collector showed up at our house.

When we first started our business, we hadn't yet secured the lease on the restaurant space, so the legal documents listed our home address. Hence, the tax collector standing at my front door as I answered it in my pajamas, covered head to toe in angry welts. The effort to juggle the business's cash flow meant we'd fallen behind on payroll taxes. The tax collector was there to help us come up with a plan to get above water. I was so thrown by him arriving at my home that I didn't fully register he was there to help (the tax man showing up at your house can trigger all kinds of fear responses, and my inner alarm bells were clanging). I asked if we could set up a time for him to come to our office, and he agreed. I closed the door and said, "Ok universe—message received!" I spent the day alone at home making lists of how we could insulate our financial exposure, manage the next opening differently, and build another restaurant without dramatically tipping our family's balance. By the time I went to bed that night, my hives had disappeared.

Most of my ideas about how we could manage another opening differently hinged on the members of our team who were ready for growth. Expansion would allow us to hold on to some brilliant young people we did not want to lose. And I knew that nurturing and growing that team was the only chance we had to move out of the phase of doing too much ourselves. We didn't have the budget to pay the salaries needed to attract professionals with a lot of experience. Growing people up into positions of leadership and teaching them the job allowed their salaries to grow along with them, as the business could afford.

Meaningful Growth

Part of my concern about growth had to do with the state of our marriage at the time. We had become stronger business partners; however, our marriage was paying the price for all the time we invested in the restaurant. In the early days of Chai Pani we said yes to every business opportunity. This was important for networking and the success of our new business, but we had no time together as a couple. Most of our important conversations were happening while we were driving because that was the only time we were alone. We'd given up date nights for family dinners and work events.

This led to us burying issues. We didn't have the time or energy to deal with any tension between us, so we plowed through. Because we weren't managing to make time for harder conversations, we got disproportionately upset with each other over small things. Breaking out in hives was my body's way of waving the white flag of surrender.

This was a pivotal moment in our evolution as partners in life and in business. Time alone (and walks along the coast of Italy) would eventually nurture our love back into harmony—but we were years away from that. We faced a critical decision. We could not flourish if we continued in survival mode.

Criteria for Evaluating Growth Opportunities

Up until that point we'd built a successful business by being totally hands-on. If we went ahead with a new location in a different city, we would significantly increase our workload. We had to do some deep work to uncover how we could open in another city without being in two places at once. As I wrote my list of what we needed in order to manage an opening differently, **it all came down to empowering and training the right team effectively**. We had to get out of the middle of the training process. The work we had done developing our core principles was a good first step toward building a strong foundation. It helped us teach what we value most. But we needed to train more effectively and identify areas of professional development so we could grow our team into positions they didn't have experience with. We had to find a different way to manage.

As I started figuring out what we needed to change, my nervous system began to settle—which allowed me to get on board with grabbing the spot in Atlanta for a second Chai Pani. I agreed to the expansion and approached Meherwan with a plan that I believed would help the business as well as protect our marriage.

Together, we identified management strategies for training others in how to maintain the quality of what we'd built. We also outlined some rules about how and when to grow, and what must be in place before adding another location.

Rules to evaluate growth opportunities:
1. We have several key "culture carriers" we've identified who want to grow with us and are ready for the challenge. Culture carriers are people who embody our company's core values—they understand what matters most to us.
   » They must be prepared for the next step in their careers, with professional development and training.
2. Everyone at leadership level is on board with the plan.
   » This does not mean that the final decision is a democratic vote. It means that we allow time for a process of discovery within our leadership team. This helps us pay attention when anyone on the core team has concerns about a move we're about to make. Fear should not drive the decision but is a nudge for further evaluation. We all have blind spots, so including our leadership team in growth conversations helps us notice what we might otherwise miss.

3. Success is aligned across all avenues of the business. The success of one location can't be at the expense of another.
    » This requires us to have a pool of people in training for leadership, so that if we take managers from one location, they have been mentoring potential leaders to take their place.
4. Growth is for the success of everyone.
    » Our whole team, and each of us as partners, needs to understand how we all will benefit from the growth of the business. Employees are presented with clear plans so they understand why we are growing and what's in it for them. Our success must equal their success.
5. We will only choose meaningful growth.
    » This requires evaluating each opportunity to assess how it fits our company's vision.

Rules we added over time after making plenty of mistakes:

6. Don't chase bright and shiny new things (added after we spread ourselves and our team thin with too many different concepts).
    » Evaluate whether the opportunity benefits our greater mission or distracts from it.
7. If it's not a "HELL YES," then we shouldn't do it.

We also made some personal commitments. Meherwan and I set aside time to be together and *not* talk about business. And we established regular outings for Aria and Meherwan to go out alone together. We also committed to traveling again as a family. Affording big trips seemed impossible at the time, but we knew we could find a way to budget for an occasional vacation if we made it a priority. And we did.

A Flat Company Chart

After evaluating the decision with our team, we decided to take the leap. We began by identifying team members who were ready for significant leadership roles. Out of our approximately thirty employees, about seven of them had been with us from the first year. Instead of shaping our business into a pyramid with a top-down management structure, we aimed to build a flat chart that relied on zones of responsibility. We began the process of removing some of our "hats" of responsibility and delegating more to the team.

The mindset of treating everyone as equals completely changes the traditional hierarchical structure. A position is not a rung on a ladder, but a specific responsibility based on a current skill set. Like any complex system, no single responsibility in our business is less or more important than another. A watch is a good analogy—no one part is less or more critical in the proper functioning of the machine. If even one tiny screw is missing, the whole thing stops working. Each part affects the others—one gear is responsible for driving another. And if the "gear" understands its place and importance in the functioning of the watch, then it understands that the gear "driving" it is also fulfilling its responsibility.

Similarly, in our model **there isn't a hierarchy of authority, there's a diversity of responsibility. Getting a job done becomes a responsibility that ultimately requires a person taking ownership. And key to this model working smoothly is hiring smart people who care about others, and communicating well with them.**

Working with Friends

Mikey was excited to expand Chai Pani to a big city and agreed to relocate to be on-site for the buildout. Mikey has a brilliant artist's mind and an interesting relationship with time management, so it was a process to learn how to manage projects well together. Managing different work styles effectively was important in our growth as leaders. Structuring the process so that it allows for people's individual genius, while still holding them accountable, can be an effective management strategy but is not always the easiest approach. Leaders often miss the opportunity to include some of the most interesting and impactful ideas when they aren't presented in a conventional way. We place a high value on creating magic in our spaces, so we invest time and resources in that process. We had to learn our way through this, but the outcome was well worth the effort.

The relationship I'd developed with Mikey was brought home to me one winter day while we hung Christmas lights. In those days it was up to me to decorate the spaces for the holidays, so I was often in there at the crack of dawn on the Friday after Thanksgiving, trying to hang lights before the holiday shopping crowds descended. I enlisted Mikey's help decorating whenever I could, because he was the only other person on the team who would obsess with me over getting the décor just right.

Mikey and I were in Chai Pani hanging decorations in the hour the restaurant closes between lunch and dinner. I was up on a ladder in the front window of the restaurant when Mikey remembered there was another box of decorations in the storage room. He asked me to hang tight on the ladder while he ran down to find them. After ten minutes of waiting, I sent someone to go find him. When no one could locate him, I abandoned my half-hung lights and went in search. I called his name and looked everywhere. The lightbulb must have burnt out in the storeroom downstairs, because it was pitch-black and I couldn't see a thing. As I navigated the darkness looking for Mikey, I tripped over something in the middle of the concrete floor. A scream that could shatter glass flew out of me when I realized it was Mikey! For a split second I thought I'd stumbled over his dead body. My shriek woke Mikey from his sleep—he had fallen asleep in the middle of the storeroom floor.

His version of the story is that the storeroom felt so peaceful that he lay down to rest his eyes for a second. He said, "I didn't mean to take a nap; something about the quiet darkness down here just sucked me in." Exasperated at having been left on a ladder (and still trying to recover from the thought of tripping over his corpse), I yelled, "Did you forget that I was on a ladder waiting for you?" Mikey confessed, "Yeah, I guess I must have forgotten what I was doing. . . . How crazy that I fell asleep! Sorry about that!"

The bond I share with Mikey deepened when I came to terms with two things: Number one, I love the guy—he is like family. And number two, despite (and perhaps because of) his idiosyncrasies, we accomplish great things together. Learning to manage friends and family is complicated. I wonder if I would have found the humor in someone else falling asleep while I waited on a ladder for them. Maybe not. But this is the thing about working with friends: We understand each other on another level. Forming a deep bond can be helpful when navigating difficult work challenges. That bond makes us work harder at the relationship than we might otherwise choose to.

There is much said about the complications of working with friends. But for us, it has enhanced our business. **Working with friends requires honest, regular, direct communication and conflict resolution as well as a commitment that you will not allow disagreements at work to impact the relationship—or vice versa.** And, going back to the idea that we aim to take what we do seriously without taking ourselves too seriously, it's a shared goal to seek out the humor in the quagmires that arise when trying to supervise humans—particularly when they are our friends.

We are in this dynamic with many people and continue to learn how to best function together professionally, and remember to laugh at ourselves too. Putting Mikey in the position of managing the buildout of the Chai Pani in Atlanta was a big leap. His design capabilities were strong, but coordinating and directing a complicated renovation on a tight budget without us there every day would be throwing him into the deep end without a life preserver. We needed a support team that we trusted to be in Atlanta to help.

Daniel Peach agreed to relocate and head up the kitchen. Daniel had been with us since day one. In the few years since opening in Asheville, Daniel had visited India, become deeply connected spiritually and culturally there, taught himself to speak Hindi fluently, and was nurturing a passion for Indian cooking. Since Meherwan would continue to live in Asheville, we needed someone on the ground in Decatur to embrace the menu with complete devotion to detail. In the early days of the first Chai Pani, Daniel was the only cook on the team who naturally woke up early, so he became the batch cook. He came in at the crack of dawn every day to make the curries. He studied and perfected them with Meherwan's guidance. He taught himself on the job how to become an excellent chef of Indian cuisine, and was excited to step up in his career and take on a major leadership role.

Matt Shepard offered to make the move as well to help with the buildout and management after opening. Matt had become our first "Amblastador" in Chai Pani Asheville. This was the term we used to identify someone manager-adjacent. We needed trusted individuals to help solve problems and represent us with guests when we weren't on the restaurant floor. This role complemented and supported the managers, allowing people to fill in shifts on an hourly basis without the full-time accountability that goes with a manager's salary. Matt was an industry veteran but at the time we didn't have a management position for him. The Amblastador role allowed him to utilize his experience and do the aspects of the job he loved most. Instead of working with standard staffing models used by other restaurants, we created unique roles like this one as needed for our growing business. To really be an outlier restaurant, we had to invent our own structures. Having Matt on board with Mikey and Daniel for the Atlanta buildout and opening would help recreate that atmosphere we had in the first Chai Pani.

Charlotte was our next recruit. At the time Charlotte had been working as a server in Chai Pani for a couple of years. She was trying to figure out her next steps and was contemplating going back to school. Mikey and Charlotte are close friends, and he recognized what a great fit she could be for this next phase of our growth. He was trying to convince her to move to Atlanta to help open the Chai Pani there. Charlotte had only worked as a server and was not a manager yet, but I trusted her. We needed eyes on the ground with the service side of the business, and she was my choice to head that up in my absence. So, I set out to orchestrate getting her on the Atlanta management team. I started by getting Meherwan on board.

Late one night while preparing Aria's lunch together for the next day, I explained we needed Charlotte on the Atlanta team. I couldn't spend Aria's school year going back and forth to Atlanta. One of us needed to be anchored at home. I knew we'd all be there a lot for the buildout, but once it opened, I'd be primarily in Asheville. We had to have people from our team who could sustain our culture in the new restaurant, and Charlotte had the potential to become a powerful leader, and *also* . . . I believed she would provide a good counterbalance to Meherwan's management style. Meherwan expressed some concerns about throwing her into a leadership role untested, but I pushed back and said, "I need you to trust me on this one. We need Charlotte."

Charlotte was interested in the position, so she arranged a meeting with Meherwan. He was impressed by her in their conversation, and also that she took the initiative at such a young age to make a solid and intelligent pitch for herself as a lead manager. This got him fully on board. She accepted our management offer and committed to move to Atlanta for one year.

With a group ready to move to Atlanta, we were securing funding for the new location. Since Chai Pani still had too much financial instability

Meaningful Growth

for us to qualify for conventional loans, we managed to raise money the same way we did for our first restaurant, but this time we needed a bigger budget. It was a cumbersome process, but it came together with multiple loans from friends and business associates. While we were securing the funding, we had to be very cautious with the finances. So, as was the case with our first restaurant buildout, we had to jugaad it.

Mikey, his brother Daniel Files, and Matt moved first to begin the cleaning out and renovation process. They stayed in what we called the "rat motel"—a dump of a place close to the restaurant—the only nearby spot in our budget. Once funding was secure, we rented a house so the crew relocating would have a place to land, and anyone coming and going from Asheville could crash there. It became known as the "flop-house."

When Meherwan and I came to town we brought Aria and our dog, Rosie. We'd rent a room in a dog-friendly hotel with a pool to help make it fun for Aria. She spent many weekends passing time in a construction zone during the buildout and playing in the doggie daycare that popped up as the renovation team brought their dogs with them for the long workdays. I tried to save time so we could explore Atlanta and be together—even if it was just a swim in the pool at the end of the day. Construction zones are not much fun for kids, but I could see how much she was absorbing from the environment around her. The team went out of their way to engage her. She invented funny nicknames for everyone and could read people with astonishing clarity. She would often be sitting quietly amid the construction, reading a book (her favorite activity), seemingly not paying attention to whatever was happening around her. Then later, she'd drop a wisdom bomb out of the blue about something she'd witnessed.

One night as we got ready for bed in the hotel, Meherwan and I were having a conversation about some issue with an employee, and we were circling the topic for too long. She chimed in (surprising us that she'd been paying attention) and said, "It seems like you're stuck on this one; maybe you should just stop going around and around about it." I responded, "Yes, that's the problem, we keep going on about it because we don't have the right answer yet." To which she responded, "How's that working out for you?" She managed to say the exact thing to make us laugh and stop spinning. Aria was wise beyond her ten years. We both missed more relaxed time together, and she sacrificed a lot of weekend play time during the stretch of the buildout. But through it all, it was clear that her brilliant mind was absorbing a lot from being immersed in our restaurant world.

We'd pulled together a great team to be on-site day-to-day and oversee the project, which prevented us from having to live in Atlanta full time. However, we had depleted our Asheville leadership in the process. This is a rookie mistake, but one that's quite easy to make. The impact of this change left us with very full plates, and Meherwan and I were back to not having enough time together. What helped us get through that phase was the longevity of our marriage—eighteen years by then. We had already made it through hard times. We had different communication styles and conflicting needs, but we had a strong anchor that kept the ship steady when we hit rocky seas. We managed to hang on tight enough to each other through those hard years. We could have benefited from some couples counseling, but scarce on funds and time, we both felt that we'd rather spend our resources on taking a trip together. It took years for us to be able to make that trip happen, but it was worth the wait (and eventually we found a great therapist too).

Meherwan finally discovered his personal limit while approaching opening day in Atlanta. His fatigue created some cracks in his otherwise good spirits and high tolerance for relentless hard work. For three days in a row, he checked out of his hotel and went to the restaurant with the intention of working a few hours and then driving the three and a half hours home to Asheville. Each day he'd get stuck until way too late to drive home, so he'd end up checking back in to the hotel. On the fourth day, he honored his goal to leave the restaurant with enough time to make it home. He stopped at his usual roadside Starbucks—the halfway spot between Atlanta and Asheville. After getting some tea to help keep himself alert, he got back in the car and continued driving. After about forty-five minutes, he saw a city skyline appear on the horizon and discovered to his horror that when he left the Starbucks, he'd driven the wrong direction and returned to Atlanta! He called me on the verge of tears at not making it home for dinner. We both started laughing and agreed he was in no state to keep driving. He surrendered and continued on to Atlanta. The hotel staff welcomed him once again, seemingly expecting his return.

Chapter 13

Mastery in Servitude

> *"No amount of prayer or meditation can do what helping others can do."*
> —Meher Baba

The opening of Chai Pani Atlanta pushed us and our team to the edge. We visited Atlanta as much as we could to guide them through the process, but they had to grow into their roles just as Meherwan and I had. Needless to say, it was a chaotic process. Chaotic is probably too gentle of a word. It was once again a full-team experience that required fierce determination to pull off.

Chai Pani in Atlanta is three times the size of the first Chai Pani in Asheville. An old, renovated garage, it has tall ceilings, concrete floors, and an expansive open dining room. The space provided us with much more room to play—in the kitchen as well as with the décor. Our design goal remained the same: to bring the energy of the streets of India into the restaurant space. And once again, we utilized color, street art, large photographs from Meherwan's hometown, and murals to transform the space. To save money, we worked with as much of the inherited furnishings as we could. We kept the janky kitchen equipment, resurfaced the old wood chairs and banquettes, and kept the hand-me-down tables. With creativity, we managed to dramatically transform the space to our aesthetic and turn the restaurant into something wonderful.

We constructed a colorfully painted wooden street cart for the lobby to serve pani puri, an Indian street food favorite. Pani puri is an explosion of flavor and texture—thin, crispy, bite-sized puffs stuffed with potatoes and peas and dunked in spiced water. One bite teleports you to the streets of India, where crowds line up to experience one of the most beloved snacks. We built the lobby to be an active space where people can gather while waiting for a table. Carrom (an Indian game similar to pool but played with your fingers) keeps people entertained. We had this belief that we could make the wait part of the fun.

The week leading up to opening, I arrived in Atlanta for the full staff training. As I opened the front doors of the restaurant, I stood in place for a moment to absorb the scene before me. Isaac was lying on the floor under a table, trying to tighten its screws. Mikey was on the roof overseeing the final touches of the hand-painted sign. Charlotte was seated at a table, buried under the files she created for every new hire. Our friend Will had moved to Atlanta to help Charlotte hire the staff, and orient Josh (Isaac's brother-in-law) as the new GM. Will had a drill in hand as he reattached a cabinet door. The sight took me right back to our first opening.

Kristine spotted me in the doorway and yelled from her perch dusting the HVAC in the very high ceiling beams, "Hey! Can you believe how great this is? I'm having so much fun—it's like a family reunion! We're having a blast!" I've always admired Kristine and her family for their work ethic (her brother Peter helped us with the first Chai Pani buildout and then MG Road). They possess a seemingly never-ending supply of strength, and tackle challenging physical tasks without allowing their aging bodies to give them pause. So, I wasn't surprised to find her up in the rafters—her tenacity perfectly fit the wild ride of restaurant buildouts. But what moved me was her joyful approach to the work that permeated the whole environment.

That kind of camaraderie had set the tone with our first restaurant buildout and ultimately created the culture for our team. I worked hard to guide them, but I was nervous whether it could be recreated in the new restaurant in the way we hoped. After checking in with everyone, I discovered with thrilling astonishment that it had.

Joey (Isaac's other brother-in-law) had found the Atlanta location for us and became an investor to help make it happen. A retired pro basketball player, his cheerful energy matched his almost seven-foot presence that lit up the room. He high-fived me and took me aside, saying, "This is just magic. I've never felt anything like it. I mean, it's totally freaking crazy, but I'm having the time of my life!"

They were exhausted and sleep-deprived—some having slept on cushions in the restaurant for a few nights to save on hotel rooms. They were scrambling to finish their punch lists—trying to pull every possible moment of productivity out of the dwindling days remaining before opening. I recognized the looks on their faces from the memory of our first opening—a rare combination of sparkly creativity, nervous energy, and physical exhaustion that morphs into a giddiness where everything becomes hilarious. Laughter is a tool for surviving the endless and ridiculous predicaments that arise in restaurant renovations. It brought me so much pride and fulfillment to witness that unfolding for them. I knew it meant that despite the seemingly impossible deadlines and work left to do, they were doing it all exactly how we *most* wanted it done. They had their priorities straight and were recreating a happy team culture that sets the tone for all that comes next.

Approaching the opening, Meherwan was back and forth to Atlanta so much that it was making him delirious—as evidenced by him driving the wrong direction and accidentally ending up back in Atlanta. The relentless travel on top of our already full-time jobs left us frayed. I felt like a single parent manning the home front while trying to squeeze in my own trips to Atlanta to oversee my responsibilities there. We were back in survival mode.

My experience of Meherwan is that he has three distinct personalities that he embodies at different times. One is a relaxed, fun-loving dad—seeking out playfulness and quick to laugh and joke. The other is a deep thinker. He puts on that hat when he has a problem to solve, and he goes into a cave of deep concentration to workshop it. His third personality exists on a frenetic frequency. This is his visionary idea-generation mode. He tackles challenges like they're riddles to solve and devours books for guidance until he uncovers a solution. He makes an action plan and then lays on a fierce sales pitch to get people on board, hoping not to encounter any debate.

Coworkers who understand Meherwan well learn to decipher his different modes and respond accordingly. But as his partner, I have a stickier time shifting gears with him. One of our biggest tension points was team meetings. At the time, we were having regular weekly meetings with both restaurant leadership teams. Fundamentally we agreed on a lot, but our styles of facilitating meetings are opposite. I have only one personality—I show up in work meetings the same way all the time, regardless of what I'm navigating internally. Meherwan's style depends on his mood. This dichotomy creates a challenge in how we relate to each other, particularly in times of tension.

During one meeting, Meherwan was questioning a decision made by the Asheville team, all of whom were relatively new in their management roles. He was in his frenetic visionary mode and was moving with intensity. The team was visibly overwhelmed by his reaction. As they sat in uncomfortable silence, I realized that the way he was facilitating left me feeling like I was strapped into a rollercoaster. I was holding my breath as we slowly ticked up an incline of tension. Then I plummeted down into the feelings of discomfort in the team. I noticed the expressions on everyone's faces. I saw their body language when they stiffened through the sharp twists and turns, and I internalized it.

The rollercoaster experience makes me want to intervene, to soften how others feel. You can imagine how well this goes over with Meherwan. It's sort of like me grabbing the wheel while he's driving. And anyone reading this who (like me) instinctively tries to create equilibrium with people when there's discomfort can imagine how uncomfortable it feels on my end. It's not a great dynamic. But here's the reality: The drive Meherwan brings to those difficult moments helps us make progress and is one reason our business is profitable and growing. Regardless of my discomfort, I recognize that hard decisions must get tackled despite whatever we personally experience in the face of change.

It took time (and many internalized rollercoasters) for us to discover that our differences were providing us with the opportunity to learn from each other's strengths. Out of concern for how we were experiencing our communication differences, we worked on it. He learned to read the room and have more sensitivity around how his message was being heard. And I learned to not get so overwhelmed worrying about people's reactions. I also try to not edit him mid-meeting—or grab the wheel.

Establishing Our Zones of Responsibility

As we grew individually and in our roles, we learned to **establish clear zones of responsibility and stay out of each other's zones**. This helped us insulate our personal relationship from the tilt-a-whirl of running restaurants. We had to be disciplined about not meddling in each other's zones. But of course there were times when things got messy. During the peak of the Atlanta buildout, despite all of our "rules of engagement," we were stuck at frustrating odds. One morning at home, we exploded into an argument about how we were both being too critical of each other's communication styles. We were stomping all over each other's zones.

Later that day we needed to attend another complicated meeting, and it was hard to see how we could do that professionally in our tense state. Thankfully, Meherwan waved a peace flag and invited me for coffee ahead of time. We've found that sometimes when we're stuck, changing locations to a neutral place shifts the dynamic and helps us work through it. We met at a Starbucks on the way to work—a spot we could safely not run into anyone we knew while we hashed it out. We tucked around a small table in the corner, firmly planted in our opposing sides. Slowly but surely, we said the hard things. We poured all our honest, mucky frustrations out, even the ones that were embarrassing to admit. Eventually this helped us relax enough to move closer to each other, until our knees touched under the table. It was hard to work through, but we did it. In the end, we both wanted to be heard. When we managed these harder conversations with grace, we could be each other's best mirrors and provide productive feedback—but this can't happen at home in our pajamas! We had to schedule time away so professional and romantic lines wouldn't get blurry. These were the moments that saved our marriage—the times when we chose to walk through the fire to find each other again. After about an hour, we were able to laugh at how doggedly we'd been holding on to our opposing perspectives.

When we left Starbucks that day, we agreed that we needed a strategy for when we found ourselves getting too reactive in meetings. We needed a way to remember the conversation we had that day, and the commitment we made to hold on to what we cherish about working together. From that day on, whenever we get really frustrated with each other in a meeting, we whisper the word "Starbucks." It helps snap us out of taking ourselves too seriously. It's a reminder to give each other some grace while we move through the hard work of running a business together. It's led to some funny moments with our team where we'd catch ourselves acting like a mom and dad trying not to fight in front of the kids. One of us would yell, "Starbucks!" the other would laugh, everyone would look at us like we were nuts, and we'd move on. It helped us return to a lightness of being with each other.

The beginning years of running restaurants together were messy. We trudged through many hard conversations and disagreements. We're both stubborn and can dig in to our convictions. We had to work at it and continue being honest with each other when things got hard—even, and especially, when we didn't have time to deal with it. Those moments were often our biggest opportunities for growth. It pushed us as a couple into a level of understanding that I doubt we would have discovered without the challenge of running a business together.

The struggle to weave our differences made us stronger and more impactful leaders. **We balanced each other by bringing our varied perspectives to the table. We also benefited from the ways that learning and growing together in life and work can change you.** We could never stay stagnant for long (personally or professionally), because work stuff would push us to deal with issues that we may otherwise have found ways of dodging. To successfully lead our team, we had to stay current with each other on the hard stuff so that it didn't start to corrode the strength of our togetherness. This required that we continuously work on our relationship. There are profound benefits to this, but that doesn't mean it's *easy* to be business partners with your life partner.

During some of the harder phases I would question if continuing to run the business together was worth it. But we'd worked through so much together—we trusted if we kept at it, we'd land in a better place. The Atlanta buildout felt like a slog. But we paid attention and did the work to learn from it—growing closer together over time, instead of apart.

Our Company Ethos

With the aspiration of having more practical budgets for restaurant buildouts, competitive salaries, health insurance for our team, and more hands to share the workload, we developed a plan to grow the restaurant group. We also wanted to share ownership stake with a few of our day-one people that had grown into leadership, and we believed that an enterprising strategy would excite them. Opening in Atlanta was a test run. We were counting on this group of young leaders who moved there to learn the ropes and be the team we needed. In addition to the anxiety of wondering if Chai Pani would be a success in Atlanta, we also worried if they were up for the challenge. We had set them up to the best of our ability, and then we took a leap of faith that they would be able to execute at a high level.

On opening day of Chai Pani Atlanta, I picked up Gustavo from work, and Aria from school, and we drove from Asheville to arrive just in time for our opening party. Gustavo had grown his career from managing the dish team to leading the food prep. A big crew from Asheville had been there for weeks to help finish the renovations and train the new hires. Ellis and Robert, managers from Asheville, and our day-one superstar James, were there to help get the doors open. Gustavo and Ellis intended to stay for opening week but actually stayed for years—they ended up being too needed in Atlanta.

Showing up to the opening party without planning it felt like an absolute miracle. It was thrilling to see our new leaders in action. After all the hands-on hard work of the first few years, I could see the path forward. We'd mentored the leadership team to be ready for growth, and this was their night to show us what they could do. It was also the test to see if the culture we'd created in Asheville was something that could be recreated.

I'll never forget the moment I knew they were truly ready for the roles we'd entrusted to them. Right before the first service of Chai Pani in Atlanta, Daniel Peach gathered the kitchen team for what I assumed would be a standard pre-service pep talk. Daniel was leading a kitchen for the first time. He'd started as an entry-level line cook and was now taking

Mastery in Servitude

a big leap. Thanks to the diversity of Atlanta, we had a multicultural kitchen crew. There were older Indian "aunties" in colorful traditional salwar kameez attire, a Black hip-hop DJ cooking as a day job, a white hippie wanting to learn about Indian food, college students from all backgrounds, seasoned Hispanic line cooks, and a tender-hearted, blue-eyed, twenty-three-year-old Daniel Peach eager to lead them.

Daniel had painted a symbol over the dish pit entrance that faced the kitchen. It's a symbol of spiritual significance for Meher Baba with the words "Mastery in Servitude" in the middle of the image. Baba's mission was to bring the religions of the world together "like beads on one string." The image is a circle of symbols from the world's main religions: a Christian cross, Zoroastrian sacred fire, Hindu Ohm symbol, Islamic star and crescent, Jewish Star of David, and Buddhist wheel of dharma. The Mastery in Servitude image holds deep meaning for us, with its focus on what unites religions and humanity—with service to others at the center. Daniel's decision (entirely on his own) to place that symbol over the kitchen showed us just how *much* he understood what matters to us. He was establishing an ethos for the team—and in doing so, helped us identify a guiding principle for the business.

Pointing at the symbol, he explained to the group that there is an opportunity offered to us every time we walk through that kitchen door and with every dish we make. **Mastery in Servitude is our guiding principle. It is our belief that if we bring our whole selves to work, and make and serve food with love, it becomes infused into every dish we send out of the kitchen.** People will feel it, and they will taste the love. That spreads out and impacts the world. We are here to be of service to our guests and to each other. It's a privilege to be of service. It's not just about making others happy, although that feels good. It's also about how that comes back to us, changes us, and brings meaning and joy to our lives. If we show up fully, that opportunity is always here waiting for us.

I stood in the kitchen listening to Daniel's speech, overcome with emotion.

The idea of Mastery in Servitude shaped our company from day one—it became our North Star. **When we think of everything that we do as an act of service, we not only help others—ultimately, we're gifted with the opportunity to master ourselves.** We understand ourselves better, we learn about ourselves, and we grow. This kid that I'd met through our first Craigslist job ad when he was nineteen years old had delivered an elegant and moving tribute to why we do what we do, without anyone asking him to. It's not easy to stand before a group of new employees and speak with vulnerability and depth, especially about a spiritual belief. In that moment Daniel made it cool to care. And, he established that he was ready to lead in the way that matters the most to us.

Meanwhile Katherine (Isaac's sister, who'd been working with us on PR) and Charlotte were putting the finishing touches on a beautifully planned party. They organized an opening night that allowed people to mingle in the space while tasting the food. The tables were pushed aside to make space for Bollywood dancing, and stations were set up around the room like street food carts. Custom food stalls had been built and decorated, each one serving a street food specialty from our menu. The vibrancy of an Indian street was brought to life inside the restaurant.

Charlotte gathered the whole team into a big circle for the last huddle before the party started. She reminded everyone that it's normal to be nervous on opening night. She asked them to remember that the main goal of the party was to welcome our guests to the fun of our environment and to establish Chai Pani as a new place in town. It was ok if everything didn't go perfectly, as long as the atmosphere remained welcoming, warm, and joyful. "That's it. Just greet everyone like they are coming to a party at your home, and have FUN!" We all cheered and hugged each other. As I went to unlock the front door for our first service,

I wiped away tears from my cheeks. Our young leaders were ready. They'd proven that they could build and nurture a team able to take what we do seriously, without taking ourselves too seriously.

Years later Daniel shared with me that after service on opening night in Atlanta, he stumbled home delirious from exhaustion. Once his head hit the pillow, he burst into tears just like Meherwan and I had on the opening night of our first restaurant. Daniel experienced all the fear, excitement, and weight of responsibility that wells up through the relentless work required to open a restaurant. The whole team of young leaders we'd put in charge had held all of it—we no longer had to hold it alone.

Give People Something to Believe In

The ethos of Mastery in Servitude is in part being of service to our people so they can be of service to others. Creating an environment that welcomes everyone and fosters diversity of opinion and background takes work. It requires care and attention. It's up to those in charge to reach across any divide and take the hand of coworkers who might be falling behind. It's a team sport, but it requires open hearts and tender care of each other to create the kind of environment where everyone feels welcome. Executing this well became my primary focus as I emerged from the hands-on running of service.

Growing a business while maintaining a positive team culture that connects with a deeper mission requires clearly articulating your company's ethos. The Atlanta expansion provided an opportunity for our young crew to rise up and demonstrate leadership. From that place, we could continue to expand not only the size of our restaurant group, but how we positively impacted our communities. **Having leaders who fully embody the company's ethos is essential when growing a business that has expansive and lofty goals.** It's important that they embrace the mission behind the goals.

SERVICE READY

We made it a priority to create an atmosphere within our restaurants that nurtures a deeper connection, within our teams by showing them the same care as our guests, and within our communities by giving back. Our "Give Back" program regularly donates a percentage of sales on a particular day to organizations doing important work. We learned how to strategically manage this even when we were not profitable by giving a percentage of sales instead of a fixed amount. This incentivizes the organization we're supporting to be invested in helping us market the event so lots of people turn out.

We believe that a good company makes the world better by existing. Focusing on being a part of the change we wish to see in the world benefits our business in ways that cannot be measured and are foundational in sustaining our culture. We put our money where our mouth is by showing up in all the ways we are able.

A couple years after opening in Asheville, we started supporting the work of the Welcome Table. Run by Haywood Street Congregation, they provide thousands of free meals every week, anchored in the belief that everyone deserves delicious high-quality food served with love. Restaurants are invited to prepare a multicourse meal that's served family-style on beautiful local pottery, at tables laid with tablecloths and flowers. This is not a rushed food line. It's organized around the goal of "including the most excluded" in an elevated experience. It's one of the most beautiful demonstrations of caring for community that I've ever witnessed, and volunteering there is one of the best ways we found for the team to experience our ethos firsthand.

On our volunteer day, we bring a group of employees to cook the meal on-site in the church kitchen and then help serve it. It's a great way to give back to our community, but it's also an invitation for our staff to experience the impact that hospitality has beyond the restaurant walls. A group of young diverse cooks stand in a preservice prayer circle holding hands with little old church ladies wearing handmade Christmas sweaters. Regardless of their differences, they stand in that circle out of respect for what they see unfolding around them, not because it's obligatory. When an environment reflects real love and inclusion, it is deeply felt. Every year our team leaves profoundly moved by the dignity they experience at the Welcome Table.

This commitment to show up for our communities has side benefits. Not only does it offer much-needed support, it also helps our communities feel connected to us. And importantly, it helps our staff feel proud of the company's mission. We choose the organizations we support by focusing on issues we're committed to, like addressing hunger and poverty, and our teams nominate charities for us to consider supporting that are meaningful to them. Seeing the impact we can make as a business is inspiring for our team, and it's a motivator for them to stay involved and stick around. They want to be a part of something important and help make a difference in the world. This touches on the most basic of human needs: to feel that our life and work has significance.

The service industry has a reputation for being transient, and there's a false assumption that it's void of substance. We work hard to dispel that notion. People might start working with us just to pay their bills, but we hope to surprise them by offering a supportive work environment, career growth opportunities, benefits, stability, and ways to contribute to making an impact in the world. They often discover, much to their surprise (just like we did), that they end up loving the work.

Flashing forward in our story to a decade after opening Chai Pani in Atlanta, our company had grown. By then, we had around 350 employees. We sent out a survey to get their input on various questions such as, "What benefits are you most interested in?" We also asked, "Why are you here?" We'd been sending annual surveys to our team for a few years and always learned important information from them. There were times when the responses weren't what we wanted to hear. Sometimes they revealed issues we were not aware of or frustrations that needed our attention. While that can feel like a punch in the gut, real honest feedback helped us correct course when we got off track. We worked hard to address any concerns, but we had no idea what kind of responses we'd get to that year's survey. It was a vulnerable time for us as a company. The pandemic had chewed us up and spit us out. Many people quit the industry, and we were struggling to attract a new generation of workers. I worried that in the mix of all the pandemic changes and stress, our workplace culture may have fragmented.

The responses we got were stunning. Across the board, the vast majority (whether from a new dishwasher or a seasoned manager) had to do with what it meant to them to be a part of something meaningful. Their answers to that simple question highlight what it is about our company that attracted them, and why they stay. I printed the responses and taped them to my wall as a reminder of what matters. Whenever I feel afraid that we've lost what makes our business special, I read their words and remember what we've built. Their answers solidify that **at the end of the day, no matter what stage of life we're in, we all long to feel a part of something larger than ourselves—to make an impact, to be of significance**.

I won't list all 350 answers to the question "Why are you here?"—but here are some excerpts:
- to make the world a happier place
- this company has supported me in times of need, and I want to support them in my own way
- food has been safety for me—indicative of a strong position and a place of comfort and escape—I want to give that back to others
- to bring happiness, joy, and relief, as well as comfort

- » I want to create a healthy world where people love each other and see one another as equals
- » honest affordable quality food
- » because I enjoy the hell out of Indian food!
- » to make others happy
- » because serving my community is far more interesting than only serving myself
- » to set a new standard for service-industry workers nationally
- » to make people feel at home
- » because a fried-chicken sandwich saved my life

Their responses reveal that **when you organize a business around a clear ethos, you end up attracting people who care about that very thing**. When everyone in your organization is empowered to engage in something of significance, suddenly the job has meaning because it's in service of something greater than making money. **Having something to believe in becomes the hook that holds them. That "something" develops into the whole team's organizing principle—a clear company ethos.**

A lot of hard work went into clearly articulating and teaching our ethos—our ultimate *why*. The first time I read the team's replies to that survey, I sat in silence and let their words sink in. I took a deep breath and said out loud to myself, "Mission accomplished."

Chapter 14

Fostering Connection, Inclusion, and Belonging

"The hero's journey: Increasingly isolated protagonist stomps around prodding evil with pointy bits, eventually fatally prods baddie, gains glory and honor.

The heroine's journey: Increasingly networked protagonist strides around with good friends, prodding them and others on to victory, together."
—Gail Carriger, *The Heroine's Journey*

After a few years of fine-tuning our work environments, it was clear that **part of what makes our particular brand of restaurant-magic special lies in how we weave together the strengths of the masculine and feminine within our work culture.** I say this not from the perspective of gender, but from archetypes. Much is written about the hero's journey, a narrative framework used to describe a structure for stories that involve a hero who goes on an adventure, faces challenges, is victorious in overcoming them, and returns home transformed. But there is less general understanding about the heroine's journey. "A heroine goes about achieving her goals through communication and information gathering. She is not a conqueror . . . she sees the skills and strengths in others and knows how best to apply them. . . . A hero must eventually go it alone . . . a heroine is the opposite."[5]

A Collective Journey

The heroine's journey is a collective one—and that's the journey we're on. Our restaurant story is not a tale about a singular hero. We are working to shake up old patterns in our industry by empowering a *heroine's journey* within our team. It's a story about *us*. Meherwan sparked the vision that set us on our adventure. I focused on creating an environment that supports the collective. My goal is that we treat each other with respect and care in a healthy and loving environment, with professional accountability. These qualities helped grow a group of people who cared enough to meet and exceed our expectations.

The word "family" is loaded. It gets thrown around a lot when trying to describe a tight, bonded unit of people. I still use it occassionally because it's the closest I've found to describe what we are, but I wish I had the word that matches what I see manifest. Family represents all kinds of things to people. For some, the association with family is not always positive. Using it to describe coworkers can also take away a boundary of professionalism that's important to maintain. The word "team" also doesn't work perfectly. When you underperform on a team you get kicked off. The environment that we aim to foster does not immediately kick someone out for bad performance. We attempt to teach them how to meet expectations and give them an opportunity to make adjustments. Or try to find a role where they can succeed. We've had dishwashers become bartenders, hosts become chefs, and servers move into management. Doing this well requires that we pay attention to each individual.

---

5   Adapted from Gail Carriger's *The Heroine's Journey*.

Fostering Connection, Inclusion, and Belonging

Being an organization that prioritizes people requires accountability *and* care. We did this by pairing the human need for belonging with the business's needs for accountability. This environment brings out our strengths. It's where people have each other's backs and show up for each other. It's a bond powerful enough to stay held together when things get nutty, or the world seems to be spinning out of control. It's a rare thing. And I don't have the right word for it. For the flow of this story, I use the words "team" and "family" quite a bit, but now you know what I mean: *an organization that fosters connection, inclusion, and belonging.*

Inventing Jobs for the Right People

About a year after opening Chai Pani in Atlanta, I met Charlotte for coffee to discuss her future. She was approaching the end of the stretch she'd committed to live in Atlanta and was at a crossroads. The restaurant was hopping and had been well received. But it had required everything that our team on the ground had to give. Charlotte's usual cheerful disposition seemed off-balance. After some fidgeting, she confessed that she didn't want to continue living in Atlanta, was tired of sustaining a long-distance relationship with her boyfriend Andrew (now husband), and was considering going back to school. She'd worked all year with no break. She knew that the restaurant needed her to put in that level of work, but she was exhausted.

Charlotte's presence in Atlanta was part of the glue holding the business together. It wasn't just her being there; it was the unique set of skills she brought to the table. Her news pummeled me.

Meherwan was running back and forth between Atlanta and Asheville more than I could, so his areas of focus were well represented. I needed a representative who I trusted to make hard decisions on my behalf, in alignment with what matters to me. Charlotte has strengths in some of the same areas as my own. She had no experience being a lead manager when she took the job in Atlanta, but she knew how I wanted things done. Helping people reach high standards while fostering a positive environment requires a particular kind of grace. She has it. She also has her own superpowers and had done an excellent job opening the Atlanta Chai Pani and impacting its success. She nurtured her team *and* held them accountable.

Growing a team of young people into leadership positions revealed to us their natural desire to design their own professional track and not feel boxed in. Many young people will not accept the "suck it up and work your way up the professional ladder" strategy for growing a career that those of us from Gen X and the generations before us were expected to follow. They look at the ladder and say, "F*ck that, the world could blow up before I reach the top." Or, "I'll only climb a ladder of my own design; life is too unpredictable to waste time in someone else's construct."

Sitting outside the café in the heavy Atlanta humidity, I tried to hide my desperation upon hearing her news. I steadied myself and focused on what I believed she needed most from me at that moment—*a choice*. Charlotte was mature beyond her years, but I recognized that she couldn't see a path forward with us that didn't feel confining or out of alignment with the life she wanted. Putting aside my panic about how the new restaurant could possibly get by without her, I gave her three options to consider. I said, "Here's what I know for sure—we need you. You are part of the fiber of this place and a significant reason that we've been able to successfully open in another city. *And* we love you, so we care deeply that you make the right decision for yourself, even if that means you need to end your time working with us. There are three paths I can see for you to continue working with us, if you'd like to."

1. "You can jump all-in. We'll offer you an executive leadership position at our offices in Asheville, with a commensurate salary." (This role and salary did not yet exist, but I would create it for her.) "You'll be part of our growth strategy

moving forward, helping us run all the businesses. This option will not, however, allow much time to attend school."
2. "A full-time restaurant-management position back in Asheville so you can leave Atlanta. Something that interests you in the restaurant space. This would have less of a long-term commitment than the first choice." (There weren't any current management openings, but we'd figure something out to keep her on board.)
3. "We'll find something part time so you can stay in the loop and earn a paycheck but still have the time you need to go back to school."

I didn't want to pressure her in this decision process, but I wanted her to know that I saw what she contributed. I told her, "You have the qualities we need to help us grow in the way that we want. I'd love for you to stay, but I will absolutely support you and celebrate whatever you choose to do next."

Lucky for us, she chose option one and took an executive position in Asheville. At the time of this writing, about a decade later, she is now the COO of our company and has grown into a powerful leader. This year alone, she was nominated for two executive leadership awards in the business community in recognition of the impact she's making.

These are the moments that built our culture. They added up and ultimately helped shift us away from the dismal retention rates that plague our industry. **When you find the right people that you want to grow, you might need to invent jobs for them.** It's all about timing. You have to catch them before they slip through the cracks or get burnt-out beyond repair. It requires prioritizing the hunches you feel and always making time for the conversation. **This takes acutely *paying attention*. It involves keeping your finger on the pulse of what's going on with your people—sensing when they need to talk and grabbing the moment before it passes. Reach out, show up, and be there at the right time. These become the moments that build a team that's invested in growing with you.**

SERVICE READY

Charlotte's decision to stay helped solidify that our business would continue to be enriched by the strengths of the feminine at the highest levels of leadership, whether or not I was in the room. Her leadership qualities bring equilibrium to our team. Visionaries need people around them who they can hear and respect. She provides that for Meherwan and will challenge him when most needed. While he tends to start flying the airplane before it's finished being built, she or I are communicating with the team about what's happening (while also making sure there are enough parachutes), so that everyone feels safe. Both roles made our company thrive.

At Chai Pani Atlanta, Charlotte had helped create a culture in alignment with our company's ethos. She'd mentored new hires and had a strong team on the ground. Isaac moved to Atlanta for a couple of years with his young family after Charlotte left, and he picked up right where she left off as a culture carrier. When Isaac returned to Asheville, the restaurant was doing great. But without him, the Atlanta store no longer had a strong leader running that business who'd been with us for years. Daniel ran the kitchen, but we went through several general managers, all of whom came with solid restaurant experience but were not as immersed in the nuances of how we wanted things done. We discovered just how essential the culture carrier role is once it was missing. Very quickly that restaurant started to suffer. Staff turnover increased, and sales started to tank. Suddenly we had big problems to fix.

Around that time, Joey Beard stepped in. Joey was one of the first investors in that restaurant, the one who found the location for us. He lived nearby and saw the need. Joey quit his job in sales (taking a significant pay cut) to jump in full time. He had no restaurant training or background, but he knew how to manage people in alignment with our ethos and bring professionalism and great energy to the environment. Within weeks of his arrival things started to turn around. The big discovery was how much his leadership dramatically changed things. Almost immediately the sales stabilized, and staff retention increased. We would never again underestimate the impact of strong leaders. Joey cared deeply about our company culture and was (literally) invested in it. This learning helped us improve our trainings to better teach people how to create a positive work environment and a culture of care.

At the time of this writing, many years after Joey moved on from that GM role, Chai Pani in Atlanta is humming along, run by some brilliant young leaders. Alice, the GM, started working there when she was sixteen. What began as her first job as a hostess on the weekends while in high school grew into a successful career. The kitchen is now run by Sahar, a mother of two, recently nominated by the James Beard Foundation for the Best Chef Southeast category for her work at Chai Pani Decatur. Together, they run a bustling restaurant while embodying our culture of care in their community and with their team.

There are many aspects of a restaurant that must work well for it to be successful; they function like the legs of a stool. An organization's culture is the seat of the stool—without it, the legs don't hold together.

Identifying Our Highest, Greatest Impact

Removing myself from the minutiae of day-to-day restaurant work would take years, but the process began when Charlotte accepted that job on our executive team. I found the person who could co-run parts of the business with Meherwan. She's able to help interpret his intentions when people need more explanation than he has time for. She can make high-level decisions that incorporate both his and my perspectives. Finding the right person to take over some of the operational parts of my job was a game changer.

I wanted to create a layer of protection for our marriage from the never-ending number of difficult conversations our roles in the business required. While Meherwan and I had returned to solid ground, the truth is that it was hard for us to hear each other clearly at work without any baggage. When we manage to, we bring out the best in each other. But that is difficult to do if we are running the daily operations together. We realized that we needed to stop doing the parts of the work that drove us both crazy when done *together*. We needed to redraw the boundaries around our roles so we could cleanly hear each other's ideas. If being in operational meetings together was our kryptonite, what if we just stopped playing with kryptonite?

It took trust for me to let go of being immersed in the day-to-day details. I made a conscious choice to do this. But I had to figure out how we could continue to design the road map together (charting where the business was headed) if I didn't stay up-to-date on all the specifics. I also had to trust that someone else could represent my thinking in the areas that mattered most to me. I had to work to de-fang the fear of what might happen if I let go of control. And I needed a way to stay engaged with, and aware of, the business's fine points without micromanaging. Was I ready for that level of surrender?

To untangle our roles and answer these questions, we focused on what the business needed most from us. Meherwan and I revisited the question: What are our highest and greatest contributions to this company? Our goal was to delegate anything taking up our time that didn't align with our greatest personal impact.

In the early days, after a particularly rough patch of working together, I'd written Meherwan a resignation letter. At the time I saw writing it as an act of love. It wasn't a threat; it was a statement that I loved him enough to set him free from the challenge that our working dynamic had become. In one of his more brilliant moments in our relationship, he recognized the sacrifice I'd be making, and how much I cared about what we had built. He didn't think it was fair for me to have to leave. He wrote me a response that read, "You can change your job however you need or want to, but you can never resign from your *real* role in our company. You are our wisdom keeper. You shine the light when and where we need it most, and you keep us true to our core. That is something no one else can do." Needless to say, I didn't resign.

Fostering Connection, Inclusion, and Belonging

Going through this process of reshaping our roles, we identified the areas that mattered most to us as individuals and matched them with what the business needed from us. We began to formulate ways to focus more time on those things—and less on everything else. By investing time teaching others how to do the things that did not *have* to be done by me, I reclaimed time to focus on my most important contributions. Ultimately, this reevaluation led me to a place of freedom and more empowerment in my work. The process was so impactful that we learned to practice it with our team.

Getting Creative to Allow for People's Greatest Impact

A few years after running Chai Pani in Atlanta, Daniel Peach came to us with a proposition. He wanted to take a sabbatical to study in India. His plan was to take six months off from the restaurant to stage[6] in Indian restaurants and homes. He wanted to work alongside the heartbeat of Indian cuisine: the mothers. He'd been saving up his money, and with the ability to live cheaply in India, he could afford to be there without getting a paycheck. His dilemma was that he didn't want to lose the opportunity to return to Chai Pani, where he hoped to share the knowledge he'd pick up.

If you want to build a work environment that fosters connection, inclusion, and belonging, these are the moments to get creative. Of course we wanted to support Daniel in his quest, but we had to find a way to make it fair for the rest of the team, as well as make it work on a practical level. How could we set Daniel free to travel for six months when others hadn't taken any significant breaks? How could we cover Daniel's absence and still have a job available for him on his return? Daniel was worth the investment of some brain cells to figure this one out, so we did.

We sent him off on his adventure with the promise that he would have a job upon his return. We could not guarantee precisely what that

---

6 A "stage" is an unpaid internship that comes from the French word "stagiaire."

job would be. We emphasized that it might take some time to get him back to a lead management position, and it could require him moving locations or cities temporarily to secure the role he wanted. As a business with razor-thin margins just beginning to get financially stable, we also couldn't guarantee him the same salary on his return. What we promised is that we would try our best. This decision required trust on both sides. He had to trust that we'd honor our commitment to find a good role for him on his return from India. And we had to trust that he'd return to us and share the wealth of knowledge he gained. By getting creative, we found a way to set him free.

Six months later Daniel did return from India—lit up to jump back in and help expand our culinary story. He ended up taking several trips like that over the years, some shorter and some longer. Not only had we supported Daniel's dream and personal growth, but his experience gave more back to our business than can be measured.

Meanwhile, James Grogan had been working hard from day one. His culinary and organizational skills, and remarkably calm and cheerful composure, earned him the opportunity to join Meherwan at exciting cooking events—giving him a chance to get out of the kitchen and into all kinds of other environments. A decade later in 2023, James and Daniel were part of the team that joined Meherwan to cook for a luncheon hosted by the State Department and Vice President of the United States Kamala Harris.

Strategies That Support a Story of "We"

If our story is a heroine's journey, a story about *all of us*, we have to do everything in our power to help grow our people in the directions that light them up. We built our business by focusing on growth from within. That means if we hired a great team player but they're not excelling, we invest time and money into their training, and mentor them into the right position. **Creating opportunities for the right people when the job doesn't already**

exist, and doing what's possible to nurture their dreams, are examples of how we grow people who care about the business as much as we do.

To break free from the old patriarchal patterns in the food and beverage industry, and write a collective story, we wove this into big-picture retention planning as well as the dynamics around the conference table where decisions get made, creating space for female leadership to make an impact.

Women in business have been taught to contort to a man's communication style to be heard. That paradigm is way outdated. The guidance to "lean in" to the man's world was a form of progress. But it often leaves women (or those with strong feminine instincts) stifling their own best ideas in the attempt to think and act "like a man." If you pay careful attention, you'll notice that often a woman will instinctively agree at first with what a man is saying, in order for him to hear what she says next. We agree so that we are given the space to disagree. We don't do this because we want to go through the inner gymnastics—we do it so that we will be heard. This is what women go through every day in the business world. And it's bullshit.

Like so many women, the world conditioned me to speak in a way that's palatable to others—versus being bold with my own voice and direct about my ideas. When a man is bold, he's viewed as a strong leader, but when a woman is bold she's often viewed as bossy or "too much." What if instead, women were encouraged to voice their ideas without expending so much energy editing themselves? What if women were empowered to "lean in" to being our own selves? And better yet, what if the "best practices of communication" incorporated the natural strengths of male *and* female communication styles?

This is what happened in our business. Meherwan and I both benefited from the balance of perspectives. Meherwan learned to lean in to feminine strengths, which enhanced his emotional and relational intelligence and built up his efficacy in those areas. As I grew in my leadership, I transformed by learning how to speak boldly with confidence from my convictions.

Even when he didn't understand what I was doing or the way I did it, Meherwan trusted my voice and wisdom. He could see it fostering a culture where people feel connected to each other, committed to us and their job, and comfortable to be themselves.

It's on us as leaders to make space for all voices—and encourage authenticity in our communications. As our organization grew, we honed these professional development skills to teach them to our leadership teams. Rules of engagement about how to best communicate clearly so that we are *all* heard is important. In manager trainings we teach how to lead meetings that hold space for quieter introverts to contribute, while also demonstrating the restraint and boundaries needed to ensure no one voice dominates a conversation. This guidance acts as a guardrail to prevent meetings from becoming overly personalized, overwhelming, or off topic. These aren't skills many restaurant workers learn on the job, so we created our own trainings around them.

We realized that to fully reach our goals we had to write our own rules—not simply adopt the best practices from other industries or models. Creating a work environment that allows people to be themselves and speak up, in their own unique voices (even when they involve emotions or, God forbid, tears), is what creates magic in a team.

It's not about agreeing on everything. Quite the opposite. It's about feeling comfortable to disagree—and understanding that being willing to debate is a form of trust, and the way an individual can make a real contribution.

Our growth was nurtured by having my attention on culture and care, and driven by Meherwan forging the path forward. In the analogy of the heroine's journey, a good heroine archetype makes space for the power of male energy but keeps it in check, guiding it toward self-mastery over conquest. That's what happened for us. We merged our strengths to build a successful business while creating a new way of being in the service industry.

We incorporated tools unique to the restaurant world by pulling from our backgrounds, past professions, and differing perspectives.

Fostering Connection, Inclusion, and Belonging

Over the years, we embedded out-of-the-box practices into our restaurant management that helped us change the game and achieve our goals.

- » **Goal:** A culture of respect where every person is viewed as an intellectual equal with something to contribute.
  - » **Practice:** Managers conduct regular "check-ins" with all employees, utilizing the art of active listening. Leaders do not just have an open-door policy; they walk through the door to be in constant communication with their teams.
- » **Goal:** The ability to have difficult conversations that address issues head-on to prevent tensions from festering.
  - » **Practice:** Professional development trainings that teach managers how to hold people accountable and have effective difficult conversations while also normalizing feelings; providing a clear structure for what to do with conflict when it comes up, and maintain healthy professional boundaries.
- » **Goal:** Build a foundation of love, care, and support.
  - » **Practice:** We teach our teams to have each other's backs—and we model this. Our Care Team is available to all employees. This is a committee that guides managers with how best to support their team members in times of crisis or difficulty. They help set up things like meal trains, fundraisers, counseling services, and access to other needed resources. It also ensures that everyone's special occasions are celebrated and honored equally.
- » **Goal:** Pair the desire for belonging with the business's needs for accountability. Our leaders recognize that their true power lies in their ability to make other people powerful.[7]
  - » **Practice:** We have a monitoring process in place for all aspects of the business. Leaders conduct quarterly reports

---

7   Inspired by Benjamin Zander's training "How to Give an A."

in the areas of food quality, operations, aesthetics, and service. The reports provide the teams on the ground with direct, honest, transparent feedback on how they're doing and what areas need improvement, so everyone knows how to reach excellence.

The Importance of Psychological Safety

It shouldn't be a groundbreaking idea to foster psychological safety in a restaurant. But remarkably, it is. The service industry, along with many others, is finally waking up to changes that are long overdue. Businesses are desperate to prevent burnout and increase connection and retention but are searching for *how* to do this in a way that's effective, especially with younger generations. The high pressure and competitive nature surrounding our collective cultural work ethic and management strategies of the past are being dismantled. Themes like work-life balance, mental health, and mindfulness strategies are front and center.

As we design new ways of doing business, understanding the importance of having a "culture" at work, and how to create one, is paramount. We are continually asked how we have held on to so many young people and turned them into leaders, growing them from within the business. Fostering the idea of a happy and healthy workplace, one in which everyone feels seen and able to contribute, became a big part of my job. Mentoring effectively so I could extract myself over time from daily operations gave me the space to focus on this deeper work. **Focusing inward on our team is what created award-winning outward hospitality.**

Chapter 15

The Elegant Solution

"If you deconstruct Greece, you will in the end see an olive tree, a grape vine, and a boat remain. That is: with as much, you reconstruct her."
　　　　　　　　—Odysseas Elytis, *The Little Mariner*

Late in the winter of 2013, Meherwan was spending long nights pacing—deep in his internal cave. We'd been married long enough for me to know that when he's in his cave, he wants to be alone. He needs uninterrupted time to think, and I try to respect that. I'd find him walking a well-worn path in our dining room—pacing back and forth while rubbing his chin. I knew he would eventually emerge to share what he was thinking.

As the nights wore on, I grew increasingly nervous. I knew we were facing financial challenges, but I was blissfully no longer balancing the books, so I didn't know how bad things were. Clearly, Meherwan did. He'd always paced at night when stressed, but this time left me with an anxious foreboding.

Our birthday was approaching, and I couldn't figure out what to do given the state he was in. Since we share a birthday, we usually plan a joint celebration. That year felt different. He was in his cave, and a party didn't feel right. I could tell that he needed to feel connected to our bigger picture so he could balance the stress of the work with some joy. He needed to remember what was most beautiful about what we'd built. I also wanted to find a way for him to feel the support and love of his team.

We'd been in business for four years, and Meherwan was becoming the leader that I knew he could be all along. But I suspected that he couldn't see that. I wanted to shine some light in his dark cave. Meherwan looked weary, like he was holding up the sky for fear it might crash down upon us. I sensed that the responsibility of taking care of everyone was a heavy burden—one he thought he carried alone.

So, I sent an email to the dozen or so people who'd been working with us for years and asked them for help making a birthday gift for Meherwan. My request was for them to write a short appreciation of him. It could be one line, a funny memory, or whatever called to them, just one thing that they appreciated about Meherwan. What I got in return blew me away. They poured their hearts out. They too had sensed that he'd been unusually stressed, and wanted to help. I made a little white box with "LOVE♫s" written on top and filled it with printed scrolls of all of their notes.

On our birthday, we curled up in bed and took turns reading each letter out loud. Both of our cheeks were wet from tears as we absorbed the stunning testimonials. One note will stay with me forever. It came from a line cook recently promoted to kitchen manager, Michael Goode. Michael was our age, a recovered addict who got himself clean and scraped his way back by working his ass off in kitchens. He'd been around a long time and had seen it all.

Michael wore all black, making his pale skin and lean frame decorated in tattoos all the more dramatic. But this guy was so freaking happy to be alive after all he'd been through. He had a contagious laugh that would boom so loudly out of the kitchen that it made people in the dining room smile just hearing it. As much as I loved Michael, I didn't expect that the most eloquent love letter would come from the guy known as "the Vampire" in the group. My favorite part reads:

> *I love my job. What's even crazier: My job loves me. Meherwan, when I say "my job," I mean "you." Whether you realize it or not, you've seen me through some of the hardest times of my life. It may not have been you that was physically holding my hand the entire time. But you created (out of thin air) the environment for some of the strongest hand-holders in my life. I can't begin to express how grateful I am. . . . I may not be the most "grounded" person you'll ever meet, but I'm no longer a lost soul. . . . You created the warm, moist breeding ground necessary for my kind of bacteria to flourish. It's more than safe to say that I wouldn't be the man I am today without you, and you have no idea how much I appreciate that. I've never loved more, or been more loved, than since I've been a part of your family (don't tell anyone—it'll ruin my dark reputation). I still work for you because I genuinely give a fuck and, more importantly, because you do. You've taught me so much. . . . Meherwan, you transcend titles. Whether I call you employer, teacher, father, brother, friend, or occasional foe . . . you are, first and foremost, my family . . . and family, as it were, is the most important thing in the world to this particular line cook/manager. I hope the anniversary of your birth is absolutely spectacular. I hope you get back even a fraction of what you give.*

These notes solidified that we'd succeeded in building a culture of which we could be deeply proud—something we should fight like hell to protect. We had given Michael something to believe in, and the recognition of that helped Meherwan climb out of his cave.

Our dear family friend Erico once said that the most confounding predicaments call for "an elegant solution." Finding one requires us to dig deep. Often, there isn't an easy answer—but there is usually an elegant solution if you are willing to put in the hard work to find it. That's what Meherwan was doing in his cave.

Finally, he walked me through the details of the crisis we were in, and it was clear that his worries had been warranted. He laid it all out, including the choices we had before us. He said, "We grew our management team too large and too fast to survive this slow winter. We can't float it, and our credit isn't strong enough to borrow the amount we'd need. I see three options:

1. We fire a significant portion of the team we just promoted into leadership roles. This would be terrible for many reasons, not the least of which because we care deeply about their well-being.
2. We look for outside funding. The timing of this is the worst because we're not currently showing the profit we will show by the end of the year, and we'd have to give too much of our business away in return. The terms would be terrible.
3. We all take a significant pay cut across the board. I've run the numbers, and if the entire leadership team cut their salaries for the winter, and you and I don't take a paycheck at all, we can even out the deficit by the end of the year. If we can convince the team to hang in there somehow for a few months of earning less, we can pay them more in the summer. By the end of the year, if all goes as planned, we will be able to make up the difference to them. But it would need to be a significant pay cut—likely more than some will be able to float without getting loans."

We approached the team with these options and asked them to consider option three. We were prepared to charge our mortgage on a credit card if we had to, and help the core team with personal loans if we could. As hard as the situation was, they believed in us. Some volunteered to not take a paycheck until we were above water. They trusted that we would do our absolute best to stand behind the promise and make it up to them. They not only wanted to help, but they wanted to be part of the solution. The team's love letters and their response to the crisis were evidence that we had built a culture that could maneuver through hard times by relying on the strength of each other.

Returning to Our Core Ingredients

We called that period our "winter of austerity." We buckled down and focused only on the essentials—the core ingredients that make us who we are: community, good food, excellent service, and care of each other.

Since we'd started our first restaurant with meager funds, we knew how to work with frugality. Relying once again on the art of jugaad to make do with what we had, we froze all unnecessary spending. Analyzing every line item in our budget, we assessed what could be cut. Instead of using a flower service, we bought flowers from the grocery store and made our own arrangements. We washed our own windows and took our trash to the dump, bypassing the extra trash pickup fee. Paint touch-ups were done in-house instead of hiring professionals. We managed to trim just enough to be able to get the budget back in balance after the pay cuts went into effect.

The thing about trying times is that *if* we pay close attention, they provide the opportunities for the most growth. The lessons for us that winter were hard-earned, but without them we would not be the company we are today. That experience helped our success moving forward. The process taught us how to remain nimble and able to cut back expenses quickly when needed. It's more difficult to run a restaurant that lean, but at times it is essential. It's important for businesses to know the limits of what's possible so that they don't overreact and throw in the towel when things get hard.

Transparency and Timely Communication

Change is never easy on an organization—particularly a change that involves a negative adjustment in people's pay structure. I don't want to diminish the fear and discomfort our people experienced as we made our way through that winter. One essential takeaway we gleaned from the experience is the **importance of strategic, honest, well-timed communication**. I don't believe it's an overstatement to say that it was the most important factor in our staff's fortitude through that difficult time. They needed to understand what was going on. They did *not* need to hear rumors from coworkers or information out of context that would cause panic. They also needed us to listen to their feelings and acknowledge that it was hard. Upfront transparency helped them hang in with us when the changes happening around them made things appear topsy-turvy.

Vulnerability is not a comfortable place for leaders. It's much easier to tell your people that "everything will be ok," hoping to save them from worry—despite all evidence to the contrary. **Leaders who share the uncomfortable, vulnerable truth with their teams build trust. From that place, they can more impactfully convey their conviction that everything will be OK.**

From learning to hold off on final decisions until we found the most elegant solution, timely and honest communication with our team, and returning to the core ingredients that define us, we learned how to make big moves without allowing the fear of failure to paralyze us.

We continued to shapeshift our way through that rough year until we made it. After that experience, we learned to view mistakes as opportunities to extract pearls of wisdom—instead of allowing them to grind us to dust. **Mistakes and subsequent lessons learned can be the push to do things better—not only to survive, but to avoid becoming stagnant.** Our hardest lessons wove their way into the fabric of our company's best practices. The trick is to allow them to shake you up—so they do not slip by in the panic and fear that can take hold when things get messy. Often we learn more from our failures than our successes.

In 2014 we designed our first non-Indian concept. It was a new direction for us, one that developed from the desire to expand. We weren't yet ready to open in another city, so we were pursuing opportunities in Asheville, eager to improve the company's financial stability. At that time, with our small team and limited resources, it felt easier to manage another restaurant in the town where the core team was based.

For this project, we entered a partnership with Elliott Moss. Elliott was a local chef who wanted to bring pasture-raised, wood-smoked barbecue to Asheville. Meherwan resonated with Elliott's self-taught chef story and loved his cooking. He was excited about bringing traditional whole-hog Eastern Carolina barbecue into a sit-down restaurant space. I had some reservations. Compared to the team we'd been growing and developing for years, we had relatively little history with Elliott, and I was concerned about introducing a new food story into our plans—we'd set out to tell Meherwan's cultural food story. I felt sure the restaurant would be super popular and would serve delicious food. I just wasn't sold that we should be the ones to go in on it with him.

Mikey, Charlotte, Meherwan, and I gathered with Elliott around a dusty table in an empty shell of an old factory—the proposed restaurant space. It was in an up-and-coming neighborhood just south of downtown Asheville, soon to transform into a vibrant brewery district. Elliott would be the head chef and manage the kitchen, and our team would run the operations of the restaurant. As we reviewed the architectural plans, I felt a tension headache coming on as I tried to stay focused. I usually get excited about the design phase, but that day I felt stressed. Once again, my body was talking to me.

This would be the first time we'd built a restaurant from the ground up instead of renovating a second-generation space. It was a different kind of beast. Complicating matters, Elliott's indoor wood-fired smokers required all kinds of special engineering. While we workshopped ideas for the design, the scope of the project set in. The blue lines of the architectural drawings started to swirl as I stared at them too long. As they blurred, I thought about the potential impact of this direction on our vision.

Despite my intuitive red flags, Meherwan was fired up about the project and had investors on board. I shared my concerns, but he felt strongly about forging ahead. The crux of my unease (beyond whether the partnership was a good fit) was my suspicion that our team, and particularly Meherwan, might not enjoy owning a restaurant where we didn't have full creative control. And while I was optimistic that it would be a good financial move, I wasn't convinced that it was the best use of Meherwan's (or our team's) energy. I worried it would prevent him from having enough time for his own creativity—something that seemed increasingly challenging as our business grew and became more complex. Ultimately, Meherwan asked me to trust him, so I did.

Offering my concerns and then rolling up my sleeves to help make it happen was a learning experience. **Beyond the paradigm of right versus wrong, there is a place to land where you move forward in peace, despite having misgivings. You can provide your input and then surrender control over the outcome. In partnerships, you don't always agree on all the decisions. But we can still believe in *each other*. We can support our partners and coworkers to help them succeed.** I dug deep to be able to fully surrender so I could move forward without tension. If I didn't, my dissent would become toxic and undermine the entire project.

I trusted that in the end, we'd either figure out how to make it work, or we'd learn important lessons from it. I got on board, hoping to be proved wrong—for everyone's sake.

Buxton Hall Barbecue was a hit. *Bon Appétit* named it "one of the best new restaurants" in its opening year in 2015 as well as bestowing us the honor of the best "Fried Chicken Sandwich of the Year." With multiple James Beard nominations and press accolades piling up for our restaurants, our reputation and reach were growing.

In its prime, Buxton was super popular and turned out excellent food. But it was a beast to manage. The space was four times the size of our Asheville Chai Pani, and that led to the need for the largest staff we'd ever managed. Nothing about it was simple. We needed someone there overnight to tend the smoking of the hogs, a full bakery department, an event staff for the upper mezzanine where we hosted private parties, and an off-site catering division. These are all things we don't have in our other restaurants. Each of them was important for Buxton, but they added complexity.

And there were other challenges. The heat level of the indoor smokers had to be very closely monitored, or the fire-suppression system would go off over the cook line, shutting the kitchen down and filling the dining room with smoke. The antique wood floors dating back to the 1930s (remnants of the building's first incarnation as a skating rink) could not be fully sealed, so water (and God knows what else) would drip through the floorboards directly into the manager's offices on the lower level, regularly frying computers and anything else in the way. Embers from the smoker would somehow sneak past the chimney's multiple protective layers of screening and land on the roof—burning holes through the ceiling that would cause constant leaks over the dining room.

Running Buxton required an inordinate amount of our bandwidth. Additionally, we discovered that some of my initial concerns about the partnership had been warranted. Our goals were aligned, but our approaches differed. In the end, despite the frayed nerves and lost sleep, Buxton turned out to be the push we needed to establish better systems of management to ensure our restaurants were running the way we expected. We couldn't have imagined just how quickly we would need those systems in place for all that was about to unfold.

Chapter 16

Designing Our Own Systems

The Birth of Botiwalla and Spicewalla

"Systems should support and reinforce a culture, but they can't replace it."
—Amy Zhou, Gracious Hospitality Management

Getting a restaurant profitable and running well, consistently, is not an easy task. With such slim margins, the volatility of the cost of goods, and a transient workforce, our industry faces many challenges. It takes good business sense and a relentless pursuit of excellence to make it work. When everything goes well, it's magic.

But that magic doesn't happen with the wave of a wand. It happens by understanding your business inside and out—down to the smallest details. It requires refining and reworking the systems and processes over and over again as your business evolves.

Many people get into the restaurant industry because of a passion for food. This is one of the key ingredients needed for success—but it's only one ingredient in the recipe. When I was deciding if I wanted to take the leap and start the first Chai Pani with Meherwan, I flashed back to our wedding day.

The budget for our wedding was a slim $5,000, and we'd invited 120 guests to celebrate with us in the hills of California's Marin County, where we lived at the time. I did all the planning and relied on creativity, my mom's cost-saving menu expertise, and our phenomenal friends to help execute the vision within our budget. Family and friends were coming from all over the world, and we had a full weekend of events planned. On the day before our wedding, the to-do list was daunting. That morning, I woke up with a high fever and terrible sore throat. What happened next would come back to me fourteen years later when Meherwan was pitching me his restaurant idea.

Meherwan found me at our dining table with tears rolling down my face. I couldn't figure out how to manage that to-do list while feeling so sick. He sat next to me and listened as I reviewed what still needed to be done. Before I could wipe away my tears, he'd created a map for the day—with a sequence of events and a plan for delegating tasks. I was impressed by how he could work around the overwhelm like he was playing a game of chess. While juggling the demands of family arriving from around the world, and the monster list of tasks, he remained focused. I felt comfortable starting a restaurant with him because, ultimately, I knew he'd bring that same degree of deliberation and problem-solving to our business. Pulling off such a beautiful event helped me trust that together we could build something really special.

Systems Create the Stepping Stones for Growth

After getting Buxton Hall Barbecue up and running, we spent a couple of years developing and refining better systems. To prepare our restaurants for more growth, we divided up the tasks. Meherwan dove deep into our financial models to workshop them and search for efficiencies and new processes to implement in our management structure. I devoted myself to writing a manual and reinventing our training systems. I spent months capturing every policy we'd developed over the seven years since we started, and getting all our out-of-the-box ways of doing things onto the page.

Designing Our Own Systems

We'd been modeling by example and relying on the core team of culture carriers that had been with us from the beginning. But with multiple busy restaurants, we needed to streamline our resources and how we spent our time so we weren't running in circles. We needed to better train our trainers and have high-functioning systems in place for them to easily follow. We would end up rewriting that training manual many times over the years, but capturing all our unique best practices in one place helped to hardwire our culture and dial-in our execution.

Systems don't replace communication—we learned this the hard way. Developing protocols to help with the management of tasks is an important part of our efficacy. It takes the burden off the individual staff and managers by automating everyday tasks, and frees them to think about the bigger picture. However, no matter how well organized, thorough, and accessible our systems may be, without a consistent feedback loop in place, invariably people will stop using them. For any system to be successfully implemented, the people charged with it need consistent, positive reinforcement. And that happens through regular, clear communication.

Our team leaders visit each restaurant quarterly and conduct a thorough review of all of the details of the department they manage. They check on everything from chipped paint to wobbly furniture, taste every dish on the menu, and observe the quality of guest interactions. These inspections provide an opportunity for dialogue about how things are going, and for the executive team to have boots on the ground in all our locations, noticing all the details and quality of food and service.

From the first year in business, a lot of interested parties contacted us, eager to help us grow. After getting a few restaurants under our belt, we began to meet with some of them and explore ideas. We toured their towns and heard their proposals. But we were still perfecting our model.

We had so much to learn, and we wanted to have a clear, systemized approach before we took on more growth.

Just when we were rounding the bend with streamlining our restaurant models and drafting a strategic plan for growth, the right opportunity came our way. In 2016, we were approached by the developers of Ponce City Market in Atlanta to come up with a fast-casual concept for a new food hall. Wearing bright-yellow hard hats, Meherwan, Isaac, and I toured the building site, which occupies an entire city block.

It was an honor to be asked. We were in good company with other chefs we respected who planned to open in the space. The deal was that we had to come up with a new brand—it couldn't be Chai Pani. They wanted only unique concepts created by well-known chefs, designed for a food hall, and not a duplicate of a restaurant already in Atlanta.

It was the perfect opportunity to develop what we'd been mulling over: a business that would have better margins than our full-service restaurants, with a simpler menu and a more straightforward execution—one that would be easier to scale as we planned further expansion. Chai Pani is chef-driven (thus highly talent-dependent), with a large, complex menu and thin margins. These aspects make it complicated to consistently run well in multiple locations. The new gourmet food hall was modeled after the Ferry Building in San Francisco and Chelsea Market in New York. It called for quick service, where people could dine in the restaurant or take a tray of food and eat at communal tables.

As we stood in the empty hall taking in the space, we all said almost in unison, "This is perfect!" It was clear this was the right setup for us to try a new concept. We were ready. From that invitation, Botiwalla was born.

We wanted the new restaurant to be connected to Chai Pani's brand (to benefit from its halo) but also differentiated. Thinking about what food he wanted to showcase, Meherwan was inspired by the tea houses and kebab stands he loves in India. He was excited to represent the sigri (grills) that pop up on the streets at night. There is another side of street food in India—the late-night scene. This includes meats sizzling over an open flame, and wafting aromas of charred masala served with crispy, crunchy, sweet-and-salty explosions of flavorful chaat.

In Hindi, "boti" means "chunk of meat," like what is grilled on a skewer. "Walla" is the term used across India to connect someone's profession or service. Someone who sells chai is a "chaiwalla," while someone who grills meat on a sigri is a "botiwalla." Our Botiwalla menu would be smaller than Chai Pani's and tightly curated for fast service at high volume.

Botiwalla opened in Ponce City Market with a lot of fanfare, and was named one of the "world's most exciting new restaurants" by *Bloomberg*. It's not uncommon for restaurants to take years to get out of the red, but Botiwalla was profitable right out of the gate, and has remained so ever since.

Meherwan carefully designed the menu to be margin-friendly and easy to teach while still hitting all our goals of craveworthy, high-quality Indian street food. I focused on designing a counter-service model that was efficient and easy to run with much less staff than our table-service restaurants, while maintaining our fun and engaging atmosphere. My coworker Teddy coined the new model "Over-the-Counter" Service, reflecting our goal to go above and beyond how we take care of our guests, even in a counter-service model.

For Botiwalla's opening party, we hosted a film festival. We screened a documentary film produced by our very own Mikey Files. The story followed Meherwan, James Grogan, and Daniel Peach (our first kitchen hires) on a street food tour of India. The three chefs toured ten cities in eleven days, eating everything in sight, with Mikey filming the adventures along the way. Mikey and his brother, Daniel, brilliantly edited the footage into a fun and lighthearted documentary. The opening party and film festival drew a huge crowd, and all of Ponce City Market was pulsing with Bollywood music.

Botiwalla was off to a fantastic start. We had a team that we trusted from Chai Pani in Atlanta who we grew into leadership positions at Botiwalla. Promoting from within the company helped us carry our culture into a new space. However, we still had our work cut out for us learning a new version of service and how to excel in this model. Pretty quickly we stumbled over the challenges of scaling our culture of Mindblasting Hospitality in a setup that offers fewer opportunities for interaction with customers, with less management staff to support the team. Meeting our hospitality goals there was complicated.

I was in Atlanta for quarterly service check-ins when I met with the Botiwalla GM to discuss the staffing challenges they were facing. She sat across from me at a community table in the busy food hall, clutching a large coffee. She reported that they couldn't attract the kind of applicants we were accustomed to finding with our table-service restaurants. The counter-service model was pulling in applications from high school kids and workers from fast-food chains who had little interest in going the extra mile for Mindblasting Hospitality.

I pushed back against the notion that this was the best we could find. The GM protested with, "You can't expect the same quality of service at Botiwalla from the talent pool we're able to attract." I was glad that the GM had identified the issue and felt empowered enough to bring it forward, but I left the meeting frustrated without a clear solution.

Over-the-Counter Service

On the drive home to Asheville, I crafted a plan. I realized we had to clarify what qualities we *most needed* in our team to determine what we were really looking for in new hires. We'd already been doing this for our table-service restaurants, but we needed an even more radical approach to bring in the right staff for a counter-service model. I still wanted our team to Mindblast our guests and each other. I wasn't willing to give up on that goal, so I had to rethink how to attract people interested in making that effort.

Designing Our Own Systems

One day as I interviewed a young man applying to be a server, I realized the problem. I loved this guy—his eyes lit up the room; he was engaging, funny, a strong communicator, and a good listener. But he had no work experience—this would be his first job. I had to make a pitch to the team about what I liked about this applicant, but my explanations were arbitrary. I was going on gut instinct. As I broke down the issue, Isaac and I compared notes about our hiring process and discovered that we were both looking for something elusive, hard to define, and even harder to measure. We were looking for "a feeling."

I tackled the challenge by rewriting our job interview questionnaire to help us gain clues about an applicant's excellence reflex, sense of humor, desire for and comfort with human connection, and love of creative challenges. While we had been prioritizing empathy and kindness in hiring from the beginning, the new interview questionnaire brought more structure to that analysis. I created a scoring system to weigh the overall quality of an applicant based primarily on the above criteria instead of previous restaurant experience or professional training. The interview was redesigned to provide opportunities for applicants to demonstrate an inkling that they would care about their work, and most importantly the people. Our interview process is less talking about work and more about life. We look for people with "identity capital"—experiences, passions, skills, and talents outside of work that can create in a person a strong sense of self. Experience counts, but not at the expense of what matters more to us.

My favorite question on the application is, "If you're going downhill in a canoe, and a wheel falls off—how many pancakes can you fit in a doghouse?" Of course the question is nonsensical, but if they respond creatively, or with humor, their application moves to the top of the pile, even if they have no restaurant experience. If their answer conveys irritation that we asked a silly question, that is a hint that they may not be a great fit. Over the years we've found some wonderful people because of their witty answers to that question—and the many wacky versions of it we've asked on our application. We also changed our job ads to reflect more clearly what we hoped to attract.

This approach meant adjusting our training to allow more time to teach *everything* from the ground up. We couldn't assume that new hires understood restaurant lingo or any tricks of the trade. We couldn't just put "sweep the floor" on a checklist, we had to demonstrate how to do it efficiently when guests are in the space. Each point of service was broken down and taught in detail. At first it seemed silly to have to explain every elemental thing, but once we reviewed why they mattered and oriented everyone to the same standards, good habits soon became second nature.

It took time, but we eventually found people for Botiwalla who liked working in that environment and were willing to learn how to execute Over-the-Counter Service the way we wanted it done. Happiness is contagious. Building a team of people with kind and cheerful dispositions, and taking care of them, fosters more joy that ripples out to customers and the community. Executing excellent service within the constraints of a fast casual restaurant is a challenge that doesn't end, but that's one of the things we love about this work. We strive to get better every day at redefining what's possible in service. In the case of the young applicant with the bright eyes who inspired me to redesign our application process, he became a beloved part of our team and grew into a lead manager position.

Scaling a culture requires effective systems alongside adaptation and flexibility. Thinking creatively about the challenges that come with growth is essential. A lot of little things collectively help sustain a company's culture—right down to how you word an interview questionnaire. Developing tools and systems that match your unique needs creates the stepping stones for growth.

The Botiwalla concept not only proved profitable from day one, but it is also the easiest of our brands to run. We'd landed on our growth engine—a concept we could scale.

Adjusting to Scale

That summer we went to Australia to visit Meherwan's brother, Jamshed, and his family. His parents met us there from India so we could all be together. We'd committed to traveling more with Aria, and it was a milestone for us to leave work for so long to take such a big trip. Since we did the complicated puzzle of using frequent-flyer miles, Aria and I flew one route, and Meherwan flew another, meeting us in Sydney. On Meherwan's trip, he spent a long layover in San Francisco. When he got to Australia, he excitedly filled me in on the visit he'd had with our close family friend Naozer Dadachanji. Naozer was semi-retired at the time after a successful career in finance and was consulting for a few businesses he thought were interesting. He offered his help with our growth plan.

With Naozer's expertise in financial modeling and business structure, his guidance was a game changer. But what excited me most was that Meherwan would have a partner he trusted to help guide us through the inevitable financial quagmires. Meherwan could share his fears and be vulnerable with Naozer; someone other than me could offer support when my husband found himself wearing down the floorboards in our dining room from stress. Our business was getting too large for Meherwan to hold the financial responsibilities all alone. We needed more experienced guidance. For that support to come in the form of someone we trust, who brings huge value and experience in an area that neither Meherwan or I specialize in, felt like a miracle.

Formalizing a role for Naozer in the company would give him the full picture. He'd know all the behind-the-scenes details and be better able to understand what we were dealing with, in order to offer specific advice. We sent him all our financials and future growth plans. He came back with an offer to buy a stake in our business.

For the eight years we'd been growing the restaurant group, we put every penny we could toward investing in its growth. That left us with little savings and the smallest paychecks we could get by on. In 2017, we sold a small percentage of our company to Naozer and his business partner (and our close friend) Katherine. The funds we received from that sale put money in our savings account for the first time since we started Chai Pani.

Naozer's insights into our growth planning proved invaluable. As we initiated him into our restaurant group, we analyzed not just the financials but the overall story and goals of each brand. During this process, the concerns I'd had about opening Buxton Hall Barbecue resurfaced. Buxton had significantly helped the financial picture. But ultimately, it devoured a disproportionate amount of our team's bandwidth and Meherwan's time. That evaluation helped us determine that Buxton shouldn't be the brand we grew, even though it generated the most revenue (when all was going well). The deep dive into each brand crystallized our plan, and we drafted a pitch deck outlining our growth strategy for potential investors. Naozer explained that he viewed part of his role in our business as helping to save us from the "bright shiny things" that were tantalizing but distracting. That guidance was much needed.

If only I had a dollar for every time Meherwan said to me, "Listen to this incredible new idea!" In 2018, he pitched me his latest vision and added the hilarious proclamation, "AND it'll be the easiest thing we've ever done!" His eyes gleamed with a particular kind of excitement, like carbonated energy. I'd come to recognize this look as the marking of another adventure. The idea was hatched in response to a conversation with one of our food distributors who was interested in sourcing the spices we use in our restaurants. Initially, the plan was to create our own spice factory where we'd house all the spices we were already importing for our restaurants and be able to offer them on a larger scale to other restaurants. This idea came together, and Spicewalla was born.

Designing Our Own Systems

Being an Industry Disrupter

In India, spices are treated like produce—retrieved fresh from the market. They do not sit stored in warehouses and kitchen cabinets for years. They are freshly bought, roasted, and ground in kitchens as part of daily meal prep. Inspired by Meherwan's childhood in India, Spicewalla's mission was to change the way we think about spices in the West.

Spicewalla started making special blends and provided a far superior product compared to most wholesale spices. By simplifying the distribution channels, the product would get into chefs' hands faster and more efficiently. Without all the markups, we could offer a fresher and higher-quality product that matched the pricing chefs were already spending on bulk spices. It all seemed like a great idea. But then we took something relatively straightforward and made it totally complicated. My dream-big husband turned it into an entire CPG (consumer packaged goods) line! The team created such great branding and packaging in cute, colorful spice tins, that the line screamed to be shared on a wider scale.

We had landed on what's known as an industry-disrupting product. Providing high-quality spices with careful attention to sourcing and freshness is a relatively new concept in this country. We'd found another lightning-in-a-bottle idea. So, the Spicewalla team started learning about different sales channels—wholesale, retail, grocery, and direct to consumer. Each unique sales channel required different-sized packaging, increasing the complexity. We began selling in retail stores, which need different distributors and container sizes than the ones used for wholesale distribution. Costco approached us about an opportunity. We were also researching how to sell on Amazon. Other big-box retail stores as well as small, independent shops wanted to carry Spicewalla.

The strategy to figure it out as we go seemed just fine until one otherwise normal Monday turned upside down when Oprah's team called! Our Kitchen Essentials Gift Pack was on the short list for her "Favorite Things" holiday gift guide. There was suddenly a long list of things that needed to be done if we wanted to be considered for her final list. All of it required a gamble—we'd have to invest in the resources needed for significant growth without knowing if we'd make the final cut. This required a massive investment of funds, company resources, and staff—none of which we had to spare. The list of requirements included things like: Onboard with Amazon and provide a baseline of supply to accommodate the busy holiday selling season at four times the growth in volume from current sales. We would need forty thousand tins to arrive in time for filling. At that point the Spicewalla staff was mainly a small crew of burnt-out line cooks who'd moved over from our restaurants, along with a couple of managers. They were filling and labeling each tin *by hand* in a tiny clean room and then shipping them off manually. We were in no way ready for the impact of the Oprah effect.

But when the queen calls, you gotta jump at your chance! It was truly a once-in-a-lifetime opportunity for a small business. We grabbed it. We divided up the roles—I took on more with the restaurants, and Meherwan basically moved into Spicewalla.

Just Start

After doing a full assessment, they figured out that there weren't enough of our unique square-shaped tins in all of America to fulfill the benchmarks for Oprah's list. They had to be sourced from overseas and expensively shipped, rapidly, to reach the US in time. Then they discovered that those cute square tins did not work in assembly-line factory labeling or co-packing equipment since the factories were designed for only round containers or bags. We couldn't change the container—the item Oprah selected was a specially designed gift box that was made to perfectly fit the square tins in neat colorful rows. The square tins were an integral part of the design. So, the tins would need to be imported and then HAND LABELED and HAND PACKED—tens of thousands of them, all in time to meet Oprah's deadline. We ramped up production at breakneck speed. People who had been working with us in the restaurants were moved over to Spicewalla, and we quickly added more to the team under the leadership of James Grogan. We relied on our motto from the very beginning of our first restaurant: Just start.

Spicewalla made Oprah's list! And the business skyrocketed. At the time, we were running a restaurant group with five locations (in two different cities) while designing an ambitious plan to scale Botiwalla, and Spicewalla had just hit the jackpot of all opportunities. No one on the Spicewalla team knew how to manage a rapidly growing CPG line. Once again, we were flying blind in a half-built plane. In 2018 (the first year of business) Spicewalla's annual sales were around $350k. Post-Oprah effect, sales jumped to $3.5 million by 2020 and have been growing ever since. The work we'd done to improve our management systems was effective and helped us ride the tidal wave. The challenge before us was how to grow without losing the culture that we'd worked so hard to create.

Teaching Our Teachers

As we refined our training process, we got better at teaching our teachers what matters most to us. The key was differentiating what makes our business unique and successful and then effectively teaching the right people in greater detail *how* to maintain it. With that in mind, we identified twelve key leadership practices that we train all managers to master. As our business grew, we started holding monthly leadership seminars to bring together the managers from all our businesses in different locations, at least virtually. Each month we cover one of these principles in depth as a way of providing ongoing professional development. We are forever students of our industry, so these principles evolve as we do. Having leadership on the ground that works toward mastering these principles is the secret sauce that helps us grow successfully without losing the magic. We aim to **manage systems and processes but mentor the people**. We teach these leadership practices with that intention.

OUR TWELVE KEY LEADERSHIP PRACTICES[8]

1. **Work Big.** Operate at all levels. Dive in but don't get stuck in the weeds. Have a bias for action and impact. Push yourself. Push others. Work and communicate with a focus on results. Remind others to do the same.
2. **Embrace Change.** Our business is growth. Therefore our business is change. Be curious. Be aware of your own biases. Challenge assumptions. Be comfortable with uncertainty and disagreement. Make bold decisions by conviction, not compromise.
3. **Be Great at What You Do.** Know the most important thing you should be doing and be great at it. Be obsessed about getting from good to great. Seek out and learn from people who are great at what they do.
4. **Take Ownership.** Rise to the occasion. Your job isn't done until *the* job is done.
5. **Be Resourceful.** Everything is figureoutable. Don't let a lack of perfect tools hold you back. Jugaad it and carry on. Time *and* money are extremely valuable resources, so do more with less. Constraints help us think differently and redefine what's possible.
6. **Simplify.** Always ask yourself, "What problem am I solving for?" Adding complexity in pursuit of efficiency uses up bandwidth and resources while delivering marginal returns. Be skeptical of anecdotes and look for the data.

---

[8] Inspired by management practices at Nike and Amazon and by *Right Away and All at Once* by Greg Brenneman.

7. **Normalize High Standards.** Be relentless with clear, consistent, and firm standards. Audit frequently, benchmark against the best, and continually raise the bar.
8. **Give Feedback.** Embrace a culture of giving and receiving feedback. Don't be afraid of it. Learn how to do it well, and do it habitually. Have the courage and wisdom to help people understand how to be successful.
9. **Become Dispensable.** Recognize potential talent and teach them to do what you do. Create a path to growth for others and get out of the way. That frees you up to try new things. It's not easy to let go, but if you don't elevate and delegate, you will not grow.
10. **Create Happiness.** We all deserve to be happy, inspired, and fulfilled by our work. Be kind. Be cheerful. Be optimistic. Know our purpose and communicate it religiously.
11. **Be Customer-Experience Obsessed.** Work backward from providing a magical customer experience. Look around and think about everything you do through the lens of their experience. Make it easy to be a customer.
12. **Profit from the Core.** Obsess on profitable growth. Stop doing things that lose money—they inevitably take a ton of time trying to fix. Think money in, not money out. What we do is not easy, but if we can deliver great products, great service, great spaces, and Mindblasting Hospitality, the money will automatically follow.

By the end of 2019 our systems were refined and dialed in to be effective in multiple locations and across all our concepts. We were ready for expansion on a larger scale.

On a personal level, I could see the light at the end of the tunnel between the chaos of building our business and finding a place of balance in my life. It felt like all our years of hard work to build our dream were finally paying off. We had a little security in our bank account and a strong team of culture carriers and leaders ready for growth, and on most days, we felt like things were running well—a feeling that's often fleeting in the restaurant industry. The work I'd done to extract myself from the minutiae of operations was paying off, and I had more time to focus on deeper work and mentoring. It took years of training people to take over all the details I was tracking, and many failed attempts at delegating, but I had finally reached a place where much of the daily operational work was being managed by others. Aria was about to graduate high school. She had grown into a brilliant and grounded young woman preparing to leave for college. I was mourning the end of us all living under the same roof, but I was excited about what was to come in Aria's life, and in my own.

To savor the fleeting time together, Meherwan, Aria, and I took a bucket-list trip to Maui. We brought Aria to our favorite places that we'd discovered twenty-four years prior, on our honeymoon. We swam with turtles, explored the island, and watched endless sunsets over the Pacific. It felt like a celebration that our family had survived the tumultuous early days of the restaurant business. We were no longer just surviving, we were thriving. The intensity of the work that was required of us in the early restaurant years left some scars, but the love between us was deep and strong. The scars are part of the story but not what defined us. If anything, they made us work harder on ourselves, which strengthened our family.

Meherwan and I began to imagine the next phase of our lives. We were gearing up to spend more time together and focus more on the areas of the business that lit us up the most. We were looking forward to growing our company in a way that provided exciting opportunities for our team, and ourselves. I wanted to devote more time to mentoring our leaders and developing an even stronger company culture.

Little did we know that the world was about to turn upside down.

Chapter 17

What to Do When Things Fall Apart

"When there's a big disappointment, we don't know if that's the end of the story.
   It may just be the beginning of a great adventure."
—Pema Chödrön, *When Things Fall Apart*

It was early winter of 2020, and Meherwan and I were having a familiar discussion (one might say debate) about our finances. We were on the cusp of big expansion plans, and I was concerned about our personal finances being so tightly entwined with our business. I felt wary about not saving more money and putting aside a solid retirement fund, and he felt clear that our money was best used investing back into our business. He believed that our business was our most powerful tool for our retirement, as it should continue to pay us long after we retire. I wasn't totally comfortable with this idea. We had everything we needed and a lot of what we wanted, but not much of a safety net.

I'd witnessed my parents giving everything they had to their restaurant, but it not providing a path for retirement, and I saw how much stress that caused. While I understood his conviction that our investment in our business would continue to grow, I was nervous about not having enough emergency funds set aside in case anything went wrong. He countered with, "But we are very well diversified with our businesses. What in the world could happen that would negatively impact all our businesses in different cities, with unique markets and concepts, at the same time?"

And the universe responded, "Hold my beer."

Meherwan was on his way back from India in February 2020 with some close Indian chef friends. News was just emerging about a dangerous virus spreading across China called Covid-19. It had just hit Italy, and emergency declarations were beginning to spread around the world. I asked Meherwan to come straight home and not spend the day in New York he'd planned on the return trip. He made it back just in time before things got really weird, really fast. We were entering a global pandemic, something the world had not seen in recent history.

Within a few weeks, California and New York City closed down businesses. Other cities and states were starting to follow. We'd seen what happened in Italy and watched in utter shock that an entire country could lock down and stay inside for weeks. It seemed impossible to imagine that happening in America—the land of the free. But here we were, facing that probability. Our employees were getting nervous about coming to work. No one knew what to do. The heartbreak hit close to home as we heard the tragic news that we had lost Floyd Cardoz, an Indian chef friend and mentor in the restaurant world. He'd been in India around the same time as Meherwan and got sick shortly after his return to New York. The loss shook us deeply.

In spring of 2020, we had five restaurants in two different cities and states, a Botiwalla under construction in a new city, Spicewalla experiencing rapid growth after the Oprah effect, and other leases secured for upcoming restaurant locations soon to be built. Hundreds of employees were depending on us for their livelihoods. The governors of North Carolina and Georgia (where our businesses were located) had not yet called for official lockdowns, but we expected them soon. There was talk of loans from the government if the whole country went into lockdown—but no one knew what the government would actually do if every business in America had to close.

We gathered our executive team around the conference table to make a plan. Our upper leadership team at the time consisted of ten people who'd worked with us for years, starting in the restaurants and growing their careers along with us. They cared deeply about what we'd built together. We ran through all the scenarios, and it felt like throwing darts at the wall. Trying to do fiscal planning around a catastrophe we couldn't grasp was impossible. Meherwan asked us to make our best guesses at how long we'd need to be closed. Most guessed two weeks; I felt the need to be more conservative and said three weeks. Everyone looked at me in horror. Meherwan said, "Well if that happens, we're screwed."

Of course, in retrospect, we were all wildly deluding ourselves. If we had known then that we were facing years of pandemic disruption, we'd have lost our minds. Knowing what I know now, I can see the gift of our naivete. Even figuring out how to keep paychecks flowing for two weeks seemed near impossible without any money coming in. It would require every penny we had to stay afloat and pay people while we were closed. We knew they needed money, so we had to find a way to help sustain them.

The one thing we all agreed on was that we would do everything in our power to take care of our people. It was our responsibility to figure it out. If it led to bankruptcy, so be it. But we would fight like hell to keep that from happening so that everyone, ourselves included, would have jobs to return to when it was over.

Meherwan was forcing us through a process of making very hard but necessary decisions. It felt like he had a flashlight in one hand and a machete in the other—whacking through our tumbleweed of problems. I realized about halfway through the meeting that he was barely breathing. None of us were. Our fears felt like a tsunami about to crash down upon us, but our collective willpower kept them just far enough away. We had to do the work to make impossible decisions and plow forward.

It became clear that closing was the right thing to do, even though it was not yet mandated by the government. We needed to keep our people safe, and no one yet understood how to do that with Covid. So, we crafted a plan. We would host an online auction to raise money for an emergency fund for our team. We'd scrape together all liquid cash in the bank accounts. We'd beg for rent forgiveness from our landlords. We'd get everything in order so we'd be ready to apply immediately for any government aid that might become available. Meherwan and I would stop our paychecks, along with others around the table if they were able.

Meherwan had facilitated the hardest meeting of his life, and it led us to a game plan. We divided up the work: who would handle communications with the restaurant teams, who would figure out the finances, who'd head up the auction, who'd research Covid and safety protocols and how to get protective gear for reopening, and who would organize giving away all the stocked food and supplies to our staff before anything went bad. I've never been more grateful for the steadfastness of our people. I can't imagine how hard that moment was for solopreneurs who had to figure it all out on their own.

The Role of Vulnerability in Leadership

I looked around at the team. Each of us was slumped in our chairs, heavy under the weight of the moment. We'd weathered a lot of storms and highs and lows together—but this felt different. It seemed as if everything we'd worked so hard for could vanish. All the people depending on us for their livelihoods could be in trouble. This dream that we'd poured our blood, sweat, tears, and love into for eleven years could crumble. I caught the grief in Isaac's eyes and the distress on Charlotte's face. I felt an irresistible urge to press pause on the meeting, and name what I saw. I knew that if we ran from the tsunami of fear, trying not to look in its direction, we'd be shaken off-balance. **We were stronger together if we faced our fears head-on and allowed the feelings in.**

I placed my hand on Meherwan's arm, signaling that I needed to say something. I took a deep breath and said, "We've just made some of the hardest decisions of our professional lives, but we did it. You all focused on what matters most: the care of our people and each other. No one had to tell you to do that, you just did. I want to acknowledge how scary this is and how proud I am to work alongside each of you while we do everything in our power to make it through this. Our people could not be in better hands. They will feel your love, and that will bring them comfort—despite the world falling apart. I want you to know that I see how heavy the burden is. You are not carrying it alone—we are in this together, and we are powerful as a collective. But I want to just take a moment to face the fears together. If we confront them head-on, we will be stronger because we're not spending all our energy keeping the feelings away."

I held back my tears as my voice quivered. Molly Milroy, our marketing director (who didn't yet know she was pregnant and thus very hormonal), rested her head on her knees and let out big heaving sobs. That opened the floodgates. We sat there, some of us allowing tears to flow and some sitting in silence, letting ourselves feel it all. I finally heard Meherwan exhale, releasing a long deep breath. I knew then we'd be ok. It felt like the whole team surrendered some of the panic. If we could remember to breathe and collectively hold each other up while facing our fears, we would not lose what we valued most.

I understood more fully in that moment what the business and our people needed most from me, and how Meherwan and I bring balance to solving problems and managing crises by contributing our different strengths. I broke the silence by saying, "We do not need to fear feeling awake to the reality of what's happening. This is really hard—that's real. And we are going to get through it together. Ok, now let's get to work."

That night I reread Pema Chödrön's book *When Things Fall Apart* to help ground me. For years my nickname had been "Chai Pani Mom." Now it was time for me to show up in the most powerful version of female leadership. My team needed guidance from a leader who could not only support them through a terrifying time, but also demonstrate how allowing our feelings to exist can increase the power and efficacy of our team. **We can face fear and looming feelings (especially the most terrifying ones) and in that process find the strength to make the best possible decisions together. Not from a place of fear, but by allowing vulnerability a seat at the table.** If the world turned into the Hunger Games, we would not participate. We would stay together and share. We would love. And we would survive.

Suddenly most of the world was in a state of crisis at the same time. We were worried about how to keep our loved ones and ourselves safe. Stores were out of cleaning supplies and toilet paper, and online deliveries were not functioning. Aria's high school was closed, and the three of us were home all day, every day, for the first time in many years. Despite the deep fear and confusion of that time, there was also surprising sweetness. In our little circle, we were grateful for the safety of our family. A big backyard to spend our days, and open spaces to walk, helped us handle those uncertain times.

The thing about that wildly upended time is that it felt oddly familiar to us. Restaurateurs spend much of their careers solving seemingly unsolvable problems. It's a muscle that we're forced to develop. Things not going as planned is just another Saturday night in the restaurant industry. **Success in a restaurant requires the conviction that everything is figureoutable.** The ability to figure things out helped us manage a disrupted world. Many industries shifted to remote work, but our industry is built around bringing people together. That's what we do! Restaurants had to adapt and manage challenges beyond measure, but the lessons learned from that experience made us stronger and more resilient.

What to Do When Things Fall Apart

Everything was confusing. As restaurants began to reopen after the nationwide shutdown, every city in every state had different rules. Health codes changed daily. We weren't supposed to open for indoor dining, so everyone had to shift to a take-out model or outdoor dining spaced six feet apart (a luxury of space very few restaurants have).

Following the rules involved a redesign of every system—from the kitchen equipment and layout to building temporary outdoor patios in parking spaces with funds no one had. The whole world was sourcing paper goods and take-out supplies as supply chains fractured. Protective gear was needed, but masks, gloves, and sanitizer were sold out. The complications were enormous, but the will to survive with our business intact and our people cared for kept us motivated. We have never worked harder. Meherwan didn't take a single day off from March 2020 until Christmas that year.

When Associates Become Comrades

Much of my time was spent researching safety protocols and sourcing protective gear and take-out supplies. I deep-dove into things I never thought I'd need to know about, like air purifier filtration density. In the middle of that confusing time, a friend invited me to join a small think tank she and her husband were forming with a handful of industry friends. The goal of the group was to share information and brainstorm ideas so we could help each other figure it all out. I leaped at the opportunity.

Rochelle and Nick run the Cast Iron Group in Durham, North Carolina, the same Rochelle and Nick who helped us design our very first logo and website while driving to South America in 2009, before they started a restaurant and brewery. When the think tank formed, we met weekly to share notes and commiserate. We always managed to laugh at the ridiculousness of the reality we were facing (alongside plenty of tears). Appropriately, they named the group "Shitnado."

What came out of that group is a model for what is possible when associates become comrades. It provided a space to work through the challenges together and support each other while openly sharing information. It was a bit of light in dark times, and much-needed support. Rochelle made a spreadsheet where she collected all the research we gathered. Nick had a buddy who imported scuba gear from China, and during the pandemic he began to supply masks and protective gear for hospitals and restaurants. We bought all the protective equipment our team needed through that scuba company. We helped each other interpret the rapidly changing and difficult-to-decipher health codes for restaurants, sourced green take-out packaging, and brainstormed creative meal-kit ideas and ways to redesign our businesses. Knowing that we were all going through the same thing, we felt less alone. It was a demonstration of the power of what community can do, and how we can survive upheaval when we come together and share ideas and information.

Reinforcing Cultural Values

To help our team stay connected, I started writing love notes to the staff. I continued sending them regular emails called "family letters" throughout the pandemic. I wrote when things felt particularly confusing or tumultuous, or sometimes just when I had a thought to share or an update on the constantly evolving protocols. I wanted to shine some light on the way forward, to help them see a path around all the obstacles they faced every day. I wanted them to know I was right there with them. When I shared my own vulnerability, it helped them to feel less alone with whatever they were dealing with.

Things were constantly changing. Restaurants started permanently closing all around us. People were scared. In the family letters I answered questions, explained what we were doing and why, and gave as much honest information as I could provide. It became one of the bridges that helped sustain the culture of care within our teams we had worked so hard to build.

The practice of sending family letters was a way of reinforcing our company's ethos. **Naming cultural values or demonstrating them with simple gestures of connection on a regular basis is important—especially in times of crisis. As leaders, we cannot assume our people know where our hearts are—we must show them.**

I never could have imagined that a year after sending my first family letter we'd still be in upheaval. Meherwan was devoting much of his time to Spicewalla. That business took off while everyone was cooking at home. I focused on Covid protocols and helping our restaurant teams navigate the constant changes. Charlotte took a maternity leave with her first baby, and I jumped back into daily operations of the restaurants to help cover her.

Aria did her freshman year of college remotely from home, so we had multiple Zoom calls going under one roof every day. In that upended time, we established some rituals to help ground us. Every afternoon at 3 p.m., the comforting aroma of freshly crushed ginger and cardamom pods warming in milk would waft through the house as we made chai just like at Meherwan's home in India. Usually, it was a big pot to see us through the remaining meetings of the day. Aria would emerge from her room for chai in between Zoom classes, and I'd get to squeeze her and hear about her day. Our home patio became Grand Central Terminal—from trainings to operational meetings, we gathered there six feet apart, with cups of chai. In the first sweltering summer in lockdown, we clustered every umbrella we could find to create shade for outdoor meetings, then gathered around fires as the pandemic stretched into the crisp autumn days.

With our daily ritual in place, Meherwan and I started a video series for Spicewalla that we filmed in our kitchen on Sundays called *Chai Time*. Meherwan would cook dishes from the restaurants or share meal-prep tips while I filmed him live on Instagram and chatted with people on the feed. Aria and her friends would come and go in the background, our dogs ran around and barked at the mailman delivering packages, and scenes from our pandemic life at home unfolded on camera. It turned into a way to connect with our community and customers. The ritual helped us realize how deeply we missed gathering in person, and that we needed every ounce of human connection we could find during those isolating times.

Meanwhile, we were juggling socially distanced restaurants and running takeout-only or outdoor dining. Everyone was tired of this mode of operation. Employees were working long and hot shifts sweating behind their health-code-mandated masks, while some customers would complain about having to put one on for five minutes to pick up their takeout order. The basics of interacting in public were bumpy and frayed. Employees were naturally exhausted. Tourists were cranky about safety protocols impacting their vacations and were sometimes shockingly rude. The nightly manager reports changed from reflections on the quality of service that day to statements like "I fear for the future of humanity." Service had never been harder.

We relied on hope, tenacity, and conviction that we'd get to the other side. This effort was aided by how our devoted local customers showed up for us. They stood in line, followed whatever health code rules of the week were needed to keep everyone safe, and supported us through the long years of disruption. They left love notes on our doors and ordered enough takeout to keep paychecks flowing.

During that time, I got a fifty-dollar check in the mail along with a handwritten note that read, "For your staff—we miss you!" I recognized the name on the envelope as one of our long-time customers. She was an older woman who ran a small farm near Asheville. She lived frugally, so for her fifty dollars was no small change. I sat there at my desk and felt a wave of love from that letter. **Countless small gestures of care added**

up to something of significance that supported *how* we showed up in service every day. They provided the recognition that the littlest things can help us hold on to our humanity. That moment lifted me up and helped carry me through the calamity that was restaurant life at the time.

When we reopened our businesses for take-out service after the initial shutdown, we had to figure out ways to operate safely and help our people feel comfortable being in person again. My goal was for each business to set up a staff area with temperature-check stations, sanitizers, masks, clean individual places to store belongings, and updated information on the latest CDC guidelines.

We had closed MG Road (the bar and lounge that was under Chai Pani in Asheville) and used it for storing the mountains of take-out supplies while indoor dining was shut down. The first time I entered that space after reopening, I was overwhelmed with emotion. Rose, the Chai Pani GM, put my guidance into action, transforming a storeroom into a welcome center for our employees. I was deeply moved by the level of care she brought to the task. It felt like a big hug for the team. She understood how to help her people feel comfortable coming back to work. Not everyone needed the same things. Each restaurant had its own unique dynamics. Rose knew her team so well that she knew just what to do. The staff were provided their own entrance through the storeroom, so they could get ready before interacting with deliveries or customers. She taped directional arrows on the floor with signs guiding people through the process and welcoming them back—simple clarity in a time when the world offered very little of that. Arriving to work felt like following the yellow brick road. Her thoughtful approach made it easier for that team in an otherwise chaotic and unfamiliar time. She Mindblasted them! *That* level of care is what kept our staff coming back to work.

SERVICE READY

After a couple of tumultuous years, we made it through the pandemic. Our industry was shattered, hearts had been broken, and loved ones lost. We had to turn our businesses upside down and inside out so many times that we lost track. Somewhere along the way we banned the word "pivot" and started using the words "reimagine" and "reinvent." This perspective focused us on creative solutions and the path forward.

In the multiple reimaginings that were needed, we paid attention to the unmet needs of our communities. Keeping our focus on what was most needed helped us adapt our businesses accordingly and keep them relevant at a time when many restaurants were struggling to stay open. Paying attention to what's needed is a practice that's been beneficial for our businesses well beyond a state of emergency. It keeps a business relevant and can help identify unique ideas and solutions that may not otherwise be discovered. We grew during the pandemic, not by sticking to our original plans but by launching concepts based on what our communities wanted.

Destruction is painful. But once everything was in shambles, we had the opportunity to choose how we wanted to rebuild. What did we want to hold on to? What was better left in the rubble? What did we want to do now that the hardest part was over?

Much of the world went back to business as usual. We tried our best to use the opportunity to evaluate how to rebuild better. We learned lessons that will be forever written in the DNA of our restaurants. From that learning, we fine-tuned our most essential core values. We wrote them on a big poster and hung it next to our conference table for constant reference. Recognizing that whatever upends us again, or distracts us when we're busy, if we focus on these six values, we will be ok.

What to Do When Things Fall Apart

1. Love of service
2. Care
3. Creating magic
4. Excellence
5. Showing up and stepping up
6. Driving meaningful growth

The pandemic taught us how to run our business not in the best of times but through the worst of them. **Building a foundational culture that can weather the storms of change is THE key ingredient.** The hospitality industry would benefit from taking a long hard look at why so many people left when the world fell apart. Those who ask the question, "How can we do better?" are leading the industry to a new way of thinking about business. We aim to keep that conversation alive.

Restaurants are one of the places where we can find each other again in tough times. The hospitality industry has the privilege of creating one of the few opportunities in the world where people from different backgrounds and beliefs can pull up next to each other and Just. Be. Together. To be in the business of bringing people together is a responsibility. And a gift. Coming together is healing, and restaurant workers get to be a part of that. THAT is life-changing. Not just for the people gathering, but for those of us who help make it happen.

Simple things that can get taken for granted—like bringing our families together over dinner, or striking up a conversation with a stranger at a bar—remind us that we can still enjoy someone's company even if we don't have everything in common. These moments create a bridge over our differences and help us remember our shared humanity. Restaurants help people find a way back to each other. In our restaurants, our tables are laid with love, and everyone is invited to gather around them.

Recipe for 4 cups of Chai Pani's Chai

- 2 cups water
- 1 inch of fresh ginger (smashed with mortar and pestle) and a sprinkle of cardamon seeds or crushed cardamon pods (can substitute with 1 teaspoon Spicewalla Chai Masala)
- 2 tablespoons black tea granules (the best kind for chai is called CTC—Crush, Tear, Curl[9])
- 2 cups whole milk

1. Add the water, fresh ginger, and cardamom (or chai spice) to a small pot and bring up to a boil.
2. Add the tea and continue boiling for another minute.
3. Add the milk, and when it comes to a boil, lower the heat and simmer for 7–8 minutes, stirring frequently, allowing the milk to get foamy. Bring up to a boil and back down to simmer two times.
4. Once the mixture gets to a golden brown, strain through a fine-mesh strainer into your favorite mug.
5. Add sugar (or honey) to taste. Enjoy!

---

9   *Crush, Tear, Curl* refers to the way in which the tea is produced. CTC black tea is preferred for a chai recipe because the flavor of the tea is so strong, it's not lost in the world of milk, sugar, and spice.

Chapter 18

Finding Where the Love Lies

"Practice is rooted in self-correction and refinement, working toward clearer and more reliable technique. But when a mistake occurs, we can treat it either as an invaluable piece of data about our technique or as a grain of sand around which we can make a pearl."

—Stephen Nachmanovitch, *Free Play: Improvisation in Life and Art*

In our little microcosm of restaurant life, emerging from the pandemic felt like returning to planet Earth after living in the upside-down. So much had changed, it was the beginning of a fresh start. It should not have taken a pandemic for our industry to recognize the need for psychologically safe and supportive work environments, but it did. Many of the cultural touchstones considered out-of-the-box when we started Chai Pani were beginning to trend. The challenge was that entire industries were trying to reinvent deeply rooted habits without having enough models to support a new way forward. Figuring out *how* to build a culture of care in a business, and then understanding what systems work for your organization to sustain that culture is critical.

The business world referred to that time as the "Great Resignation." People were hopping around, seeking new opportunities, and industries struggled without a consistent work force. Many restaurants had to start from scratch and hire a whole new team. Our restaurants didn't suffer as much as some, as we were able to hold on to many of our people. I credit our managers for much of that retention, and the heroic efforts they put into supporting their teams during the crisis. It's what helped many people stay connected to their work during those hardest days. But even with decent retention, our teams were suffering. They'd lost some of the joy of bringing people together. To find balance again, their voices needed a platform, their hearts needed connection, and their minds needed a sense of safety.

In the attempt to "get back to business," many places were missing a key ingredient. The feeling of being cared for is what creates psychological safety. Without it, all the other initiatives (like raises and benefits) aren't enough to help people feel good about going to work when times are hard. **When people have gone through a collective trauma, the feeling of safety and care is the most important priority.**

As the world emerged from the pandemic, I eventually hung up my hat as our Covid safety czar and focused on the path forward. I wanted to reflect on what we learned. Some of the learnings were hard ones. We had worked relentlessly to save the businesses and create new ones to keep people employed. But we struggled to keep up with the level of communication that everyone needed as we raced to solve constant problems. Check-ins had slipped because it was hard to find the time. Without that focused opportunity to be heard, people felt more disconnected and confused about our collective *why*. From this realization, I saw my number one job as ensuring that our culture of care remained strong as we transitioned back to a new normal. We had to rebuild our infrastructures and systems that had held us together. The scaffolding had fractured when everything was upside down. It didn't crumble, but there were cracks that needed mending.

When the pandemic first hit, and all our restaurants struggled to reopen in a takeout-only model, Botiwalla was already set up for it. It adapted quickly and held on to its profitability through all the disruption. It also had the least amount of staff turnover. This was a great indication that Botiwalla was the concept to scale once we could get back to our growth plans.

Our table-service restaurants (two Chai Panis and Buxton Hall Barbecue) had a harder time shifting back and forth between the different modes of service required by the ever-changing safety rules. Those businesses also had the most turnover. Many of the new staff in those restaurants were hired during the pandemic while we were operating only take-out service. Because of that, we had a large percentage of staff who'd never worked in a table-service environment. Much work had to be done to recalibrate our businesses. Staffing became so competitive during the pandemic that we had to increase our pay structures beyond what the businesses could afford. The pandemic loans helped to bridge the gap, but we had to find a path forward without depending on more loans. The revenue models for our restaurants had totally changed. Costs of goods were way up, supply-chain problems impacted expenses, pay was up—the entire financial structure had to be redesigned.

Creating Go Forward Plans

We analyzed the processes needed to get back to profitability, happy teams, and excellence in execution. Meherwan devoted himself to finding a clear system we could follow to manage all the moving parts. He came across a process called a "Go Forward Plan,"[10] and then he tweaked it to fit our needs. Finding systems and ideas from other businesses and adapting them into the restaurant space helped us land on solutions that worked best for us.

---

10   From *Right Away and All at Once* by Greg Brenneman.

Meherwan gathered the executive team around the conference table—the same one that our tears landed on when we made the decision to close our restaurants at the start of the pandemic. He laid out a structure we could follow to get each business high functioning and profitable again. His voice was grave as he explained with conviction, "This work will be hard. I know we've all just come out of a time that required so much from us—so much adaptation, so much change. Getting these businesses back on track will take everything we have to give. We can't keep running in circles playing whack-a-mole while racing to put out fires everywhere. We gotta get strategic and shift from reactive work to proactive work. So, today we begin the process of creating a detailed road map to recovery for each one of our businesses in order to save them from going under." The faces around the table reflected the overwhelm we experienced upon hearing his declaration, but also the recognition one feels when someone speaks a necessary but inconvenient truth.

So, we got to work. We broke down a Go Forward Plan for each business. Our executive team became the "Go Forward Team" to honor our commitment to this goal. It became our primary focus, requiring us to press pause on everything else.

The Go Forward process took months. Each business faced unique challenges and needed an individualized approach. **We asked ourselves a critical question for every issue: What problem are we solving for?** Asking this pivotal question was essential in finding the answers specific to each challenge. Some restaurants needed to increase sales, others had plenty of business but were losing money due to staffing and cost of goods increases. We brainstormed individual solutions so that the results would fit each business's particular needs. We devoted ourselves wholeheartedly to the process, and it worked. After six months of deep work, we had most of our businesses back on track. Ultimately, that work led us to implement more effective systems that we likely would not have found without the crisis pushing us.

We also experimented with management structures and incorporated some best practices from the Entrepreneurial Operating System® (EOS)[11] and other models. The process was time consuming, but after its completion, we are a more effective management team. We have clearer lines of communication and better-defined roles. As each of our responsibilities got crystallized, we wasted less time with too many people trying to solve the same problems. We were able to reach our goals, and our restaurants are now more efficient, with improved margins. **There is no paint-by-numbers way to run a restaurant well. It requires adapting systems to land on what works. If we didn't turn our brains inside out to solve our challenges, we would constantly be trying to fit a square peg in a round hole.**

Utilizing Metrics

One of the big discoveries of the pandemic was the importance of learning how to provide Mindblasting Hospitality in a digital world and gig economy. Our restaurants are built around bringing people together, and when we couldn't do that, we had to reimagine ways to connect with our communities. Learning how to embrace delivery and takeout was important.

Prior to this, we often didn't accept take-out orders during busy shifts at Chai Pani in Asheville because the kitchen was too small to manage it well and still provide timely food for dine-in guests. We believe that the people who waited in line to dine in person deserve the best possible experience, so we were prioritizing them. One busy lunch rush, a neighbor who worked at a gallery across the street tried to call in an order for takeout. Isaac answered the phone that day (the whole staff was slammed with a packed house and a long waitlist) and explained that takeout was turned off because the kitchen had reached capacity.

The caller got really frustrated and snapped at Isaac, saying that he

---

11 www.eosworldwide.com.

was a regular who orders from us all the time, especially in our slower seasons, in part to help support neighbors through the winter. With his temper flaring, he went on to yell that it was unfair because he was manning his workplace alone and couldn't leave his post to dine in the restaurant. Before hanging up on Isaac, he vented that the unpredictability of not knowing if and when he could order from us was inconsiderate.

Ever-calm Isaac remained unruffled by the man's anger, but he realized that the guy had a valid point. So he went about trying to make it right. Not because the caller was pushy or angry, but because his argument made sense. So, Isaac personally packed up the meal that he had wanted, filling the to-go containers with extra abundance. And then, he hand-delivered it across the street. The guy was immediately embarrassed upon seeing Isaac arrive with a food bag in hand. They had a nice chat, and Isaac told him that he understood how he felt, and while he wasn't sure exactly how to solve the problem, he was going to try.

This began a deeper analysis of our approach to takeout. Importantly, it helped us realize that, in essence, offering takeout was a service to our community. It was a way of honoring the devotion our regulars had bestowed on us through the years. So even though it was really complicated to figure out, we tried.

Emerging from the pandemic and completing the Go Forward Plans for each business, we focused on our management principal "Profit from the Core." Part of this was learning to more accurately measure what our community wanted and how to work with the detailed metrics. The metrics we collected revealed that delivery and takeout were not going away in the post-pandemic world, and there was some good opportunity in there if we could figure how to excel in it.

We utilized the metrics by:
1. Looking very closely at the data:
    a. How often is online ordering turned off and for how long?
    b. How many orders have missing items?

Finding Where the Love Lies

    c. How long are the delivery drivers waiting on orders to be ready?
2. Working closely with the teams and developing strategies to support their ability to offer takeout as often as possible and with excellence.
3. Implementing systems to ensure orders are complete:
    a. Environmental SOPs (standard operating procedures) with detailed build-lists on how to pack bags
    b. Multiple marking systems to ensure orders are complete
    c. Stickers to indicate that a drink is in the order
4. Responding to reviews on delivery apps.
5. Sending offers to loyal take-out customers.
6. Running promotions in the slow season to give added value to customers.

Although customers aren't getting the full dine-in experience, we still strive for Mindblasting Hospitality, even when we don't control 100 percent of the guest journey. They may not get the aesthetics, music, and vibes—but they CAN get Mindblasting food! It's a big way we can spread our love and philosophy beyond the walls of our restaurants. Takeout and delivery allow us to maximize our revenue while making relatively few operational changes. However, not every restaurant has the space to accommodate it and the steep delivery fees have to be kept in balance for it to work.

To approach the next phase of growth in our company, and extract personally from the weeds, we began to manage our teams with a "highly aligned but loosely coupled" approach. We provide context over control.[12] Teaching managers *why* certain processes are in place is important, so

---

12 From the Netflix culture deck, jobs.netflix.com/culture.

they understand the purpose behind them. They then get the goal that we're aiming for. That makes us "highly aligned." Being "loosely coupled" means the team is free to think outside the box and come up with even better ideas to accomplish the same goal.

Metrics play a role in this process because they help empower managers to make informed decisions. We spend time teaching them how to utilize the data effectively and what to be looking for. Then we set them free. This means we have to be unafraid to allow managers to reinvent the wheel. We trust that they have their finger on the pulse of their spaces and people more acutely than we might. They can't just go rogue; they run their ideas by us. This approach involves spending time fielding ideas (some that might not be worth trying), but in the end it's worth the effort. Some of our best ideas and systems have come from them.

Bright Shiny Things

After all the deep and detailed work, our businesses were humming again, and we could revisit our plans for growth. We were blessed with many ideas that showed great promise for success, but we were pulled in too many directions. We'd added new concepts over the years, and multiple brands. We realized (the hard way) that we could not do it ALL, at least not well and not at the same time. To plan for growth, we needed to tighten the criteria we used to evaluate *what* to grow and, importantly, what to let go of. **Landing on a great idea, or finding a promising venture, also means learning to evaluate the opportunity cost.**

This was brought home for us when we made the hard decision to shut down a popular business. How do you close a restaurant that everyone loves? Nani's Rotisserie Chicken was an idea born in the pandemic in response to how people wanted (and needed) to eat. It was a grab-and-go concept featuring high-quality, pasture-raised chickens, rotisseried to mouthwatering perfection and paired with healthy comfort sides—veggies in light, bright marinades, salads, mixed grains, and pastas—designed to feed a family. The recipes were inspired by my mother's home cooking, hence the name Nani (meaning grandmother in Hindi).

We opened Nani's in a space around the corner from Chai Pani in downtown Asheville. Our intention when we secured the space (pre-pandemic) was to create an annex kitchen for the ever-busy Chai Pani and, while we were at it, serve a quick grab-and-go item or two out of the small storefront. We wanted to ease the pressure on the Chai Pani kitchen as well as keep people who couldn't get a table happy. It was a great plan until the pandemic put everything on hold. The landlords kindly allowed us to hang on to the unfinished spot until things got back to some kind of normal. The pandemic forced us to figure out the best use of that space while restaurants were stuck in take-out mode. From that reimagining, Nani's was born.

In 2022, Nani's was nominated for "Best New Restaurant" by the James Beard Foundation. With no parking, the location wasn't ideal for grab-and-go, but it served its purpose during the pandemic of providing nourishing take-out food. Everyone on our team loved it and survived those hard years on its delicious meals.

When the summer of 2022 rolled around with Chai Pani winning the JBF "Outstanding Restaurant" award, things went bananas in our tiny 1920s building. Lines of people circled around the block hours before service, hoping to get a table. We were slammed every hour of service every day of the week. Our kitchen was imploding under the pressure as the volume pushed them to the brink.

One day during the peak of that busy time, I went into the Chai Pani walk-in looking for something. It was so full that the produce bins were stacked on pallets in front of the metro rack shelves, leaving just enough room for one body to squeeze in—and requiring a game of Tetris to reach anything on the shelves. I happened to notice a single potato stuck randomly between two boxes on a shelf. As I was leaving, I asked the manager what the heck the potato was doing there. Chefs follow strict organizational systems in the walk-in, so it stood out to me. She yelled in a blur as she raced past me, "There literally is not another square inch in this place to put that damn potato!"

We were up to our eyeballs in business. The locals who had seen us through the pandemic could no longer get tables, tourists driving for hours to dine with us couldn't get in, and we had to turn off takeout because the kitchen could not possibly produce the amount of food needed—or find a place to store the necessary supplies. We held firm to our no reservations policy because we feared that reservations would change the entire nature of the rowdy, casual, affordable street food place we had built. Inserting reservations in the middle of such busyness would mean that we'd be instantly booked out for six months. People had planned trips to our town just to visit Chai Pani, and if they didn't know we required a reservation, they'd be out of luck. There was no easy solution. Right after winning the award for the most outstanding restaurant in America, we were quite far from excellence. Suddenly, it became way too hard to be a guest at Chai Pani.

My moment of realization was that potato in the walk-in. Anyone running their own business has likely had a similar moment: the realization that things are just not right. You have a problem that needs a solution, but you can't figure it out, so you're just doing your best to keep afloat, until one day—bam! A potato speaks the truth, and you have to confront it. We kept expecting things to calm down, but they didn't. So, potato in hand, I marched upstairs to our offices, interrupted Meherwan in a meeting, and said, "We have to call an emergency meeting. Chai Pani needs our immediate support with the chaos downstairs. Our team is crumbling under the pressure." He knew this; we all did. But the potato on the shelf rang the alarm bell.

After bringing the team together for some brainstorming, we made the hard call to return to our original plan for the space that had become

Finding Where the Love Lies

Nani's. With sad hearts, we ate our last perfect rotisserie chickens, shuttered Nani's doors, and did a rapid thirty-day transformation of the space. Nani's kitchen was reorganized, and the team was trained to support the Chai Pani kitchen. We took what had been Nani's front of house and made it a retail storefront for Spicewalla. Mikey worked his design magic in one month, turning it into a spice wonderland.

As hard as it was to close a beloved concept, the process taught us something important. Despite Naozer's best advice to avoid "bright shiny things," we had spread ourselves too thin. When you're growing and successful, exciting opportunities get presented all the time—and Meherwan's wild imagination was full of new ideas. Our challenge was that we wanted to do too many of them. And when the pandemic hit, we needed revenue and our people needed jobs, so we created businesses that fit the needs of that time. While that helped us survive, it was time to return to our leadership principle "Profit from the Core." The first part of that principle (as referenced in chapter 16) reads, "Obsess on profitable growth. Stop doing things that lose money—they inevitably take a ton of time trying to fix. Think money in, not money out." That was the guiding principle we focused on as we faced the hard decisions before us.

We were juggling too many concepts, and that diversification led to challenges with our ability to refine each business to the best version of itself. It's harder to perfect that many menus, and optimize the sourcing, along with honing financial models when each concept is unique and facing different challenges. We began an important process of questioning why we got into this business in the first place, what we loved most about it, and what we wanted to focus on moving forward. Our executive team came together to rethink what we wanted for our future.

Over a decade earlier, back in 2012, I led a visioning process with our core team after taking a course from Ari Weinzweig's ZingTrain program. That process helped crystallize our mission. The first time I led the group visioning session, we had just shifted our "corporate" offices from the closet-sized room in the restaurant to a few small rooms above Chai Pani. Charlotte, Isaac, Mikey, Meherwan, and I had moved from working hands-on in the restaurants to being full time in the office. Daniel Peach and James Grogan oversaw culinary operations. It was a small but dedicated crew.

We had gathered in our "conference room," which was really a hallway. Sitting around a beat-up old coffee table in hand-me-down chairs, we were there to do some visioning. We were ready to dream bigger, thinking ahead to where we wanted to be in five and ten years. We then worked backward from the vision to determine how we needed to grow our team, and ourselves as individuals, to get there. Meherwan wrote at the top of the page, "Ten locations in ten years."

At that phase of our restaurant story, just putting that declaration in writing felt audacious. The process of dreaming big filled the room with nervous excitement. It was a moment frozen in time that would keep coming back as a pivotal point in the trajectory of our company. Writing it down helped us believe we could do it. Soon, instead of feeling like a wild and crazy idea, it just became what we were doing.

Back to 2023—it was time for the team to reevaluate where we were headed. We'd reached another pivotal moment in the story we wanted to write for our business. It was time for some visioning. Our executive team again gathered around the conference table. The setting has changed from the early days. The hand-me-down furniture has been replaced, and we now have offices spread over three floors in the building next door to the original Chai Pani, with departments for design, finance, HR, the executive team, and a group of rock-star administrative assistants who help keep everyone organized. Isaac is the VP of Growth, leading all of our buildouts. Charlotte is our COO. Mikey is the Brand Director. Daniel Peach is our Culinary Director, based in Atlanta. James Grogan is the Director of Sales at Spicewalla. Those faces from day one are still the faces I see every day. We added more wonderful people to the circle around our table. We've grown as individuals, but most importantly, we've grown even closer together. One thing that remains constant is the depth of care this team has for our people.

The Power of Visioning

Creating a vision as a group is a powerful process. **Visioning helps us decide what we want, write it down, and make a plan to get there.** There are different visioning processes to guide organizations. But essentially, it's a way of collectively imagining what future success looks like. It's more than just a mission statement for the business, it's a specific description of what success will look like regarding a particular goal.[13]

Following the steps of the process helped us realize that we had been using the terms "mission," "vision," "ethos," and "purpose" sometimes interchangeably, without enough clarity. Each of these descriptors are important to us, and they impact our business. But without enough distinction between them, we weren't utilizing them effectively. We started the visioning process by identifying and differentiating our purpose, core values, niche, and goals. This helped us create a vision that was clear and possible for us to attain. We think of our ethos as the foundation that holds the vision together. That granular clarity made it easier for us to formulate a strategic plan about specifically how to accomplish the vision.

We were inspired by the idea of creating BHAGs: big, hairy, audacious goals.[14] This refers to a "bold challenging goal that pushes an

---

13 Adapted from https://www.zingtrain.com/article/why-and-how-visioning-works/.

14 From the book *Built to Last: Successful Habits of Visionary Companies* by Jim Collins and Jerry I. Porras.

organization to surpass itself."[15] When we completed the process, we hung our vision on the office wall to use as a guide throughout the year. Putting a vision in writing is important. It's a reference point we come back to regularly. This process helped us draw a road map, so we collectively know where we're going. A road map helps ensure that our hard work is moving us in the direction we want to go.

For our visioning in 2023, we followed the guidance of the *Harvard Business Review*'s article on visioning.[16] We emerged from the process with important clarity about our direction, which brought us to a big realization.

From that exercise, we wrote the following vision:

THE CHAI PANI RESTAURANT GROUP VISION

VISION = PURPOSE + CORE VALUES + OFFERING + ENVISIONED FUTURE[17]

A. **PURPOSE:**
   » To serve the world through food, love, and care.
B. **CORE VALUES:**
   » Love for service and hospitality (being of service to everyone we interact with).
   » Commitment to excellence (fanatical attention to quality and consistency).
   » Care (for each other, our guests, our community, and those in need).

---

15   Ibid.

16   From *Harvard Business Review*, "Building Your Company's Vision." https://hbr.org/1996/09/building-your-companys-vision.

17   Ibid.

- » Showing up and stepping up (being there and getting it done).
- » Creating magic (Mindblasting food, service, and spaces).
- » Driving meaningful growth (for our business and our people).

C. **OUR NICHE:**
- » Delicious, approachable, fun, value-oriented Indian food served in beautifully curated, joyful, immersive spaces.

D. **OUR BIG HAIRY AUDACIOUS GOAL:**
- » To be one of the most loved and respected restaurant groups in the world known for changing the perception of casual *Indian food.*

This process helped us map the details for *how* we would reach our vision while holding on to what we value. We clarified what we love the most about what we do, and what we want to spend our time on moving forward. In thirteen years, we'd come so far toward reaching our objectives and goals that we felt we had in many ways accomplished them. After much reflection, we made a pact to say no to bright and shiny things that did not fit into our master plan. Before that deeper dive, we had a very clear sense of what we did, but visioning helped us crystallize our *why*.

This process of **adjusting the road map has been crucial for us. It has helped us remain connected on a deeper level with our work and why we're doing it. Effective visioning requires dedication and regularly revisiting the road map and goals.**

The framework of our vision that had emerged focused on our *Indian* concepts. Our team was not ready to launch our ambitious Botiwalla expansion plan if they were also trying to master the many diverse concepts we were juggling. By narrowing our focus, we can increase our chances of success, balance, and joy along the way. Deciding to focus fully on our Indian concepts meant releasing the others.

With that clarity, we decided to close the other Nani's we'd opened in Atlanta and find roles for that team in our other restaurants. We also sold the Buxton Chicken Palace kiosk (another concept born in the pandemic) to its manager, setting them up to be independently run. This left Buxton Hall Barbecue.

We had parted ways with Elliott Moss, the founding partner and chef, buying him out of his share of the business. Buxton had struggled the most out of our businesses to survive the pandemic disruptions. All of our other businesses were able to return to profitability, but Buxton had not. It was draining money every month. The answer was clear—it was time to let Buxton go. But a directional change like this comes with incredibly hard decisions.

So there we were, facing a gargantuan task of closing a popular restaurant with a large staff. A long list was staring back at us from the whiteboard—all the difficult tasks that had to be done to close. As we worked our way through the list, I felt the group growing increasingly tense. I'm pretty allergic to sitting through meetings dodging unspoken landmines. I sensed that everyone was worried about how our staff was going to feel, so I paused the process and addressed the elephant in the room. "Where on this list is the care of our staff?" Meherwan responded (slightly annoyed that I'd interrupted the flow of the meeting) that we have to look at *every* task through that lens. He had assumed it was a given, but he hadn't identified that for the group. Just him clarifying that expectation allowed us to take a big collective breath and think more clearly. Before proceeding, I wrote at the top of the list, "FIND THE LOVE." This one step sharpened our resolve to think about each task through the lens of how to best take care of the people involved.

Over the years of training our managers, I've taught them to ask themselves a question when faced with a challenge: **Where does the love lie?** It's a thought experiment that helps us focus on what matters most. It puts the notion of care at the top of our mindset and prioritizes it in decision making. Learning how to make the best decisions is how we hone our craft. If we weave this question "Where does the love lie?" throughout all the hard decisions, then by doing so we are inserting a connection to something bigger than ourselves into the mix. It's a way of asking: **How do I accomplish the business objective, while also focusing on what best serves our people?**

The first bullet point on our list about "finalizing the timeframe for closure" was rewritten to "Find the timeframe that will best take care of that team and then fix the closing timeline around that." Point two shifted from "Figure out how to tell the team we're closing" to "Find as many opportunities and positions in our company to offer the team and then begin conversations with them." Clarifying our mission to find the love totally shifted our experience. We trusted that we would find the way to do what we had to do (close the restaurant) while *also* taking good care of our people.

It's easy to misunderstand this concept of focusing on the love as just being nice all the time. Quite the contrary. **Sometimes real love lies in finding the courage to say the hardest parts—sharing our difficult truths and making the challenging but necessary decisions.** The importance of this has been a lesson hard-learned in our work as well as in our marriage. When Meherwan and I found the courage to tell each other the hard truths, things always got better. But it took us time to discover this. It's not easy to disrupt a seemingly peaceful situation to address hidden things lurking beneath a calm surface. But we've benefited profoundly by doing just that.

Practicing this is at the heart of *how* we weave our ethos into day-to-day life at our restaurants. Doing the right thing for our people requires us to make hard calls. If we do that in a way that sustains our values and takes care of people, then we honor our goal to be a people company that happens to serve awesome food. It's not about perfection, or never making a mistake. It's about how we handle our mistakes, correct course, and take care of each other along the way.

Chapter 19

Storytelling with Food and Culture

"To other countries I may go as a tourist, but to India, I come as a pilgrim."
—Martin Luther King Jr.

Our team landed in India in the middle of the night in a city that never sleeps. One by one they exited the Mumbai airport, merging into the crowd, the air thick with the smell of burning sandalwood and cow dung. Their faces wore the long hours of travel as well as bewilderment at the sensory overload. The Mumbai airport is the gateway to the chaotic wonderland of the city. More sound, color, smells, people, and action cohabitate in one square foot than anywhere else on earth.

I love the energy of the Mumbai streets—the way they flow like a rushing river winding its way to the sea. The chaos has an organic system that allows twenty million people to get where they need to go. People navigate around bullock carts, rickshaws, and thousands of cars. Dogs scramble around your legs and cows meander right down the middle of the road. Your body is guided by the flow while engulfed in stimulation, punctuated by an impossible amount of honking horns. You feel it down to your toes. I was excited to be back in Mumbai, and to share this one-of-a-kind experience with my coworkers—all of whom were in India for the first time.

Connecting Leadership to the Company Ethos

It began with a dream back in 2012. After pinching pennies to recover from a particularly rough winter, we needed a motivating light at the end of the tunnel. In our annual planning session, we decided on a staff trip to India. To change the perception of Indian food in America, we wanted our team to better understand the culture they were representing. We set a goal to take them to India so that they could experience firsthand the story our restaurants are telling.

But we couldn't fathom how we'd afford it. We finally realized that we just had to **decide what we most wanted to do, then work backward from there**. The realization came when Meherwan calculated how much money we wasted on lost pens. He added up the expense of supplying pens that inevitably disappear with guests and in server aprons, along with the never-ending supply of Sharpies for the kitchen that vanish after one use. The amount we spent on pens in one year added up to the cost of one plane fare to India! We had to stop losing pens, and get the team invested in *why* paying attention to that detail mattered. We figured out how to cut all waste and unnecessary spending on a million little details, and the team cared about that process because the goal was getting to India.

That knowledge is power. By vigilantly focusing on curbing waste and loss, we could eventually do what we wanted to do. After this discovery, we applied this frugal mindset to our wish lists. When we wanted to crack the code on how to afford health care for our staff, we analyzed the budget to find where fat could be trimmed. We negotiated better rates from food distributors, which became easier as our business and buying power grew. When you serve thousands of pounds of chicken a week across all restaurants, saving a few pennies on product ends up saving thousands of dollars at the end of the year. We utilized the training we got from our frugal beginnings, and the mindset of jugaad, to be sure that we never spent on unnecessary things. That was our path to getting what we needed and wanted most.

On the first trip in 2013, Meherwan took his two head chefs, Daniel and James (and Mikey as videographer), on a food tour of India. The trip's impact was palpable, so we scrimped and saved to open the opportunity to more people. Meherwan now leads a food tour every year, with the goal that all our managers get a chance to go at some point. Isaac also leads a tour every year that *any* staff member who's worked with us for more than a year can apply to attend. It's an all-expense-paid trip for six to eight people at a time.

In 2023, our team really deserved to celebrate getting the business through the pandemic. Recovering from the financial hit of the shutdowns was a huge accomplishment, and returning to these trips was our reward. That January, we had two tours happening in different parts of India at the same time. The one led by Meherwan started out in Mumbai en route to his hometown of Ahmednagar. Isaac led another, from Goa up to Delhi. Our two groups came together to attend Daniel Peach's wedding in central India, near his fiancée's hometown of Pune.

I met up with the group at Elco Market, a popular street food joint famous for its pani puri. I'd joined the team (five of our restaurant managers and Meherwan) in Mumbai to take them to the Slum Innovation Project, an organization our restaurant group supports. After a night's rest in a nice hotel to recover from travel, we took them to explore another side of India. It's a land of extremes, where billionaires' mansions tower over one of the world's largest slums, and hipster Brooklyn-style coffee shops stand next to crumbling ancient temples.

On their first day in Mumbai, we set out to visit a community center in the slum known as Dharavi. We met up with Nawneet, a gem of a man who focused his San Francisco Film School thesis on making a documentary about children in the slums of Mumbai. After filming in India, he found that he couldn't leave. He devoted his life to helping the children growing up in that neighborhood build a better life. He created a community center that provides a safe haven for children to gather, study, and get access to school supplies, Wi-Fi, computers, tutoring, and mentorship. Two of the young women we helped sponsor with education scholarships showed up to meet our team and give us a tour.

We wound through the maze of dark alleys just wide enough to walk single file through muddy passages. The midday sun sizzled above, but the lanes were dark as night—shadowed by towering shanty homes made of salvaged sheet metal and tarps. Over a million people live crammed together in an area of a few square kilometers, without running water or plumbing. These are not encampments—they are homes where hard-working people pay more than they can afford to live.

One of the young women, now a college student, proudly brought us to her home, up three flights of vertical fire-escape ladders that require holding a flashlight in one hand while pulling yourself up the metal rungs with the other. At the top of the stairs (which she climbs with giant buckets of water on her back), we entered the single eight-by-ten-foot room where her five family members live. It was clean and organized. Every inch had a well-designed purpose. There was electricity and, thanks to her skilled carpenter father, a window built into the sheet-metal wall that allowed air in but kept out the monsoons. Our team squeezed into the space and stood in silence, absorbing the reality of this family's day-to-day life.

She looked up at me and said, "Do you like my home?" The question was innocent and full of pride. She had no idea the lens through which this group of Americans was seeing it. She welcomed us with the same hospitality, so common across India, that she would have if her home was a palace. In India guests are considered next to God, and are treated as such. Visiting India forever changes your notion of what genuine hospitality is. Our group was moved to tears.

We spent a few more days exploring Mumbai and then met up with

Charlotte and James, who flew in for Daniel's wedding. We piled into a big van for the drive to the city of Pune, a place Meherwan visited regularly throughout his childhood. We joined Isaac's crew arriving from South India and spent the day taking them to Meherwan's favorite spots. They experienced the vada pav cart, famous all over India for its mouthwatering interpretation of the vegetarian burger-like street food specialty. They went to the Irani bakery that inspired Botiwalla's design, which still looks exactly the way it did when Meherwan frequented it as a young boy.

I separated from the group to run some errands. As I wandered down MG Road, I saw in the distance my coworker Teddy standing amid the cacophony of honking horns, swerving rickshaws, cars, and push carts piled high with goods—a typical action-packed street corner in India. He was chatting with Erin, Chai Pani's front-of-house manager, and Megan, the kitchen manager. There they were, in the middle of the mayhem, looking completely at home. I felt full of pride that we'd found a way to bring them there.

Before they continued their ten-day tour of India, eating their way from street-corner dives to fancy five-star hotels and the most important stop at Meherwan's mother's kitchen, we headed to Daniel's wedding. The cultural immersion of being in India was topped off by a magnificent three days of back-to-back wedding events set in an ancient fort. Fifteen people from our restaurant group made the trip. We were welcomed with showers of marigold petals, garlands of tuberose flowers, and trees lit up with twinkly fairy lights covering the expansive property. Walking through the medieval gates transported us back in time. The weekend was a feast of beauty and love. No one does weddings quite like India!

The night before the wedding ceremony, Daniel, Charlotte, James, Isaac, Meherwan, and I stood on the fort's rooftop under an orange sky, watching the blazing sun wash over the Indian countryside. We looked at each other in disbelief. We had been together on the Chai Pani adventure from the beginning. That moment at Daniel's wedding felt like a dream come true. It was a feeling of accomplishment, where just being there together was the best reward for all the years of hard work. It took a lot of intention, creativity, and planning to manifest that dream into reality, but we'd done it.

Bringing our team to India is more impactful than we could have imagined. At the end of the trip, we ask everyone about their highlights and what they would be taking away from their visit. On this trip, every single one of them named the tour of the home in the slum as their personal highlight. The staggering warmth of Indian hospitality leaves an imprint on your soul. After this trip, Megan posted a beautiful note about her experience, and this part has stuck with me:

> *It made me re-fall in love with my job. Seeing the vision and inspiration makes me want to share this overflowing love I've felt since landing in India . . .*
>
> *I'll never be the same after that.*

We bring our teams to India so that their hearts can be broken open by the generosity of spirit and the warmth of the people. The trip is our way of teaching them a part of our own story that influenced who we are and why we do the things we do. We take them to the places that motivate us to believe that what we do matters, that every act of grace and every plate made and delivered with love creates a ripple out into the world. We immerse them in the place that has personally brought us closest to the source of enchantment in our world (call it God, love, peace, or whatever it is for you). Often, it offers people an opportunity to find that source within themselves. This awareness functions as a bridge to our philosophy of Mindblasting Hospitality. Feeling intrinsically motivated to seek out the love and be a light in the world is at the heart of it. It's hard to teach. Understanding and, better yet, experiencing the inspiration behind our business is one of the best ways we've found to help people "get it."

Leaders who have tapped into that source are more effective because they understand the importance of having a powerful ethos as a business. The experience of being in India teaches something that's hard to define. It's a gift we can offer. A deeper understanding of our *why* helps our managers weave it into their leadership. **Businesses that invest in their team understanding their why foster a work culture that becomes self-sustaining.**

From the scent of fresh roasting spices wafting from our kitchen to the warmth reflected in the eyes of the people from Meherwan's hometown captured in the photos that line the walls, it's about transporting our guests to a land that we love. Our restaurants are the canvas we use to paint a picture of India. India is a technicolor, cacophonous, one-of-a-kind experience. The more our staff experience it firsthand, the better they help us tell the story. Aligning a restaurant space with another culture's story is a creative challenge. **Guests notice minute details, even if unconsciously, and that builds a story in their imagination as they move through the dining experience.** We want that story to be a true, authentic representation and celebration of India.

The Necessity of Reinvention and Trusting the Process of Change

After we closed Buxton Hall Barbecue, we were faced with the decision of what to do with the space. We'd invested a lot of money and time in that building, from the initial buildout and equipment to endless repairs and improvements. We thought about selling it, but it would be difficult to get a good return on our investment. Plus, we loved that building.

It is a mammoth ten-thousand-square-foot space: a large dining room and full bar, a lobby big enough for retail, a mezzanine level with a small bar, a huge open kitchen, and an entire lower level for prep including overflow kitchen space, storage, and offices. Meanwhile, right around the corner, Chai Pani was squeezed into its one-thousand-square-foot dining room, with a tiny kitchen, not enough storage, and only enough room to fit one table large enough for more than four people. The space felt blessed after getting our start there, and we could not imagine moving. But it was a constant struggle to manage the demands on Chai Pani in that space, not to mention the number of guests who were left disappointed after not being able to get in. We'd built the annex kitchen around the corner, but even with that there wasn't enough kitchen space to do catering and special events or consistently offer takeout. The solution became clear. Chai Pani was busting at the seams, so we would relocate it to the Buxton space.

Change is never easy. But if our years in this industry have taught us anything, it's that **remaining stagnant is the worst possible thing for a restaurant. Change and reinvention are vital aspects of many businesses, especially restaurants. If we allow fear of the unknown to keep us frozen, we will never accomplish our dreams.** We all feared what could go wrong by moving Chai Pani. What if we ruined the magic? What if people didn't like the larger space? What if we lost the intimacy and connectedness people felt in the original location?

Because we have navigated big changes so many times, we now trust the process and confidently face our fears head-on. When we held the team brainstorm about moving Chai Pani, we made a long list of everyone's fears. Then we came up with solutions for every single one of them. That list shaped our plan for *how* to move the business without ruining the magic. I cannot overstate how powerful it is to write down the fears and get them out of the corners of our minds. **Fears control us from the shadows. Once out in the light of day, workshopped and managed with creative solutions, their hold on us lessens.**

Storytelling with Food and Culture

Representing a Culture with Authentic, True Stories

Buxton had been closed and cleaned out, ready for its next evolution. In early 2024, Mikey, Meherwan, Isaac, and I went to envision its next chapter. There's something stirring about an empty restaurant after it's been shuttered. The walls still talk, echoing all the celebrations and memories that happened there. It feels a bit like someone's house the day after a big party—no matter how much you clean up, the feeling of the party remains. The challenge before us was how to transform that location into one that tells the story of Chai Pani. We wanted to highlight the historical aspects of the building and for it to feel like the restaurant had always been there.

For the Buxton design, we'd preserved the murals that line the cinderblock wall because they are regional folk art dating back to the 1930s. The first public record of the building that we could find was as the Asheville Skating Club, known by local old timers as the Black skating rink, a remnant of the city's segregated past. The murals depict images of summer and winter sporting events, so the folklore is they were painted on the walls of the skating rink in honor of the Olympics that took place in 1936. These murals are an important part of Black history in Asheville, so we wanted to protect them. That worked well when we built Buxton Hall Barbecue, as it was a celebration of traditional barbecue in the South.

But now, the mission was to transform this place into a celebration of the streets of India. We had a design challenge before us. We walked around in silence, each of us lost in our imaginations. I commented on how the old textures of the walls reminded me of crumbling Victorian buildings in Mumbai. Meherwan said, "You know, these murals are like the black-and-white sporting images that you see in gymkhanas, the ones from old Bombay." Gymkhanas are found all over India and are similar to country clubs focused on sports, where people can play, or watch a cricket match while enjoying a meal. They have a distinct look, with verandas adorned in pergolas, often wrapped in dramatic bougainvillea, overlooking the sport fields. They date back to the time of British rule, with remnants of Victorian design mixed with the layered texture of old Indian buildings. They remained long after the British left and were reclaimed by Indian communities and culture. They usually have trophy walls, where black-and-white photographs commemorate sporting events that took place there.

Mikey lit up. "It TOTALLY looks like a gymkhana! Oh my god!" Meherwan added, "It's a gymkhana hosting a Bollywood wedding, serving Indian street cart food!" We all cheered in response, "YES! That's IT!" This is where our collective years in India helped us understand the story we want to tell—and then tell it with authenticity. No one else in the area might understand what a gymkhana hosting a Bollywood wedding looks like, but we did. That knowing gives us the confidence that we can do justice to the story we want to tell in our restaurants. That trust leads us to creatively think outside the box. Nimble thinking allowed us to adapt our design vision to preserve the integrity of the original art, while highlighting the images alongside a design story true to India.

Jeremy's crew got to work with renovations, while Isaac masterfully coordinated all the moving parts. Mikey came up with a design that took the Chai Pani aesthetic to the next level, allowing his creativity to stretch beyond the small walls of the original space.

I designed the floor plan and was ecstatic to have space for all the large-party seating we could ever need. I found a way to break up the cavernous dining room into smaller cozy spaces, defining four separate "rooms" (visually) while keeping the line of sight connected to the party atmosphere of the space. We knew our roles so well by then that little communication was needed. There are challenges with every buildout, but this one felt dynamic and exciting, despite the hurdles. Compared to the chaos of our first buildouts, the progress we'd made with the process felt palpable.

One day I was sitting outside the restaurant, taking a break from laying out the floorplan with giant cardboard cutouts in the shape of the tables I was designing. I was on a conference call with Meherwan, Isaac, and Charlotte. Charlotte called the meeting to discuss how much longer the renovation was taking than planned, and how far over budget we would be. Charlotte and the executive team were working backward from our renovation timelines to hire and train new people, coordinate the PR and opening parties, and liaise with everyone involved in the relocation. Needless to say, it was a heavy lift. Everything Charlotte said was spot-on. Mikey's design was taking a lot longer than he'd planned, but what I saw unfolding from his imagination was enchanting. I knew it was going to be worth the wait.

I was in the middle of explaining why I thought we shouldn't scale back in order to stay on budget when Mikey pulled up in his pickup truck, the back of which was dragging under a tower of giant tree limbs. I paused my call and, mildly amused, yelled, "Mikey, why the hell are you carrying around a tree?" He leaped out of the truck to excitedly explain his vision for reconstructing the tree inside so it wound around the stairs up to the mezzanine with fairy lights and flowers draped from its branches. We exchanged a few ideas (and my concerns) about how he planned to do this in a way that prevented bugs and rot from infesting the tree limbs. I thought to myself, "No one else other than Mikey would have the audacity to see this through." I loved everything about it. The creativity, the originality, and especially Mikey's interpretation of how to recreate a gymkhana inside a restaurant was pure creative genius. So, I got back on the call and said, "This wait will be worth every penny. We gotta figure out how to float it a little longer, because Mikey is over here building a magical wonderland."

The day before opening in the new space in May 2024, we held a huge party for friends and family. To commemorate the move from the original location to the new one, our manager, Marla, had the genius idea of hosting a processional like an Indian wedding. We hired a rickshaw from a local tuk-tuk company, decorated it in flower garlands, and used it to lead a parade from the old space to the new one. We gathered in front of the original Chai Pani, the building that started this wild and wonderful adventure. I had the same butterflies in my belly that I did fourteen years earlier on opening day. I walked down the sidewalk to see so many friends—old and new—gathering in front of Chai Pani, drinking chai and handing out balloons to kids.

Our close friends and employees gathered together to move Chai Pani from the building that had blessed a dream. Tears were shed, and hearts were flooded with memories. I looked around that group and saw people who started working with us in their late teens and early twenties now married with children running circles around them. We loaded up the rickshaw with some of the next generation. This included Charlotte with her toddler, Jules, Angi and her daughter Mabel, Molly Milroy's son Finley (the one she was pregnant with when the pandemic hit), Mikey with his newborn baby, Giorgio, and myself. We squeezed into the rickshaw with Bollywood music blasting and led the parade through downtown Asheville to the new location a half mile away. Behind us Meherwan led our community, dancing and singing, to our next home.

We entered the new Chai Pani to a huge crowd gathered inside. Longtime customers, friends, fellow restaurateurs, employees, landlords, farmers, and food suppliers, all came together to celebrate. Employees who'd worked with us years ago returned from all over the country to surprise us. Many success stories were launched from one brave dream. One creative venture ended up manifesting so much connection and joy—and became a training ground for us all.

The space is breathtaking. One minute you're standing on a street in Asheville, and the next you are teleported to another land. It's an explosion of color that engages all the senses. You enter through cascades of marigold garlands, inspired by Daniel's wedding in India. The dining room is anchored by an indoor pergola wrapped in fuchsia bougainvillea, adorned with homemade lights hanging like flowers from the vines. Another riot of marigold garlands centers the back of the dining room. The gymkhana trophy wall frames the original historic murals. The mezzanine that overlooks the dining room transports you to a madcap, hot-pink, enchanting land where guests can snack on pani puri, get a drink, or play a game of carrom while waiting for a table. In its new home, Chai Pani can breathe and expand into a fuller story. Outside of actually being there, it's the most accurate portrayal of the feeling of being in India I've ever experienced.

My dear friends Raina (our first manager) and Mehera (whose photos still grace Chai Pani's walls) wrangled all the original crew into a big family photo. That picture makes me emotional whenever I see it—it's my *why*! The thing about restaurants is that they attract people with passion and big hearts. That photo is full of interesting and successful people—some off on their own adventures, some still a part of ours. But all are forever the heartbeat of our story. They helped us become a business that grew while holding on to a culture of love and care. With all the ups and downs, this has been the ride of our lives. It would not have been the same without the people we've shared this journey with. They taught us how to build a culture that matters. And now, we grow for them, and all that we built together.

I left the new space that night with a thought echoing in my head: Chai Pani was all grown up now. This improbable little restaurant that thrived against all odds, won the James Beard "Outstanding Restaurant" award, and faced countless challenges along the way, was ready for a new chapter—ready to be the best version of itself.

A lot of ingredients went into the recipe of Chai Pani's success: great food, the belief that everything is figureoutable, having a clear story and telling it with authenticity, and bringing people together who work hard to create an ethos of care. Our core principles are all interconnected—each one helps the others. For a recipe to shine, individual ingredients must be assembled with care. When the recipe is made with love, it's felt in the final product. Chai Pani had that most essential of ingredients—the one that made all the others come to life and truly shine.

It is, in the end, a love story.

Epilogue

Then Came the Flood

"If everything around seems dark, look again, you may be the light."
—Rumi

In late September 2024, we went to bed under a tropical storm warning. Hurricane Helene had carved a path inland up from Florida after rapidly gaining strength in the warm waters of the Gulf. The forecast had the storm headed our way, but weakening by the time it reached the mountains. This was an extremely large storm system whose circumference stretched across multiple states, indicating that lots of rain would fall by the time it passed over us. However, it's unusual for the mountains of North Carolina to receive significant impact from a hurricane. Many people moved to Asheville because it's tucked in the mountains hundreds of miles away from the coast and the front lines of natural disasters. So, we went to bed prepared to lose power for a couple days and maybe deal with some localized flooding near the river. In an abundance of caution (with Meherwan thinking I was overreacting), I didn't drain the tub after my bath that night just in case we lost water and needed it for flushing the toilet.

SERVICE READY

Then forty trillion gallons[18] of rain fell from the sky. In its path over the Southeast, Hurricane Helene dumped an incomprehensible amount of rain across the region. On Friday morning, we woke to the sound of trees thumping as they fell to the ground around us. High winds and pounding rain tore through the skies. We didn't know it at the time, but all around us the rivers were surging, creating torrents of water that flooded far beyond every historic line in recorded history. Areas in the hundred-year flood zone were prepared for a couple of feet of water but got submerged under twenty-seven feet of raging river. The storm and flooding left behind a wide path of destruction and caused an estimated two thousand landslides. Entire small towns, buildings, bridges, farmland, and millions of ancient trees were washed away. Over one hundred lives were lost. Hurricane Helene permanently altered the landscape of the region. It is now considered a geological event and one of the worst storms in US history. The Appalachian region will be marked by "before" and "after" the hurricane of 2024.

By midday Friday the skies had cleared, and it was eerily quiet. We tentatively stepped outside to assess the damage, with no idea of the devastation that had occurred. Trees were down *everywhere*. Some were resting on houses. Our neighbors across the street had a tree inside their kitchen. Miraculously everyone in our immediate area was ok. I clambered over the tower of trees blocking our street to try to see more, and discovered our entire neighborhood was buried. Giant trees were uprooted—some cracked in half, tumbleweeds of tangled wires and power lines draped across them—cars crushed, and the road invisible. I stood in shock.

We were on our own. Power, water, and cell services were all down. If our neighborhood looked like Armageddon, we could only imagine the areas closer to the river. There was no emergency service on the way, or any way for them to reach us. We had to band together to dig ourselves

---

18   The Weather Channel. "See: https://weather.com/storms/hurricane/news/2024-10-01-helene-and-other-storms-dropped-40-trillion-gallons-of-rain-on-the"

Epilogue

out. The neighborhood got to work carving a path. The eighty-one-year-old across the street and the father who had a tree in his kitchen both had chainsaws. Meherwan joined them in cutting through the toppled trees so we could reach the main road.

Without functioning communications, we relied on reports from neighbors and a battery-operated radio to get news of what was unfolding. A few local DJs were trapped at the radio station, so they became the hub of communications as people called in with spotty service. For a few hours that morning the backup generators for our cell towers provided some service, giving us a little bit of news of the storm and allowing us to send messages out to let friends and family know we were safe. We learned that water and power lines had been decimated across the region. Thousands of people were missing. One meteorologist said that that level of destruction in our mountain region from a hurricane was a one-in-five-thousand-year event.

Charlotte was away when the storm hit. Pregnant and juggling a toddler at the time, she wisely stayed out of town. The only person on our team with reliable service, she was able to operate as our lead communicator. She sent messages to the full staff so that when they got service, they'd have information from us and be able to reach someone about their jobs. The goal was for her to account for everyone and determine who needed help. We were terrified for our employees and had no way to find out if they were ok. It was a long couple of days of worrying. Our Spicewalla factory is close to the river, so we were concerned about that location. All three of our restaurants are on high ground, so we'd never had flooding concerns, but as damage reports trickled in about the severity of what had occurred, we had no idea what to expect.

Friday night we settled in by candlelight. Aria was safe in DC, and we had a dry roof over our heads with some food in the fridge cooled by leftover ice packs. With our immediate surroundings safe and close friends accounted for, our minds were on the many who weren't and how to reach them. At 9:30 that night there was a knock at the door. My old friend

SERVICE READY

Brooke and her husband were standing in the dark. They'd been visiting us from California the week before and rode out the storm at a friend's house nearby. They spent all day trying to drive out of Asheville to get to a wedding in Virginia. After nine hours of being rerouted on detours and closed roads, they discovered that all roads in and out of Asheville were blocked from landslides or flooding. Miraculously, they managed to make their way back to our house and squeezed their rental car through the tunnel that had been carved out of the downed trees and power lines. This is how we discovered that Asheville was completely cut off.

On Saturday morning, we tried to drive downtown, but all routes were blocked. Isaac got on his bike and was able to reach each restaurant in town to assess damage. The new Chai Pani space had some roof leaks but was intact. We'd recently opened a new Botiwalla in West Asheville that was undamaged. The Spicewalla factory was flooded, so Michael, the COO, scrambled up a team who could get there, and they managed to save the supplies and stock. Surprisingly, our original restaurant location on Battery Park Avenue had power. We'd recently moved Chai Pani to its new home a half mile away and had renovated the Battery Park space to become a Botiwalla. Mikey was in the final phase of hanging pictures ahead of the grand opening scheduled for the weekend the storm hit. The location that launched our restaurant adventure fifteen years earlier was about to be reborn.

Rumor spread in the neighborhood that the Publix grocery store a few miles away set up Wi-Fi access in their parking lot and was operating on a generator with limited supplies. Meherwan rode his bike to Publix to try to reach our people. The lines to get into the store were hours long, but he got a few messages out from the parking lot. Each message took over fifteen minutes to send. But he managed to receive Isaac's note with the status report on the businesses and an update from Charlotte. There was still a long list of people whom she had not yet heard back from.

I rode my bike to the nearby fire station to ask if they knew a route out of town so we could go gather water and supplies. The two firemen

Epilogue

on duty had no information to share, or knowledge about when we could expect emergency responders to arrive with water for the community. As I rode away, I realized that we would have to become the leaders we needed.

Overnight, strangers became friends and communities banded together. Neighbors gathered to cook potlucks on camp stoves, supplies were pooled, scarce water was shared, and the cars that had gas became communal vehicles used to collect supplies. The entire area moved into a state of collective compassion and support.

A message reached me that our friends at WCK (World Central Kitchen, an emergency aid organization run by famed chef José Andrés) had reached out to see if we were ok, and they wondered if we had power at any of our Asheville restaurants. They wanted to see if we could help prepare food for the emergency response.

This wouldn't be the first time the little restaurant space where our story began would have to reinvent itself. Richard, Chai Pani's GM, sent out a message to all staff that everyone who was able to reach downtown should gather at noon on Sunday at the old Chai Pani location. Only about a dozen were able to get there. With communications down, movement restricted by blocked or flooded roads, and limited gas supply, most people were trapped where they were. Some were being evacuated or were dealing with damage to their homes.

Having power and some spotty Wi-Fi in the restaurant felt like a luxury. We opened the doors for staff to gather, charge their devices, get some bottled water, and connect. People wandered in wearing muddy muck boots—dazed and in shock. As they plugged in their devices to get messages out to loved ones, we scrolled through the images and devastating news received from friends. Stories of lives lost, children ripped from a mother's arms as they clung to the roof, pulled into raging waters. Witnesses described a tidal wave washing over areas far away from the flood zone. Small towns now flattened or missing. Heroic accounts also trickled in. An entire neighborhood was saved by one guy in a kayak with an axe, cutting into attic walls so people could escape.

Few words were exchanged in our greetings other than, "Are you ok? Are your people ok?" My main priority was to create a safe space for everyone to gather so that they would not feel alone. There was no fixing this, nothing that could take away the heartbreak and shock. There was only the offering of some comfort by not being alone in it. Together, we would help hold each other up and figure out how to move forward.

Clustered around tables in the front of house, we listened to updates on the radio and wrote notes on giant posters we hung in the front windows with all the info we could gather on where to find resources. With very little information to go on, we let people know that without water, we would not be able to open anytime soon. We had no estimate yet on when water would return, but the reports were bleak. We assured everyone that we were scrambling to develop a plan to help them through this catastrophe.

I presented the idea of cooking for WCK while we were waiting to return to business. Most people looked at me with foggy bewilderment, clearly wondering, "What are we supposed to cook with? How will we do this with no water?" We sat quietly mulling the idea together.

My years of cooking at the Youth Sahavas—the place that sowed the seeds of inspiration in me to want to be in the service industry—flashed to the front of my mind. I knew from that experience how to get resourceful to make food in large quantities under extraordinary and unconventional circumstances. Our community was stranded and needed help—we had to do what we could. We're restaurateurs, we show up every day to get food to the people—*that's what we do*.

So I said with confidence, "Let's gather all the product from our restaurants that can be salvaged and find anyone willing to volunteer to make some sandwiches. The first WCK helicopter leaves this afternoon to drop food and water in areas that are completely cut off. They need

Epilogue

help. We can do this! And because we can, we should. Who's in?" Richard, the GM, was enthusiastically nodding his head with a "Hell yes!" Others concurred. Meherwan nodded as if in a trance. His mind was on the 213 local employees who depended on us for their livelihoods. I didn't know yet how much WCK would compensate for the food, but I knew it would help pay at least a few people while offering some much-needed assistance for people in need.

The gift our restaurant group provided us was the resource of our people. We could divide and conquer the work and each focus on what we knew how to do. After getting the buy-in from the team gathered there, I got in touch with the representatives from WCK and said that if they could find water for us, we would start cooking.

As restaurant workers, we know how to mobilize fast and feed people. We're nimble and used to things not going as planned. We adapt quickly because we've had to learn how. We were built for times like this. Restaurateurs across town were on the ground serving free food before any government aid got there. Friends from a nearby restaurant, Curate, also jumped in to help WCK. They had some prepped kabobs that they offered us, so we decided to make sandwiches with Curate's lamb and what we had on hand. Friends and strangers saw the lights on in the restaurant and began wandering in. Mikey and his brother, Daniel, were there and quickly switched gears from hanging art for the planned opening to gathering food supplies. Youth Sahavas friends Matt Shepard, Ben Goodrum, and Charlie Eaton showed up to see what they could do. Next thing I knew, I was crouched next to Charlie's dog in the back of a pickup truck with a giant tub of lamb skewers. This way of functioning was very familiar to us—this was just like Youth Sahavas! This, we knew how to do.

Meherwan got the kitchen cranking. Daniel Files and I organized a sandwich assembly line in the front of house. We blasted some music, got in a rhythm, welcomed strangers (including kids) who showed up to help, and worked fast. Having busy hands calmed our nervous systems.

SERVICE READY

Moving our bodies toward a purposeful goal gave us a path forward. Our many years of jugaading it in that little restaurant space flooded back to me: our wild start, the pandemic disruptions, and the chaos after the JBF award. This little restaurant could now give back to a community that had given us so much.

Within a few hours we made 720 lamb and paneer (cheese) sandwiches on pav (an Indian-style soft bun). The WCK crew filled five-gallon water jugs from local breweries (who had stored potable water for brewing) for us to cook with. Their team showed up to pick up the sandwiches Sunday afternoon and were greeted by cheers. We were grateful for the chance to help, and for WCK's organization systems that got food distributed so quickly to people in need. They showed up with a flag for us to hang in the window, and we made the arrangement official, agreeing to keep cooking for their emergency food drops.

By Sunday (two days after the storm) we had heard from most of our staff that they were safe, but some had still not responded. Four days after the storm we received the following message from our executive assistant, Allison, whom we had not been able to reach. She lived in Lake Lure, one of the areas that had some of the worst flooding. She'd finally found some Wi-Fi to send a message out:

> *We're ok. . . . But if you hear of anyone wanting to bring supplies to Lake Lure/Chimney Rock, tell them not to risk it and focus on communities closer to Asheville. The National Guard will take the supplies, but you'll be turned away. Shit is still really bad here, and they've pulled a lot of bodies out of the lake. . . . The Army engineers confirmed the dam is stable for now, so we should be able to get out tomorrow. I'll keep you posted if anything changes. Love you guys.*

This kind of information gave us a clearer picture of what people were dealing with.

Epilogue

By Tuesday, word spread that we were making food for the helicopter drops, and more people started showing up to help. Nick, Chai Pani's chef de cuisine, made it into town from his farm and got to work helping me. We reorganized the space around making bulk meals for WCK with enough left over to give other organizations and neighbors that needed food. We decided we would not even think about a path to reopen for business until the area was out of the immediate crisis. Without water or electricity, and with very little supplies, people were struggling to find food, and many areas were still completely cut off.

After helping get us started, Meherwan posted up at home with a borrowed generator, using his cell phone as a hot spot to get online and fill out every tedious insurance form and aid application. He worked around the clock to ensure we all had a business to return to. That freed me up to dive full time into food production and community organizing. The restaurant was functioning as a community hub helping direct supplies and support where needed. One day as I was leaving home in my new role as disaster aid coordinator, Meherwan said to me, "You were made for this. I'm so proud of you, and of our team. This mission is in our business's DNA, and now it really shows." His appreciation buoyed me. We are fully aligned about what matters most and we share the same clarity about our company's purpose. After years of learning our way as business partners, we'd made it to a place of deep respect for our different strengths.

Having a strong business ethos prepared us for the moment, and we were rising to meet it. Fifteen years of witnessing the essential role restaurants play in communities came full circle. Beyond offering much-needed food, we were providing a place for our people to gather. I turned half of the dining room into a staff area with charging stations, computers, and Wi-Fi access so they could hang out together and charge their devices, get online, and fill out FEMA and other aid forms. I made a station with snacks and water bottles that grew into a minimarket of free supplies as people kept showing up with goods to donate. Most of us were living on those snacks and a family meal the kitchen made every day. Charlotte sent daily emails with information for the teams about grant money, how to apply for aid, our own fundraising efforts, and updates, but many staff still couldn't access them at home without internet. We posted those emails around the space to ensure everyone got the information. People would wander in overwhelmed, read the signs and love notes I taped to the wall, connect with each other, and then settle in and start to relax. It became a community center for our staff and other volunteers.

One young woman, a server in Chai Pani, said to me after a day of volunteering, "I feel so much better when I'm here. I can't *not* be here. I need to do this work right now to get through this." I felt the same way. Everyone did what they knew how to do. I realized that the whole thing, all the food production and emergency aid, was also a front for hugs. We were offering an important service, but in-person connection felt just as essential. The WCK flag in our restaurant window drew people in. Some wandered in looking to be of service, and some came in need of help. The needs were daunting, but helpers kept showing up. We all turned to each other, and in doing so we felt held through the disaster. It was a way of focusing on the light—we found that light in each other. It was clear to me that what our people needed most was to feel cared for. When everything falls apart, this goal becomes the most important role for leaders. It is not only what helps people feel better, but also what made our company culture strong.

It seemed like everyone around us had banded together to mobilize. The need was too vast for aid organizations to manage alone. It was going to come down to every single person doing what they could to help the greater good, and each other. That started to happen.

To offer support, our Atlanta restaurants organized a call for water donations, and before they could blink, the Chai Pani patio in Atlanta was piled high with gallons of water. They started filling U-Hauls with

Epilogue

the water and drove them to us once the roads reopened. Daniel Peach made multiple trips, as did his dad and several managers and friends from Atlanta. Stores were slowly reopening but would usually run out of water within hours. Finding water for your household was a time-consuming task that often involved standing in endless lines. Being able to offer water to our neighbors and everyone on our team was a huge support. You know things are upside down when the seventy-year-old father of a cook can get a U-Haul full of water to a cut-off neighborhood before the national guard does.

Miraculously, our whole team had been accounted for and was safe. But a week after the storm, entire communities were still trapped by landslides and washed-away roads. Power was still out for most of the area, as was water and internet service. Massive support started flowing in from city, state, and federal agencies. The roads were packed with long lines of service vehicles, army four-by-fours, and every type of tractor and bulldozer imaginable, and convoys of twenty to thirty emergency vehicles at a time moved into town. But the scale of need was beyond measure. The area's familiar background birdsong was drowned out by a constant buzzing of chainsaws cutting trees, Chinooks and helicopters flying overhead, and generator engines humming.

Two weeks after the storm, fall weather arrived, and we lit fires to stay warm, still waiting for electricity to return. The stars lit up the night sky without light pollution dulling their brilliance. We didn't stare at a TV. Instead, we read by candlelight and went to sleep early. I jumped out of bed every morning and rushed in to manage the emergency response. I couldn't imagine getting through that time without the companionship of my people and the community. It carried me.

Whenever I was away from work, a piece of my heart felt missing. I couldn't sit back and witness the young people who work for us getting crushed again. Their hearts had been smashed by the pandemic and a world that feels so often upside down and tumbling out of control. I couldn't save them from the suffering, but I could shine some light on a path forward and offer them a way to feel connected to something that mattered. All that was in our control was how we responded to the trauma, offering what we could. That resilience makes a community strong. I was fueled by the energy of the response and the outpouring of love.

In the second week after the storm, I was sitting in a booth in the front of house planning the WCK menu when a blur dressed in black rushed past me. The man ran into the kitchen yelling, "Where's your back door?" Ben, diligently chopping vegetables, looked up to see this stranger with an unlit cigarette dangling from his mouth. When the guy blew out of the kitchen, Ben chased after him through the front of house. I realized I needed to find out what was happening, and jumped up to chase them down the stairs. When I caught up, the guy was examining the back door. Without any introduction, he said, "Can I cut a hole in this wall?" We were in very weird times, so I responded, "Probably." Catching my breath, I continued, "Can you first tell me who the hell you are and what your goal is here?"

Meet the renegade special-ops plumber, Ruston, who announced that he was there to get us hooked up with water. His pickup truck outside the window with a WCK logo on it helped me connect the dots. I told him that two plumbers had already been out to see if a cistern for potable water could be connected to our building, and both had determined it wasn't possible with the building's 1920s configuration. Ruston looked at me with a twinkle in his eye and said, "Baby, I can hook up a water tank hanging off a cliff in Nepal! I can get you water. What fucking plumbers said it can't be done?" At which point some tears escaped my eyes. The idea that we could connect a tank of potable water and stop running around town filling five-gallon water jugs to be able to keep cooking left me overcome with hope.

I hugged him and thanked him, and we became fast friends. It was obvious immediately that he was a master in the art of jugaad. I started

Epilogue

calling him the "pirate plumber," and he provided us with weeks of entertainment as he tore through Asheville, helping WCK get water to the masses in unconventional ways. He was from New Orleans, so he knew a thing or two about trying to save a town in the aftermath of a hurricane.

The pirate plumber fit right in with our tribe of misfits and out-of-the-box thinkers otherwise known as restaurateurs. The way that service workers naturally plugged right in to the emergency response and aid organizations is an indication that we share similar get-it-done energy and the skills needed to tackle extreme challenges.

Weeks after the storm, dried mud fields covered empty spaces where buildings used to stand. Shredded platic, car parts, and machinery dangled from trees. A train car was wrapped around a treetop, bent in half as if it were made of clay. Swaths of barren brown land covered hills that once exploded with fall color. Traumatic stories continued to emerge as cut-off areas got reconnected and more people evacuated. Asheville is a town with two degrees of separation between most of us. Everyone here has been directly impacted by the storm or knows someone who lost everything, or someone they love.

The storm left profound destruction, but in the wake of it, the people of Western North Carolina were changed. We'd been woven together in a way that shows the potential all communities have to take care of each other. I believe we will forever be stronger together after the storm. You never unknow neighbors who become family overnight. The Appalachian region is full of tenacious and feisty people deeply connected to the place they call home. The culture here is rooted in the mountains (some of the oldest in the world) and the river that runs through them, with a deep history of farmers, creatives, and entrepreneurs who have dwelled in this area for hundreds of years. But what I witnessed after the storm took my breath away. People showed up for each other with a generosity of spirit and unrelenting work ethic that I have never experienced.

We had little access to outside news and were focused on the immediate needs in front of us. In the absence of that drumbeat, reminding us of how divided we supposedly are, we discovered that when we only have each other, we have all we need to survive. What happened in the wake of the flood is something I didn't believe was possible in our current political climate. For a few weeks, our differences washed away. It turns out that there truly is more that unites us than could ever divide us. I wish it didn't take a disaster for us to know this. It lit a spark in me to carry this forward into our work once we had the opportunity to reopen.

I didn't stop to rest for four weeks, and neither did the community. The experience helped me come to an even deeper awareness of what it means "to mother." It's about being a lighthouse—powerful and essential—shining light that guides people home through the dark.

On the morning of October 28, a school bus drove down my street, navigating around the piles of debris that still spilled onto the road from every yard. The sight of something so normal shocked me. Schools were finally reopening after digging their own wells to get water. Homes got decked out in Halloween décor that peeked out from behind twelve-foot-high towers of downed trees. The kids needed the normalcy of Halloween. We all did. We moved into a new phase of the recovery.

We began to evaluate what strategies would be needed for our businesses to recover from this catastrophe. They'd been closed for weeks, and there was no long-term way to sustain our people without getting paychecks flowing again. So, we organized around making that possible. Meherwan came across a strategy called the "OODA loop," an acronym used by the Air Force. It's a decision-making model that utilizes four steps: observe, orient, decide, and act. The idea explains how agility in observing and reacting to unfolding events rapidly can help organizations respond more effectively. We got our businesses back open by following that process. Once again, we found inspiration from outside the restaurant world and adapted it to land on a path forward.

Epilogue

- » O: We observed what was needed.
- » O: We oriented to the new conditions of no potable water and an entire community in need of food, work, and coming back together.
- » D: We made the costly but essential decision to invest in expensive, tanked-in potable water for all the businesses.
- » A: We took the actions necessary to get our businesses reopened.

We decided to not worry about making the right decision. Instead, we committed to make the decision right. We had to trust that as a collective, we would keep at it and do whatever it took for us to eventually get it right. Our people deserved that, and we'd worked too hard for too long to do anything less.

WCK was wrapping up their restaurant partnerships, so the timing was right to shift toward reopening our businesses. The reimbursement from WCK helped inch a handful of employees through that time and covered our cost of goods. In four weeks of preparing food for the emergency response, we made over twenty-five thousand free meals. Two days after the hurricane hit, we hung the WCK flag in our window and shifted full time into aid relief. Four weeks later we hung a grand-opening banner in the same window, and the original Chai Pani space was officially transformed into a Botiwalla.

As power returned, we reopened all three of our restaurants, the spice factory, and the retail store. The businesses that reopened spent crazy money to tank in exorbitantly expensive water. This was the cost of being able to employ people and help save the economy of our town. The math was upside down and will be for some time. But we were grateful to be able to open our doors and get people back to work.

We're all thinking about how to alchemize the pain we've witnessed into what we want to move forward with. A question rattles around my mind: "What can we hold on to that we never want to lose from this experience?" One practical lesson was the indisputable need to be better prepared for disasters. The hard reality is that running businesses in the age of climate change is going to require a new playbook. This disaster taught us that we *all* should be preparing for the unexpected, in whatever ways we can. In response, we made a "break glass in case of emergency" plan for our business that has a level of protection and protocols in place that we never before thought would be needed.

I'm profoundly grateful that our business has its roots in Asheville. What we built and grew our company into was shaped by the people and culture of this place. The community's response to Hurricane Helene confirmed this.

We learned from the experience of destruction and how our industry was leading the charge in the recovery. The hospitality industry embodies the mission *to be of service*. It's what we do best, especially when it's needed the most. But we need our communities as much as they need us. Like a forest, the roots of our trees are interwoven; we rely on each other to stay standing. Independent restaurants need protection and support: improved representation and advocacy locally and nationally, safeguards from fraudulent insurance, and emergency assistance to help recover after catastrophes. We are the heartbeat of our communities—the dollars we bring in go right back into the local economy in the form of paychecks to employees, farmers, and suppliers. When we go out of business, the economic ripple effect is catastrophic on the entire area. We have work to do to make our industry more financially secure and sustainable. When the public has our back, we step up with our whole hearts, with an offering—of *resilience*. We show up rain or shine, natural disasters or pandemics, with the mission *to serve*. Navigating unprecedented times is in our DNA. Whatever the future holds, fostering resilience in all industries, governments, and communities worldwide will be essential—something the hospitality industry models every day.

A Love Letter to the Hospitality Industry

"Don't ask yourself what the world needs. Ask yourself what makes you come alive, and go do that, because what the world needs is people who have come alive."

—Howard Thurman

The heart of being a restaurateur is rooted in how we bring people together, not just in the best of times, but in the worst. My years on this wild restaurant ride have taught me that bringing community together is one of the most important roles that hospitality workers play. Those of us who are in the business of hospitality consider ourselves lucky that what we call "work" is also a vehicle for delivering connection and belonging. *People need to gather.* Love is contagious; we catch it from others. Gathering is one of the most important human experiences—especially in times of division and disruption. There is strength and comfort in community.

In many parts of the world, people gather in squares and parks, otherwise known as "third spaces," a place outside of home and work to congregate. In America, it's restaurants and bars. We provide something rare in this culture: places where people of all backgrounds and beliefs come together around a shared experience. It's part of the glue that binds us, part of what holds us together despite our differences. Small acts of hospitality give us the strength we need to get through life. And, I believe, in these wobbly times, experiences of coming together are what humanity needs more than ever.

There are no barriers to entry in the restaurant industry. Everyone is welcome; you don't need a permission slip or a degree. The stage is open for anyone from any background or experience level to get out there and do something extraordinary. With all of the challenges in this industry, we don't focus enough on how remarkable it can be.

What I didn't expect when we started this restaurant adventure is how much I would end up loving it. Not just the people I work with, but the entire industry. Falling in love with this industry has changed me. It helped crystallize not only my vision of how I see the world, but how I see myself.

The wonderful and terrible news is that in order to really master being a great restaurateur (and I suspect this is true of mastering most things), we must *be truly ourselves.* Among the ten million lessons this industry continues to relentlessly teach me, that's at the top of my list. This work has demonstrated to me that we exhaust ourselves if we try to be like anyone else. We must figure out who we are and what we can uniquely contribute. The truest version of ourselves and our vision is what's needed to create something memorable.

My personal growth toward becoming more myself was made possible because of this industry. The business of hospitality has the power to be a great changemaker in the world—and within the individuals who call this their "work." If we're paying attention, it changes us. I found that what I was learning about myself freed me to try on new roles and step out from behind the curtain.

In the middle of every challenge we've faced, I learned something that surprised me. I discovered that I truly, madly LOVE my work, and the people in it—even in the hardest of times when the amount of work is overwhelming. When things fell apart, I was needed back in the restaurants with my boots on the ground. I found the work invigorating at times when logically it should have been exhausting. This is the greatest indication to me that I've landed on the right fit.

A Love Letter to the Hospitality Industry

The gift that our restaurant odyssey has given me is the ability to find my own voice, and trust it. When we started our first restaurant, I viewed my job as a supporting role, helping my husband manifest a dream. Along the way I uncovered my own strengths and leaned into them. It turns out that I was doing something revolutionary behind the curtain all along. I shaped a company culture that people want to be a part of. I realized that I could be just as much of a creative force from behind the curtain as I could out in front of it. There is a powerful impact to be made when focused solely on a company's culture and creating a place of dignity. Our surprising discovery was that creating a strong culture wasn't the byproduct of a successful business—it was the primary component that made it successful in the first place.

I'd been saying for years that starting a restaurant released Meherwan's inner "mad artist," but it had done the same for me. In the end, this work became my dream too. It fostered in me a process of self-discovery that helped unleash my own creativity and confidence. It doesn't matter what your role is—whether it's on stage under the bright lights, or behind the scenes. If you are bringing the power of your own strengths and radical vision to your work, that is what disrupts the status quo. That is the creative process.

A friend recently met a famous chef in Chicago. He got a tour of the spectacular kitchen, which included a specialty giant oven imported from Europe. As the chef explained, when the oven arrived they discovered that it didn't fit through any of the doors, and it couldn't be disassembled. So, being inventive restaurateurs, they tore down a wall of the building to move the oven into the kitchen. THEY TORE DOWN THE WALL! This speaks to the heart of who we are as restaurateurs. We are innovators, and we get shit done. We don't let obstacles, lack of money or experience, and certainly not walls stand in our way. We jugaad it. We take on challenges like solving a puzzle. The thrill of figuring out how to seat four hundred guests in a forty-seat restaurant on a Saturday night? We love that. Feed a community without power or water after a hurricane? No problem. We're good at solving the seemingly impossible. We do it every day.

There is much to glean from the hospitality industry, but *resilience* is a quality that industries worldwide could learn from us. Whenever there's an organizational mess, like an airport during the holiday rush, I play a game in my mind of imagining what a restaurant operator would do to improve that situation. I envision an inspired mindset that would manage the chaos with grace. Imagine an airline breaking the mold by handing out free hot chocolate, having extra people work the crowds and cheerfully answer questions, having gifts for tired children, and giving upgrades just for being a nice person. That is what restaurateurs would do. We organize the chaos, then we turn the difficulties into opportunities to demonstrate care and earn customers for life. What if an airline consistently surprised and delighted their customers? It's not rocket science—it's hospitality.

For the service industry, this idea is a way of life. We aren't perfect people—we're full of cracks. We embrace the character and grit that our life stories provide us, which makes for a stronger team and a more interesting product. We know the importance of the right details and rely on them to demonstrate how much we care. WE TEAR DOWN THE WALL in order to install the best oven because that's the thing that will set our food apart. Most restaurants have limited resources, so we learn how to utilize them where they make the most impact. Making people happy is our religion. A good restaurateur is an artist; an exceptional one finds the cracks in order to know where to shine the light.

In her poem "Good Bones," Maggie Smith writes:

> *. . . Life is short and the world*
> *is at least half terrible, and for every kind*
> *stranger, there is one who would break you,*

A Love Letter to the Hospitality Industry

*though I keep this from my children. I am trying
to sell them the world. Any decent realtor,
walking you through a real shithole, chirps on
about good bones: This place could be beautiful,
right? You could make this place beautiful.*

Those of us in the industry of hospitality show up every day with the intention to make this place beautiful.

I am eternally grateful to be a part of this tribe. Not everyone falls in love with it—some run like hell from its wild ways. For many, like myself, we run away only to discover that it still has its hooks in us many years later. When it clicks, it gets under our skin, and we feel inexplicably lit up by a crowded dining room. When given the chance to bring our full selves to work in a nurturing, supportive, and creative environment, hospitality workers shine light so bright that it can dispel any darkness.

When I decided to write this book, I was motivated by two things. I wanted to capture our story for our team. Meherwan and I can't be in all the locations working alongside everyone sharing our origin stories, our *why*, but I didn't want this to be lost or forgotten. And I wanted the world to know the real story of everyday restaurateurs. Our story is not unique; it's similar to so many other independent, underfunded, bootstrapped restaurants built the hard way—with a lot of love, resilience, commitment, and work. I don't see that version of the story represented often, and yet it's unfolding around us every day, all over the world.

The tenacity of restaurant workers is something the world needs to know more about. When we embody our potential, it's love in action. I believe in this business, and that inspires me to keep trying to figure it out and continue learning from it. The love runs deep, with a passion that motivates me to do crazy things for my people—like open more restaurants! We grow our business so that every person who works with us has the opportunity to thrive.

SERVICE READY

At the time of this writing, we have three flagship Chai Pani locations: Asheville, Atlanta, and Washington DC. Spicewalla is thriving and growing. And Botiwalla has four locations, two more under construction, and has begun its ambitious expansion plan with the first phase underway. It's just the beginning of a larger-scale growth vision for our business, and the impact we can make in our communities and in the lives of our people.

This industry helped me come home to myself and find the thing I was born to do. The gift of the restaurant work ethic is how it teaches us to move toward fear to do what makes us come most alive—to do the thing that makes your heart pound even while you're standing still, despite fearing you might fail. That's what is required to make great art of any kind. It doesn't always happen overnight, but one step at a time, we can build something we believe in. That's what it takes to create a business that helps make the world a better place. And that's what it means to be *service ready*.

Acknowledgments

I did not start this project knowing how to write a book. But I knew the Chai Pani story was a good one, and I wanted to share it. Countless people made this book possible. It turns out that years in the restaurant industry developed my muscle for managing fear and stepping into the unknown. That muscle was celebrated by remarkable friends and strengthened by some brilliant teachers—all of whom helped me write this story.

David Black, what started out as an intention to capture our story for my inner circle turned into so much more because of what you saw in it. To call you my agent falls short of the role you played in shaping this book. You not only helped me believe it should be shared with the world, you pushed me to discover the parts of my story that most needed to be told. Your belief in me brought this story into the best version of itself. I don't know how I got so lucky to receive your wisdom and guidance, but I'm forever grateful.

Kara Watson, and the outstanding team at Scribner, thank you for taking a chance on a first-time author and shining light on a scrappy little restaurant adventure. Kara, you guided me with remarkable patience on how tell the full story with clarity—and how to use the delete button! Your trust in me gave me the courage to lean in to my own voice. Thank you for focusing your talent, magnificent mind, and dedication to the craft of telling a personal story. This book is what it is today because of you. It's an author's dream to work with the Scribner team and a true

ACKNOWLEDGMENTS

honor to stand under your brilliant halo: Addie, Alyssa, Sophie, Brianna, and Emma.

Thank you to Jaya Miceli at Scribner and Michael Files for collaborating to bring the Chai Pani aesthetic to life in the form of a gorgeous book cover.

Thank you Kelsey, Sarah, and Chloe for being dazzling powerhouses of PR and champions of sharing this story. And to Tina and Kimmie for ushering this story out into the world with your tender, loving guidance.

My deepest gratitude to Cara, Laura, Maddy, and the entire Spicewalla team for your profound support and creative genius. And, for showering ALL of your collective goodwill (and treats) on helping me launch this book baby.

To the magician otherwise known as Allison, thank you for holding our lives together with unrelenting care and unreasonable cheerfulness.

John J. Geoghegan, we first met when I signed up for your class hosted by The Book Passage. When you picked my elevator pitch to share with our class, it lit the spark that gave me the courage to start this book. Thank you for being such a clear and supportive guide. You became my first editor and advocate, but the impact you had on me colored way beyond those lines.

To Frankie Bolt, thank you for introducing me to the heroine's journey and editing parts of this book with exceptional vision, and your radiant heart.

One of the great gifts of my life is my circle of women friends—I don't know how anyone does life without the likes of them. To my Sunday Sauna Soup Sisters, life is so much funnier, and has way more love and beauty with you in it. You help me to be me. When I showed up a mess after unleashing an inner rebel mermaid, instead of wondering if perhaps I needed therapy (or a long nap), you celebrated me. For my writing group (aka the truth parade), Pamela, Amber and Mehera K: you helped put my pen to paper and gave me the courage to write (and live) with unwavering

ACKNOWLEDGMENTS

honesty. Raina, thank you for always seeing the real me and loving me, long before I knew how to love myself. Brooke, for nudging me to jump off mountains (literal and metaphoric!). Annie, for always encouraging me to write. And Mehera Busfield, for always encouraging me to laugh.

Thank you to Mehera Kleiner for being my creativity doula, and for helping me see that all of this was possible. Stepping into a new phase of my career felt blurry until you helped me see it all with crystal clarity. Not only did you drag me to an island in the Aegean Sea to immerse in the creative process, but you were the best possible companion as I learned to write a book. I'm eternally grateful.

Sarah, from the beginning of my restaurant adventure, you reminded me that there was something unique that I could contribute. You helped me find it. Thank you for reading this story with such intention, intuition, and your wildly intelligent mind.

Many friends helped me walk the intimidating process of revealing a very personal story with the world. There's too many to name here, but you know who you are, and you have my deepest appreciation. A special shout to Matty, Misha, Angi, Naozer, and Peter Coyote for helping me see parts of myself that were hiding.

I'm not sure why I had the courage to tackle the complex intersection of a restaurant adventure with a spiritual journey and a marriage.... but here we are! Many brilliant readers helped me find a balance between memoir, restaurant drama, and business takeaways. Some of you took the time from your very busy lives to read the whole book, some read an early section. But all of you contributed and shaped this story in impactful ways. Thank you to all my readers already mentioned here, as well as: Cheetie, Teddy, Kat, Chai, Buck, and Jamie.

To our first restaurant investors who took the ultimate risk with us: Buck and Mehera, Jacko, Billyji, Peter, Ann, and Isaac—would this story ever have happened without you? And to all the investors who came after, thank you for helping us continue the dream.

ACKNOWLEDGMENTS

There's a special kind of magic that happens every time we take on a new restaurant buildout. Some sneaky fairies conspire to send in extraordinary people who also happen to be dear friends. They have built all our restaurants by pouring their stunning love and care into our spaces. Thank you to Zack, Charlie, Joe, Jonathan, Will, Kristine, Angela, Peter, Matt, Luna, Sean, Paul, Shannon, Aria, Amar, Julia, Ben, and all of Jeremy and Mikey's teams in all of their evolutions through the years. You are all part of what made this story special.

To my OG day one crew! Thank you Isaac, for dancing in the field with us first, remaining our island of calm, and a model for leading with grace. Mikey, for bedazzling everything with unbridled creativity and your wondrous love. Charlotte, for being my partner in creating a heroine's journey for our people. Thank you for keeping your focus on what matters most while always bringing superb depth, care, and wisdom to work. To Daniel, for your devotion, and eternal curiosity that embraced the culture of India as well as an ethos of the heart. Gustavo, for bringing your heart the size of Texas and fierce dedication to this work. And James, as you embark on your own venture, I will be cheering you on, but you will forever be the only one I want to work every event with. I would not have wanted to be on this wild ride without this crew. You are miraculous humans, and I can't believe my good fortune to call you family.

To my worldwide Baba community, you are a fabulously eccentric tribe that have enhanced my life beyond measure. I'm deeply grateful to have been raised in your embrace.

Thank you to my mother, for being the embodiment of strength, and modelling how to follow one's truest self. You are an eternal badass—and a model for creative sparkle in the restaurant industry, and in life.

And to all my parents and siblings (step, in-law, and everything in between) for being pillars of strength in each of your own unique ways.

For my muse Aria, you are the greatest blessing of my life. You've

ACKNOWLEDGMENTS

always been the most gifted writer in our family, and you inspire me every day. Whatever you choose to do next, the future is bright with your spectacular mind focused on making a positive impact in the world. E.E. Cummings said it best, "you are my sun, my moon, and all my stars."

Meherwan, thank you for your wild and crazy and wonderful ideas—and convincing me that we can do them. And for being my rock of solid strength through all the storms of life. We came into this life together, and the greatest gift is to be by your side as we continue to squeeze all the life out of every day we have left. You are my beginning and my ending.

And, to the entire Chai Pani Restaurant Group and Spicewalla family, all my coworkers currently in the mix, and everyone through the years—I am eternally proud to work alongside you. You all made a dream become reality. This book is for you.